WOODSMITH CUSTOM WOODWORKING

Weekend &
Evening Projects

CONVERSION CHART

WEIGHT EQUIVALENTS
(ounces and pounds / grams and kilograms)

US	METRIC
1 oz	28 g
16 oz (1 lb)	454 g
35 oz (2.2 lb)	1 kg

CONVERSION FORMULA
ounces x 28.35 = grams /1000 grams = 1 kilogram

LINEAR EQUIVALENTS
(inches and feet / centimetres and metres)

US	METRIC
$1/16$ in	0.16 cm
$1/8$ in	0.32 cm
$3/16$ in	0.48 cm
$1/4$ in	0.64 cm
$5/16$ in	0.79 cm
$3/8$ in	0.95 cm
$7/16$ in	1.11 cm
$1/2$ in	1.27 cm
$9/16$ in	1.43 cm
$5/8$ in	1.59 cm
$11/16$ in	1.74 cm
$3/4$ in	1.90 cm
$13/16$ in	2.06 cm
$7/8$ in	2.22 cm
$15/16$ in	2.38 cm
1 in	2.54 cm
12 in (1 foot)	30.48 cm
1 ft^2	929.03 cm^2
$39\frac{1}{2}$ in	1.00 m
1 yd	91.44 cm
1 yd^2	0.84 m^2

CONVERSION FORMULA
inches x 2.54 = centimetres
100 centimetres = 1 metre

TEMPERATURE EQUIVALENTS
(fahrenheit / celsius)

US	METRIC
32° F (water freezes)	0° C
180° F (water simmers)*	82° C
212° F (water boils)*	100° C

*at sea level

CONVERSION FORMULA
degrees fahrenheit minus 32, divided by 1.8 = degrees celsius

VOLUME EQUIVALENTS
(fluid ounces / millilitres and litres)

US	METRIC
1 tbsp ($1/2$ fl oz)	15 ml
$1/2$ cup (4 fl oz)	120 ml
1 quart (32 fl oz)	960 ml
1 quart + 3 tbsps	1 L
1 gal (128 fl oz)	3.8 L
1 in^3	16.39 cm^3
1 ft^3	0.0283 m^3
1 yd^3	0.765 m^3

CONVERSION FORMULA
fluid ounces x 30 = millilitres
1000 millilitres = 1 litre

WOODSMITH CUSTOM WOODWORKING

Weekend & Evening Projects

By the editors of *Woodsmith* magazine

Time-Life Books

Weekend & Evening Projects

Picture Frame Clock

Note Board

IN THE SHOP   90

Shop Tote

FRAMES, MIRRORS & CLOCKS

Ranging from a clock that fits in your hand to mirrors that hang on the wall, the projects in this section are meant to draw your eye. Each one provides a way to polish your skills in the few hours it takes to complete.

Laminated Picture Frames

The secret to making these picture frames is building up a blank from several layers of wood.
You can mix different types of wood to create a look that complements whatever you're framing.

P art of the appeal of a small picture frame is that it's usually a quick, easy project to build. But at first glance, these two frames may not appear all that simple.

Both frames look like they were assembled with lots of tiny pieces or blocks, which must mean a lot of time-consuming setups and fine-tuning. But that's not how they were made.

Actually, both frames follow the same general procedure. And it's not that complicated.

LAMINATED BLANKS. Each frame is built in three basic steps. First, pieces of different types of wood are glued into a

"sandwich" to make a wide, thick blank. Then narrow pieces are ripped from the blank like strips of bacon. When these pieces lie flat, you can see the layers of the sandwich. These pieces are then mitered to finished length and assembled into a frame.

There's one thing to note about the size of these picture frames. They're designed to accept standard photos with precut mats (see Sources, page 126). The larger gridwork frame (on the left in the photo above) is sized to hold an 8 x 10 matted photo. The smaller accent strip frame (on the right) is the right size for a 5 x 7 matted photo.

WOOD. To highlight the details in each frame, I chose woods with contrasting colors. One frame uses mostly cherry with maple trim. The other uses more maple than cherry. You can probably find a variety of ways to customize the look of these frames by using some of the pieces from your scrap bin.

MITERING. One of the keys to making "picture perfect" frames is tight-fitting miters at each corner. This is one of those operations that take a bit of time and patience to set up, but the end result is well worth the effort. There are a number of tips to help you with this beginning on page 14.

GRIDWORK FRAME

It may look like you'd have to cut a lot of tiny squares to make the individual blocks in this frame. Actually, all you need to do is cut a series of evenly-

spaced dadoes in a strip of wood. (If the dadoes faced outward on a cabinet, this strip would be called dentil molding.)

I cut the dentil molding profile on the router table, using a simple indexing jig (see the Shop Jig box below).

FRAME BLANK

To build the frame, I prepared a single blank with three layers of wood. Later, the four pieces of the frame will be ripped from this blank. This way, all the pieces end up identical, and you'll save quite a bit of setup time.

I laminated the blank for the frame from two pieces of $3/4$"-thick cherry and a thin strip of maple. But the two cherry pieces start out as one extra-wide piece *(Fig. 1)*. That's so the dentil profile only has to be cut on one piece.

ROUT DENTILS. After the cherry piece is cut to size, the next step is to cut the dentil profile on it *(Fig. 1a)*. (Here's where you'll need the indexing jig.) Then rip the blank in half.

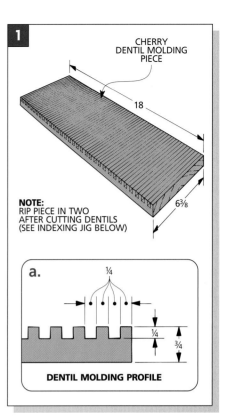

1

CHERRY DENTIL MOLDING PIECE

18

$6^3/8$

NOTE:
RIP PIECE IN TWO
AFTER CUTTING DENTILS
(SEE INDEXING JIG BELOW)

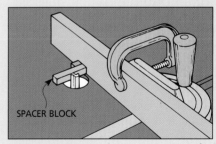

a.

¼

¼

¾

DENTIL MOLDING PROFILE

SHOP JIG .... Indexing Jig

One thing I like about the gridwork frame (shown above) is the open spaces in the frame pieces. These evenly-spaced openings are easy to cut with the help of a simple indexing jig. All you'll need is an auxiliary fence attached to your miter gauge and a couple of small pieces of scrap, as shown in the series of drawings below.

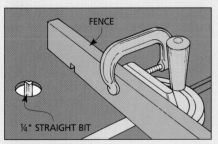

FENCE

¼" STRAIGHT BIT

1 To make the jig, clamp a fence to the miter gauge. Then rout a $3/16$"-high notch in the fence with a ¼" straight bit.

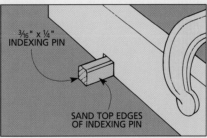

$3/16$" x ¼"
INDEXING PIN

SAND TOP EDGES
OF INDEXING PIN

2 Now cut an indexing pin to fit the notch. Sand edges so workpiece can be set on and off easily. Glue pin in place.

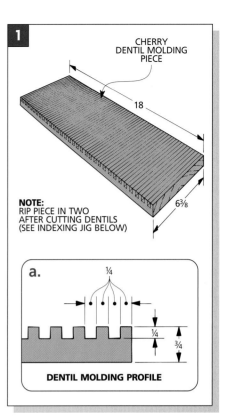

SPACER BLOCK

3 Next, move the fence so the bit is ¼" from the pin. (Use a spacer the same width as pin.) Then reclamp the fence.

REMOVE CLAMP
WHEN SCREWS
ARE INSTALLED

4 With fence still clamped in place, drill pilot holes and screw the fence to the miter gauge. Then raise the bit ¼" high.

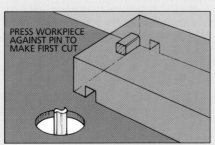

PRESS WORKPIECE
AGAINST PIN TO
MAKE FIRST CUT

5 To cut dentils, lay the workpiece face down, keeping it tight against the fence and pin. Cut the first dado.

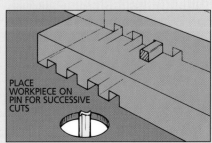

PLACE
WORKPIECE ON
PIN FOR SUCCESSIVE
CUTS

6 Place the just-cut dado on the indexing pin and make a pass. Repeat process along the length of the board.

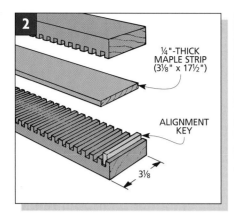

2

¼"-THICK MAPLE STRIP (3⅛" x 17½")

ALIGNMENT KEY

3⅛

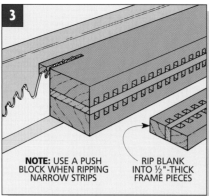

3

NOTE: USE A PUSH BLOCK WHEN RIPPING NARROW STRIPS

RIP BLANK INTO ½"-THICK FRAME PIECES

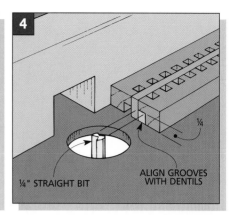

4

¼" STRAIGHT BIT

ALIGN GROOVES WITH DENTILS

¼

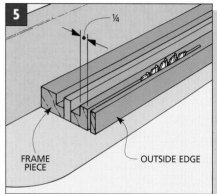

5

¼

FRAME PIECE

OUTSIDE EDGE

LAMINATE BLANKS. Next, cut a ¼"-thick strip of maple to size and glue it between the pieces of cherry *(Fig. 2)*. Avoid using too much glue — you don't want to clean up a lot of excess between the tiny squares.

KEY. To make sure the dentil profiles were aligned when assembling the blank, I used a small alignment key cut from a piece of scrap *(Fig. 2)*. This key should fit snug between the dentils and allow the cherry pieces to contact the maple strip fully.

FRAME PIECES

When the glue has dried, you can rip the blank into ½"-thick frame pieces *(Fig. 3)*. (I cut five so I'd have an extra.)

GROOVES. The next thing is to rout two grooves through the dentil molding to help set off the maple strip *(Fig. 4)*.

The key to doing this is to position the fence so the edge of the bit aligns with the maple strip. Then, after routing the first groove, all you have to do is rotate the piece end for end because the maple strip is centered between the two pieces of cherry.

If there are slivers of the cherry still visible on the maple, then nudge the fence and repeat the cuts.

TRIM OUTSIDE EDGE. There is one final step to creating the design. I trimmed the outside piece of cherry to leave the face ¼" wide *(Fig. 5)*.

CUT RABBETS. Before mitering the frame pieces to length, I routed a ⁹⁄₃₂"-wide rabbet on the back inside edge of each piece *(Fig. 6)*. This will hold the glass, mat, and backing materials.

Note: The depth of the rabbet depends on the thickness of the materials you're going to use.

FRAME ASSEMBLY

All that's left is to assemble the frame. The first thing to do is cut a 45° miter on one end of each piece. The miter should divide an opening between the dentils exactly in half so that you end up with a full opening at each corner *(Fig. 7a)*.

SHOP JIG .... *Miter Gauge Setup Jig*

Instead of resetting and readjusting the miter gauge each time I want to cut miters, I built a jig to set the miter gauge to exactly 45° every time.

CLEAT. The jig consists of a base and a triangular cleat *(Fig. 1)*. First, cut an 8"-square piece of plywood for the cleat. (Check that the corners are 90°.)

Now, set your miter gauge to exactly 45° (refer to page 15). Then use the gauge to cut the cleat to form a triangle.

BASE. Next, cut the plywood base and rip two grooves in it to fit the runner on your miter gauge *(Fig. 2)*.

Note: To make the jig accurate for both angles, the grooves must be par-

allel. So when cutting them, keep the same edge of the base against the fence.

ASSEMBLY. Now, with the miter gauge still set at 45°, set the miter gauge runner in one of the grooves *(Fig. 3)*. Clamp the cleat in place, flush against the miter gauge. Then screw the cleat to the base.

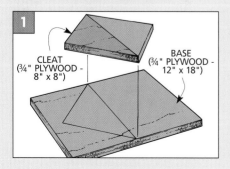

1

CLEAT (¾" PLYWOOD - 8" x 8")

BASE (¾" PLYWOOD - 12" x 18")

2

8¾

2½

CUT GROOVES TO FIT RUNNER ON MITER GAUGE

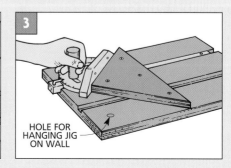

3

HOLE FOR HANGING JIG ON WALL

This clamp uses wedges to press two mitered pieces together. And it will clamp frames of various widths.

The clamp is just a piece of plywood with a square block and two cleats glued and screwed to it (see drawing).

As you assemble the jig, there are two important considerations. First, the *inside* corner of the block must be exactly 90°. And second, the inside edge of each cleat must be parallel with the inside edges of the block.

A pair of wedges fits between the workpiece and the cleat. They apply pressure in two directions at the same time. When the inside wedge is tapped forward (see photo), it pushes the joint together while the glue dries.

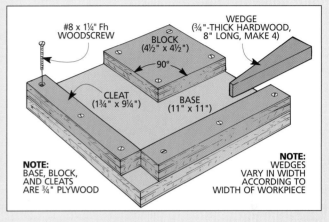

Note: Some tips for setting up your table saw and miter gauge to cut miters are in the Technique article on page 14.

Next, miter the second end to the proper length. (To fit a standard 11 x 14 mat into the rabbets in the frame, you may need to trim the mat a little.)

ASSEMBLE FRAME. I assembled the frame in two steps. First, I glued the pieces into two halves, using a jig like the one shown above. Then I joined the two halves with a band clamp.

Note: When gluing end grain to end grain, I seal the wood first with an initial light layer of glue. When it's dry, I apply more glue and assemble the joint.

FINISH. It's best to finish the frame before adding any hardware. (I applied a couple of coats of wiping varnish.)

If you have a large enough container (and plenty of varnish), you can soak the frame. This way, the finish gets in all the little openings. To allow the varnish to run off, hang the frame up to dry.

TURNBUTTONS. After the finish was dry, I nailed eight turnbuttons to the back of the frame to help keep the glass, mat, and backing materials in place *(Fig. 7b)*. (For Sources, see page 126.) Pre-drilling the holes will prevent the wood from splitting.

HANGER AND PROP STICK. Finally, I centered a saw tooth hanger on the back of the frame *(Fig. 7)*.

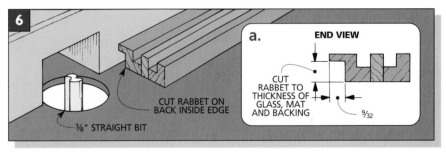

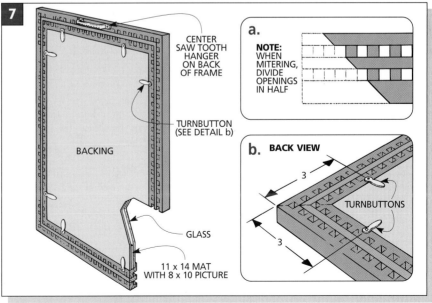

If you want to set the frame on a desk, cut a prop stick from a piece of scrap like the one shown for the accent strip frame (refer to *Fig. 11b* on page 13). Cut the prop stick to size so it will fit in an opening in the dentil molding.

ACCENT STRIP FRAME

This frame is made somewhat like a club sandwich. Three pieces of maple act as the bread around thin cherry accent pieces. Like tomatoes, these accent pieces can slide around — especially when glue is added. So the challenge is keeping everything aligned. To do this, I cut shallow dadoes and rabbets in the pieces of maple to hold the cherry accents.

FRAME BLANKS

The frame is built from two blanks. One is for the long sides (13" long). The other is for the short sides (11" long). Each frame blank is glued up with three pieces of maple, plus the cherry accent pieces (refer to *Fig. 7*).

MAPLE PIECES. Start by planing each piece of maple to thickness *(Fig. 1)*. Then cut the pieces to width and length. Next, since all the pieces of the frame are symmetrical, I marked a centerline on each *(Fig. 1)*. (Many of the measurements will be made from these marks.)

ROUT DADOES. Now, shallow dadoes can be cut on the faces of the maple pieces. The easiest way to do this is with a dado blade. But most dado blades leave small valleys and ridges in the dado. So instead, I used the router table and the miter gauge.

Note: To make identical cuts easier, I added an auxiliary fence to the miter gauge and used a stop block *(Fig. 2)*.

Each piece has two $1/32$"-deep dadoes cut near the center *(Fig. 2a)*. Because they're measured off the center of the workpiece, you only need to set the stop block once. After routing the first dado, simply rotate the workpiece end for end and repeat the cut.

Note: Since the middle piece of maple in each blank is sandwiched between the other two, rout dadoes (and rabbets) on both faces of the middle pieces *(Fig. 1)*.

ROUT RABBETS. When the dadoes have been cut in both sets of maple pieces, go ahead and cut wide rabbets on the ends *(Fig. 3)*.

CHERRY PIECES. With the pieces of maple complete, I made two $1/4$"-thick

cherry blanks *(Fig. 4)*. All the accent pieces will be cut from these blanks.

I ran into a bit of a problem with the accents near the center. They're so small it's hard to tell which is the face and which is the edge *(Fig. 5a)*. To help keep the faces always pointed in the same direction, I marked across the face of each blank with a pencil *(Fig. 4)*.

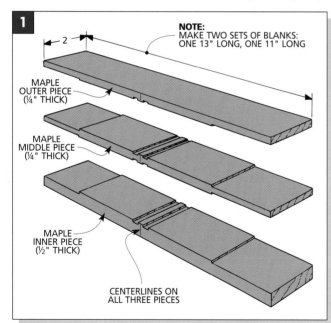

1

2

NOTE: MAKE TWO SETS OF BLANKS: ONE 13" LONG, ONE 11" LONG

MAPLE OUTER PIECE (1/4" THICK)

MAPLE MIDDLE PIECE (1/4" THICK)

MAPLE INNER PIECE (1/2" THICK)

CENTERLINES ON ALL THREE PIECES

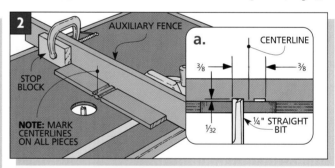

2

AUXILIARY FENCE

STOP BLOCK

NOTE: MARK CENTERLINES ON ALL PIECES

a. CENTERLINE

3/8 3/8

1/32 1/4" STRAIGHT BIT

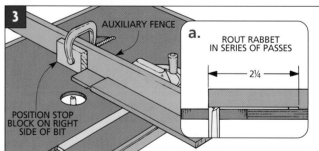

3

AUXILIARY FENCE

POSITION STOP BLOCK ON RIGHT SIDE OF BIT

a. ROUT RABBET IN SERIES OF PASSES

2 1/4

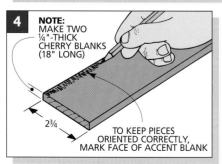

4

NOTE: MAKE TWO 1/4"-THICK CHERRY BLANKS (18" LONG)

2 3/4

TO KEEP PIECES ORIENTED CORRECTLY, MARK FACE OF ACCENT BLANK

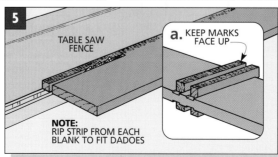

5

TABLE SAW FENCE

a. KEEP MARKS FACE UP

NOTE: RIP STRIP FROM EACH BLANK TO FIT DADOES

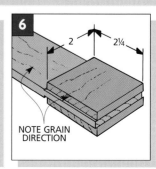

6

2 2 1/4

NOTE GRAIN DIRECTION

Then keep the marks on each accent piece face up during assembly.

The accent pieces are cut to fit the center dadoes *(Fig. 5)*. To do this accurately, I cut a test piece from some scrap. When it fit the dado, I ripped a strip off each blank, then cut them to length.

With the leftover pieces of cherry, I cut the accent pieces to fit in the rabbets in the ends *(Fig. 6)*. Note that the grain on the accents runs perpendicular to that on the maple piece.

ASSEMBLE BLANKS. When all the accent pieces were cut, I glued up the two blanks for the frame *(Fig. 7)*. But don't use too much glue. It's hard to remove the excess in the tiny spaces around the accent pieces.

Note: I offset all the cherry accent pieces on one side of each frame blank *(Fig. 7a)*. This way there's one straight edge to set against the fence when ripping the pieces to size *(Figs. 8a and 9a)*.

FRAME PIECES

When the glue is dry, shave one edge of each frame blank on the table saw to get a nice, clean edge *(Fig. 8)*.

RIP FRAME PIECES. Then rip each blank into three $\frac{1}{2}$"-thick frame pieces *(Fig. 9)*. (I cut three from each blank so there would be a couple of extra pieces.)

Next, before cutting the miters, I routed a $\frac{9}{32}$"-wide rabbet along the back inside edge of each piece to hold the glass, mat, and backing materials *(Fig. 10)*. The depth of the rabbet should match the thickness of the materials you're going to use.

FRAME ASSEMBLY

The blanks are now ready to be mitered into a frame *(Fig. 11)*. Take extra care here. Since the pieces are symmetrical, the cuts must be measured from the *center* of each piece *(Fig. 11)*.

ASSEMBLE FRAME. To glue up the frame, first I assembled the pieces into two halves, using hand pressure. Then I joined the halves with a band clamp.

PROP STICK. The frame is almost done, but it needs something to help it stand up. I made a prop stick from scrap to fit between the center accent pieces *(Fig. 11b)*. (Start with an oversized blank. It's much safer when ripping.)

FINISH. Now all that's left is to apply a finish and nail the turnbuttons in place to hold the mat and picture *(Fig. 11)*. ■

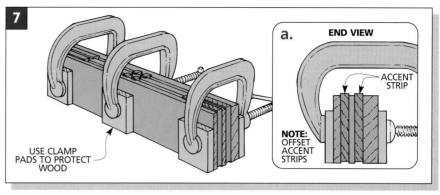

7

USE CLAMP PADS TO PROTECT WOOD

a. END VIEW

ACCENT STRIP

NOTE: OFFSET ACCENT STRIPS

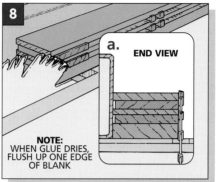

8

a. END VIEW

NOTE: WHEN GLUE DRIES, FLUSH UP ONE EDGE OF BLANK

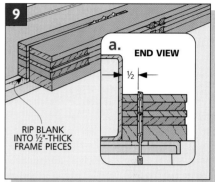

9

a. END VIEW

$\frac{1}{2}$

RIP BLANK INTO $\frac{1}{2}$"-THICK FRAME PIECES

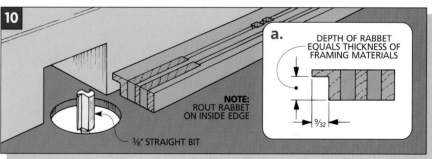

10

a.

DEPTH OF RABBET EQUALS THICKNESS OF FRAMING MATERIALS

NOTE: ROUT RABBET ON INSIDE EDGE

$\frac{9}{32}$

$\frac{3}{8}$" STRAIGHT BIT

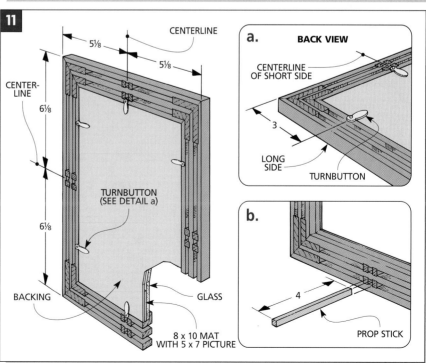

11

$5\frac{1}{8}$

$5\frac{1}{8}$

CENTERLINE

CENTER-LINE

$6\frac{1}{8}$

$6\frac{1}{8}$

BACKING

TURNBUTTON (SEE DETAIL a)

8 x 10 MAT WITH 5 x 7 PICTURE

GLASS

a. BACK VIEW

CENTERLINE OF SHORT SIDE

3

LONG SIDE

TURNBUTTON

b.

4

PROP STICK

TECHNIQUE . . . . Perfect Miters

Making a frame with tight miters is easy in theory. "Just cut a 45° angle on both ends of each workpiece. And make sure opposite pieces are the same length." But, cutting *exact* 45° angles and pieces *precisely* the same length isn't quite so simple.

On the table saw, the joint requires accurate setups. This includes starting with a clean, sharp blade. And the blade must be parallel with the miter gauge slots and square to the table.

That's just the beginning. On these two pages, you'll find some other tips I use to get both the exact angle and the right length.

One other thing. Once you've taken the time to get your miter gauge set to cut perfect miters, you can eliminate a lot of the setup time in the future by making the jig shown on page 10.

TRUING YOUR TRUNNION

Before you cut even a test piece, you need to check your saw for proper alignment. When you rip or crosscut on a table saw, the blade should be parallel

with the miter gauge slot. A misaligned blade will push the wood to the side. This can throw off critical cuts.

CHECK BLADE. To check that the blade is parallel to the slot, unplug the saw and raise the blade all the way up. With a felt-tip marker, mark one of the teeth. Now rotate this tooth to the front of the insert plate and use a combination square to measure the distance from the tooth to the slot *(Fig. 1)*.

After measuring the distance at the front, rotate the marked tooth to the rear of the insert plate and measure again. The distance should be the same. If not, it's time to adjust your saw.

TRUNNION. To adjust the saw, the trunnion assembly has to be shifted in relation to the table. (The trunnion is the heavy casting mounted under the table that holds the blade.)

Note: On cabinet-type saws, it's the table that has to be shifted.

Doing this takes a bit of "brute force." First, reach under the table and loosen the mounting bolts *(Fig. 2)*. Next, I use a block of wood and a hammer to "convince" the trunnion to move *(Fig. 3)*. (It might take a few good whacks.) Now, re-tighten the bolts and check if the blade and slot are parallel.

Be patient. You may not get it perfect the first time. In fact, tightening the bolts may move the trunnion back to where it started (almost like it has a memory of its own). If this is the case, "overshoot" the adjustment slightly before tightening the bolts.

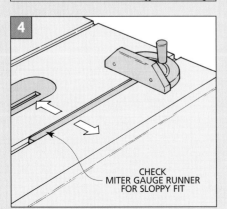

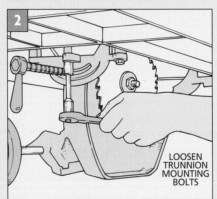

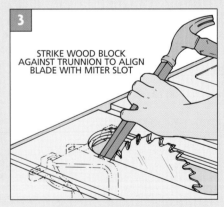

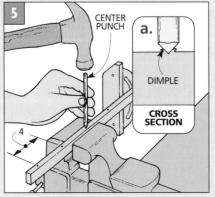

MITER GAUGE TUNE-UP

I learned long ago that most miter gauges can use a good tune-up to improve accuracy. When cutting miters, it's a necessity.

MODIFYING THE RUNNER. I start by checking how well the runner on the miter gauge fits the slot on the table saw *(Fig. 4)*. It's surprising how much side-to-side play there can be. And a loose fit can change the angle, ruining the accuracy of the setup.

To widen the runner, I use a center punch *(Fig. 5)*. The punch creates tiny dimples with raised areas. To fit the runner to the slot, dimple it in several spots about 4" apart.

Note: If the fit becomes too tight, simply file the dimples down a bit.

AUXILIARY FENCE. Another problem with miter gauges is that the face can be too small. It might not give adequate support as the workpiece is pushed through the saw blade.

For more support, I add an auxiliary fence *(Fig. 6)*. You can use solid wood or plywood, but it must be straight and of consistent thickness.

The auxiliary fence I use extends past the blade. This way, it reduces chipout. And the kerf from the blade can help when lining up a cut. One caution: if the face of the fence is angled away from the blade, the cut-off piece will be trapped and may kick back.

SANDPAPER. With miters, the piece can slide along the angled fence slightly as the cut is being made. This prevents a clean, square cut. To help secure the piece, I attach adhesive-backed sandpaper to the fence to "grab" the piece *(Fig. 6)*. Make sure the strip is long enough that the workpiece doesn't rock if it extends past the sandpaper.

STOP BLOCK. I also secure the workpiece with a stop block *(Fig. 7)*. For the first miter, I use the square end of the block. For the second miter, I flip the block around. This end is mitered to 45°, so it cradles the mitered end of the piece and protects the tip of the miter *(Fig. 7)*. A notch in the edge prevents sawdust from building up *(Fig. 7a)*.

SETTING THE MITER GAUGE

After the miter gauge is tuned up, I set the angle. Unfortunately, this can involve quite a bit of trial and error.

SET ANGLE. To minimize any hassle, I don't use the markings on the gauge to set the angle — the lines are too thick.

Instead, I use an adjustable triangle that has hairline markings *(Fig. 8)*. (They're available at art supply stores.) When using an adjustable triangle, be sure it's not resting against the teeth on the blade. This can change the angle enough that the joints won't be tight.

CHECK ANGLE. After the angle is set, don't assume that it's perfect. Test it by mitering a couple of scraps, dry-assembling them, and checking the corner with a try square *(Fig. 9)*.

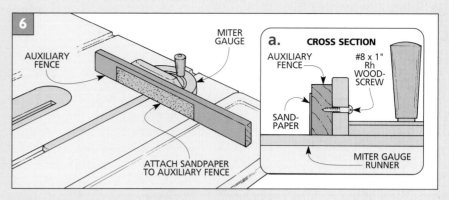

6 AUXILIARY FENCE MITER GAUGE

a. CROSS SECTION
AUXILIARY FENCE   #8 x 1" Rh WOOD-SCREW
SAND-PAPER
MITER GAUGE RUNNER

ATTACH SANDPAPER TO AUXILIARY FENCE

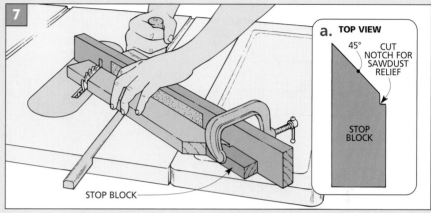

7 **a.** TOP VIEW
45° CUT NOTCH FOR SAWDUST RELIEF
STOP BLOCK

STOP BLOCK

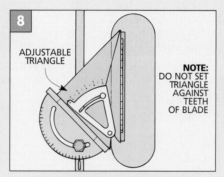

8 ADJUSTABLE TRIANGLE

NOTE: DO NOT SET TRIANGLE AGAINST TEETH OF BLADE

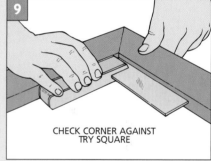

9

CHECK CORNER AGAINST TRY SQUARE

Note: The wider the test piece, the easier it is to see any error.

ADJUSTING THE ANGLE. Once the miter gauge is close to 45°, it's very easy to over-adjust and end up with the opposite error. If the angle is just shy of being perfect, I "tweak" the miter gauge using a shim (see the Shop Tip below).

Once the miter gauge is set perfectly, you might want to build the jig shown on page 10 so you can skip the trial and error the next time.

SHOP TIP . . . . *Card Shim*

As you get closer to a perfect fit, the adjustments to the miter gauge need to be very small. To do this, I loosen one of the screws that holds the auxiliary fence in place. Then I slip a playing card (or business card) between the fence and the miter gauge before tightening the screw.

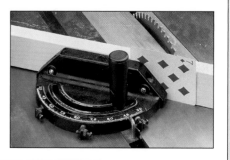

Desk Clock

This clock is the perfect size for your desk, dresser, or end table. And building it takes hardly any time. All you need are a few pieces rescued from the scrap bin and an inexpensive clock movement.

Almost every woodworker I know has at least one box full of small scraps he can't bear to part with. They're too small to be of use in a large piece of furniture, but too big to throw out. This project helps you find a home for at least a few of those scraps.

The best part of this Desk Clock is what you *don't* need to build it. You don't need a lot of wood or hardware. And you don't need a lot of time, either. But best of all, you don't need any special tools. Let me explain.

This clock uses an inexpensive battery-operated movement that fits into a hole in the front face. (Several sources for these movements are listed on page 126.) The problem is that the body of my clock movement was 2⅜" in diameter — much bigger than any drill bit I had in my shop.

I didn't want to buy a special bit to build the clock, so I designed my way around the problem. Instead of using a single, thick blank, the main body of this clock is built from three pieces that are glued together. This way, the hole for the movement can be cut with either a jig saw or a band saw.

SHADOW LINES. The shadow lines on the face and sides of the clock are another design consideration. The lines

on the side help hide the joint line where the front and back pieces of the body are glued together.

MOLDINGS. The cap and base of the clock feature a black trim that contrasts nicely with the mahogany. At first, you might think these are mitered pieces of ebony. But actually, it's just another piece of mahogany that's been painted.

DESIGN OPTION. I've also included an alternate design for the clock that is a bit taller and features tapered sides. The construction is almost identical to the clock shown above. You can find the details about building this option in the Designer's Notebook on page 19.

EXPLODED VIEW

OVERALL DIMENSIONS:
$4\frac{3}{4}$W x $2\frac{1}{4}$D x 6H

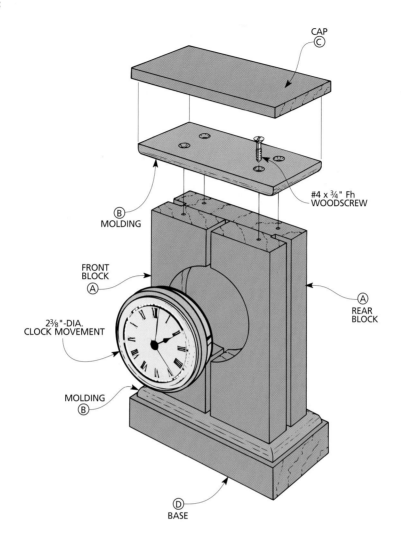

CAP
Ⓒ

#4 x ¾" Fh
WOODSCREW

Ⓑ
MOLDING

FRONT
BLOCK
Ⓐ

Ⓐ
REAR
BLOCK

$2\frac{3}{8}$"-DIA.
CLOCK MOVEMENT

MOLDING
Ⓑ

Ⓓ
BASE

MATERIALS LIST

WOOD
A Front/Rear Blocks (2) $\frac{3}{4}$ x 4 - $4\frac{1}{2}$
B Moldings (2) $\frac{1}{4}$ x 2 - $4\frac{1}{2}$
C Cap (1) $\frac{1}{4}$ x $2\frac{1}{4}$ - $4\frac{3}{4}$
D Base (1) $\frac{3}{4}$ x $2\frac{1}{4}$ - $4\frac{3}{4}$

HARDWARE SUPPLIES
(8) No. 4 x $\frac{3}{4}$" Fh woodscrews
(1) $2\frac{3}{8}$"-dia. quartz clock movement

CUTTING DIAGRAM

$\frac{3}{4}$ x $4\frac{1}{4}$ - 16   (.5 Bd. Ft.)

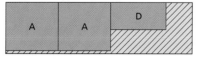

| A | A | D |

$\frac{1}{4}$ x $2\frac{1}{2}$ - 16   (.3 Sq. Ft.)

| C | B | B |

BODY

The body of the clock is built up from two thinner pieces of wood.

FRONT AND REAR BLOCKS. To build the body of the clock, begin by cutting the front block (A) and rear block (A) to length and width from ³⁄₄"-thick stock *(Fig. 1)*. (I used mahogany.)

Then on the face of the front block, lay out a circle that matches the diameter of the body of the clock movement you're using *(Fig. 1)*. (The one I used was 2³⁄₈" in diameter.)

Before cutting out the circle on the front block, I cut shallow rabbets on the sides of both blocks *(Fig. 1a)*. This way, when the blocks are glued together, these rabbets will form shadow lines that hide the glue joint.

HOLE FOR MOVEMENT. Now you're ready to create the hole for the clock movement. The first step is to rip the front block into two pieces *(Fig. 2)*. The goal here is to create a ¹⁄₈" gap that's centered on the front face.

This is a simple procedure — just rip the block down the center. But it's easy to be off a hair. So using the same setup, I made a second pass with the cutoff piece *(Fig. 3)*. This pass ensures that both pieces match perfectly.

With both pieces ripped to the same size, you can now cut the hole for the clock movement and sand it smooth *(Fig. 4)*. I did this on the band saw, but you could also use a jig saw.

ASSEMBLY. Now that there's a hole for the movement, it's time to put the pieces back together *(Fig. 4)*. To do this, simply glue the two halves of the front block to the rear block. Note that the two halves of the front block aren't glued to each other. Instead, the blocks are flush at the sides (as well as the top and bottom ends).

TOP & BOTTOM

The body of the clock is now complete. So next, I worked on the top and bottom of the clock. These are nearly identical. Each consists of a layer of molding and a rectangular cap or base *(Fig. 6)*.

MOLDING. To make the molding (B), I first cut two ¹⁄₄"-thick blanks to finished dimensions — ¹⁄₂" larger than the body of the clock in both width and length *(Fig. 5)*. (My molding blanks ended up 2" wide and 4¹⁄₂" long.)

The next thing you need to do is rout a ¹⁄₄" roundover around one face of each molding piece *(Fig. 5)*.

Note: The router table works best here. But it's a good idea to take a couple of precautions. Because these molding pieces are so small, I added an auxiliary fence to reduce the opening around the bit. Also, to reduce chipout, use a backing board and rout the ends of the molding first.

PAINT. Before going on, I painted the molding to match the trim around the clock movement. (It's much easier to do this before it's assembled.) I gave each piece a couple of coats of black paint, being careful to avoid the outside faces of the blocks (refer to the Exploded View on page 17). This would prevent a good glue bond when the cap and base are added later.

At this point, you can drill shank and pilot holes and screw the molding pieces to the main body of the clock *(Fig. 7)*. They're centered on the body both side-to-side and front-to-back.

CAP AND BASE. Now, all that's left is to add the cap and base.

The cap (C) and base (D) are nearly identical *(Fig. 6)*. They're ¹⁄₄" larger in

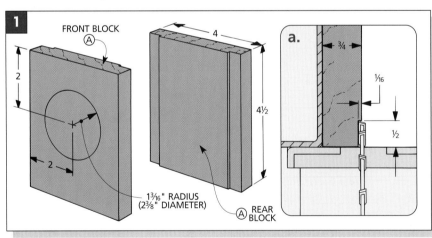

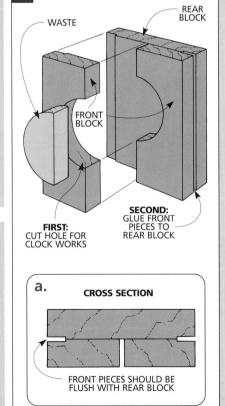

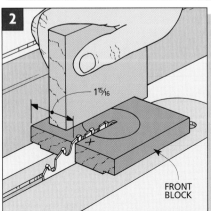

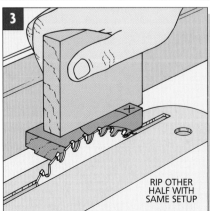

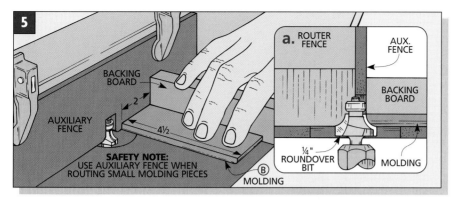

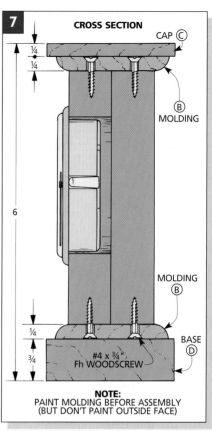

length and width than the molding. (Mine ended up 2¼" wide and 4¾" long.) But the pieces aren't the same thickness. If they were, the clock would look "top heavy." So the cap is cut from ¼"-thick stock, while the base is cut from ¾"-thick stock.

Now the cap and base pieces can be glued to the molding. You want to avoid squeeze-out here, so spread the glue thin and stay ½" away from the edges.

Finally, before pressing the clock movement into the hole, I applied a couple of light coats of tung oil to all the parts of the clock case. ■

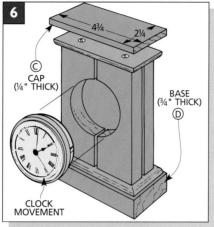

DESIGNER'S NOTEBOOK

This version of the clock is taller, tapered, and broader at the base.

CONSTRUCTION NOTES:

■ The first parts of construction are the same. The front and back blocks are cut to size and the opening for the clock is created. Then the front and back blocks are glued together *(Fig. 1)*.

■ When the glue has dried, lay out and cut the tapers on the sides *(Fig. 1)*.

■ Now you can cut a kerf centered on the thickness of each side *(Fig. 2)*.

■ Next, rout a ⅛" chamfer on each of the long edges of the case.

■ The base (D) and bottom molding (E) are made the same as before, but they are slightly longer (see Materials List).

TAPERED CLOCK

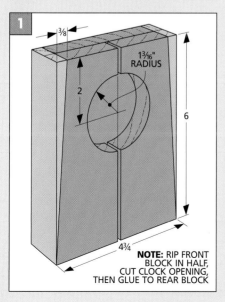

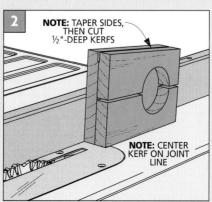

MATERIALS LIST

CHANGED PARTS

A	Front/Rear Blocks (2)	¾ x 4¾ - 6
B	Top Molding (1)	¼ x 2 - 4½
D	Base (1)	¾ x 2¼ - 5½

NEW PARTS

E	Bottom Molding (1)	¼ x 2 - 5¼

Maple Mirror

Look as closely as you like — the cherry accents in this Maple Mirror fit their openings perfectly. The secret is in the construction of the top rail. It guarantees you won't see any gaps.

What I really like about this mirror are the five square cutouts along the top rail of the frame. No big surprise here. These recessed accents are what catch your eye as soon as you look at the mirror.

But these details are kind of deceptive. They look simple (and they are). But creating them requires quite a few steps (none of them difficult).

CUTOUTS. I wanted to use a contrasting wood so the squares would stand out even more. But instead of trying to cut inlays to fit into a square perfectly, I just cut squares in a piece so the cherry shows through from behind.

Here's how I did it. The first step was to cut the squares in a piece of $\frac{1}{4}$"-thick hard maple. Then, to create the contrast, I inlaid a piece of cherry into a second maple piece that was $\frac{1}{2}$" thick. When the two pieces of maple were glued together, the cherry inlay was visible through the cutouts.

There's another thing to keep in mind when creating these square accents. Because they're identical, they have to be cut accurately. So you have to work carefully to make sure each edge of the opening is clean and square and that all five cutouts line up in a straight line. This isn't hard to do, either.

JIG. To make sure all the accent squares align and that their edges are crisp and square, I used a simple jig made from some pieces of scrap (refer to the Shop Jig article on page 23).

The jig serves two purposes. First, it's used to lay out the squares. Then later it serves as a guide for the chisel as you clean up the edges.

MORTISE AND TENON. The frame is joined with mortise and tenon joints. This is a strong joint that helps the frame support the weight of the mirror. If you haven't cut mortise and tenon joints before, there's an article on page 47 that will walk you through it.

EXPLODED VIEW

OVERALL DIMENSIONS:
37½"W x 2D x 26H

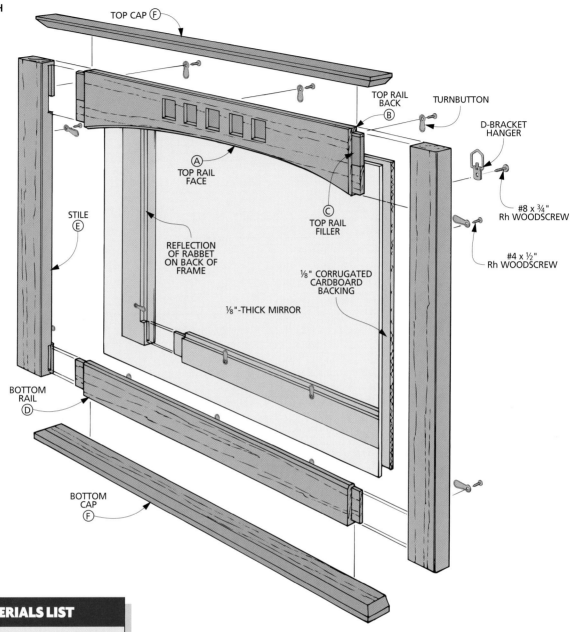

TOP CAP (F)

TOP RAIL BACK (B)

TURNBUTTON

D-BRACKET HANGER

TOP RAIL FACE (A)

STILE (E)

REFLECTION OF RABBET ON BACK OF FRAME

TOP RAIL FILLER (C)

⅛" CORRUGATED CARDBOARD BACKING

⅛"-THICK MIRROR

#8 x ¾" Rh WOODSCREW

#4 x ½" Rh WOODSCREW

BOTTOM RAIL (D)

BOTTOM CAP (F)

MATERIALS LIST

WOOD

A	Top Rail Face (1)	¼ x 4¼ - 32½
B	Top Rail Back (1)	½ x 4¼ - 32½
C	Top Rail Filler (1)	½ x 1¾ - 32½
D	Bottom Rail (1)	¾ x 2½ - 32½
E	Stiles (2)	1 x 2½ - 24½
F	Top/Bottom Caps (2)	¾ x 2 - 37½

HARDWARE SUPPLIES

(10) No. 4 x ½" Rh woodscrews
(2) No. 8 x ¾" Rh woodscrews
(2) D-bracket hangers
(10) Turnbuttons
(1) Picture wire (5 feet)
(1) ⅛"-thick mirror, 19⅞" x 31⅛"
(1) ⅛" cardboard backing, 19⅞" x 31⅛"

CUTTING DIAGRAM

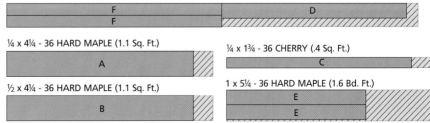

¾ x 4½ - 72 HARD MAPLE (2.25 Bd. Ft.)

F
F

D

¼ x 4¼ - 36 HARD MAPLE (1.1 Sq. Ft.)

A

½ x 4¼ - 36 HARD MAPLE (1.1 Sq. Ft.)

B

¼ x 1¾ - 36 CHERRY (.4 Sq. Ft.)

C

1 x 5¼ - 36 HARD MAPLE (1.6 Bd. Ft.)

E
E

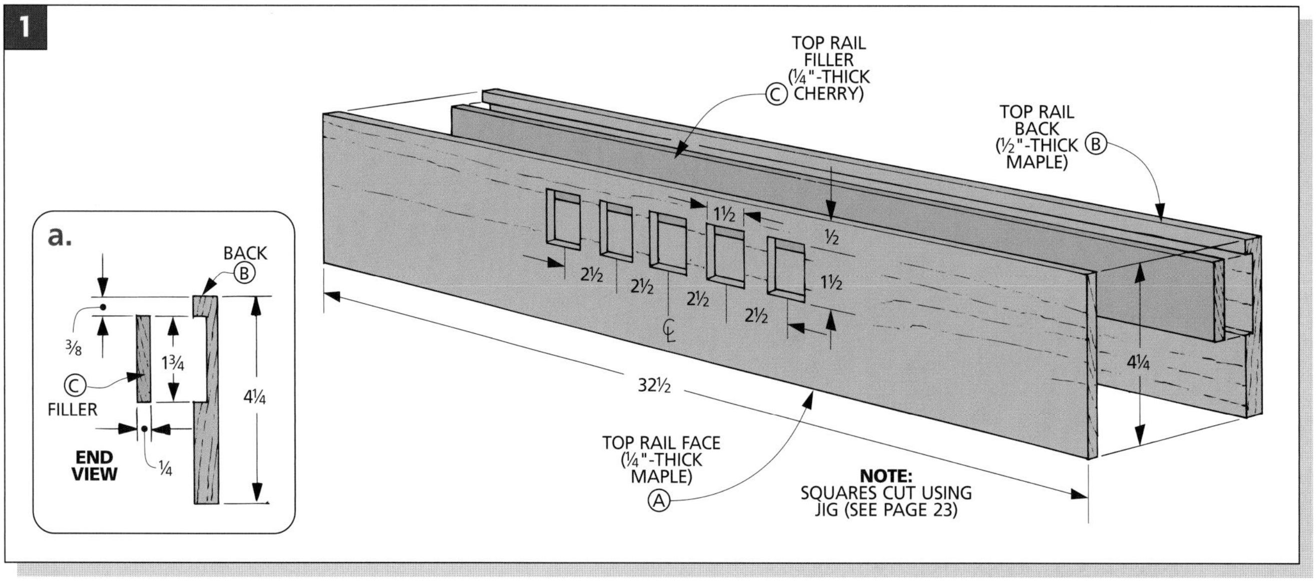
1
TOP RAIL FILLER (¼"-THICK CHERRY) C
TOP RAIL BACK (½"-THICK MAPLE) B
1½
½
1½
2½
2½
2½
2½
℄
32½
4¼
TOP RAIL FACE (¼"-THICK MAPLE) A
NOTE: SQUARES CUT USING JIG (SEE PAGE 23)
a.
BACK B
3/8
1¾
C FILLER
4¼
¼
END VIEW

FRAME

With most frames, I work on the rails and stiles all at once. But the top rail is the trickiest part of the mirror, so I started with it first.

TOP RAIL. What I wanted was a top rail with five shallow, square cutouts and some cherry in the background of the cutouts for contrast. To accomplish this, I decided to build the rail in three layers: a $^1/_4$"-thick maple face, a $^1/_2$"-thick maple back, and a $^1/_4$"-thick cherry filler *(Fig. 1)*. Later, these three pieces will be glued together. But for now, I worked on just the face piece and its accent squares.

TOP RAIL FACE. The first thing to do with the top rail face (A) is to cut it to final size *(Fig. 1)*. Then I laid out the centerlines of each of the five squares *(Fig. 1)*. (The middle square is centered along the length of the piece.)

ACCENT SQUARES. The accent squares are $1^1/_2$" in height and width. To make these squares identical, I used a simple jig (see the Shop Jig article on the opposite page). It's basically just a board with a square opening and a lip. But instead of cutting out the square

DESIGNER'S NOTEBOOK

Spindles in the top rail turn a contemporary look traditional.

CONSTRUCTION NOTES:

- The first thing to do is to cut the upper and lower top rails (G) to size *(Fig. 1)*.
- To make sure the spindles will be straight up and down, clamp the upper and lower top rails together and lay out the hole locations across both pieces at the same time *(Fig. 1)*.
- Now drill the $^3/_8$"-dia. holes to accept the tenons on the spindles.
- Next, cut the spacers (H) to size and glue up the top rail assembly *(Fig. 1)*.
- The tenons are the same as on the Maple Mirror *(Fig. 2)*.
- Since the rail isn't arched, the rabbet for the mirror is the same on all four sides. Also note that the piece of mirror is smaller.

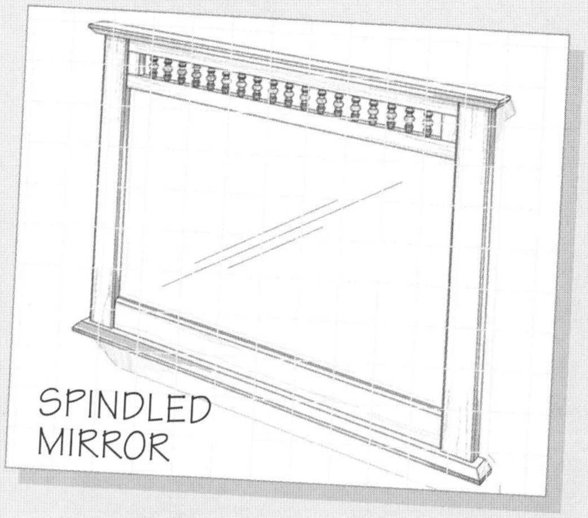
SPINDLED MIRROR

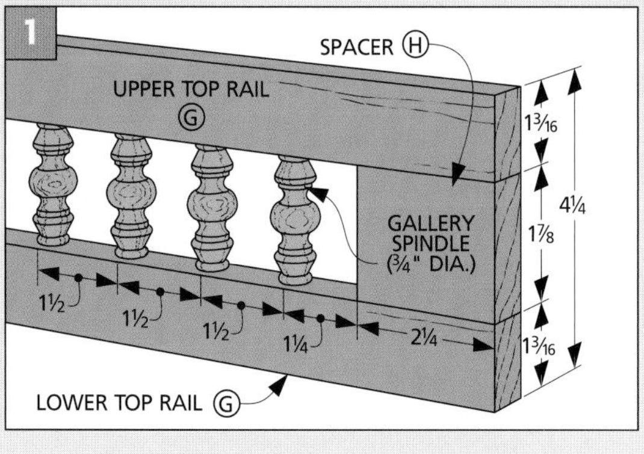
1
SPACER H
UPPER TOP RAIL G
1 3/16
4¼
GALLERY SPINDLE (¾" DIA.)
1 7/8
1½
1½
1½
1¼
2¼
1 3/16
LOWER TOP RAIL G

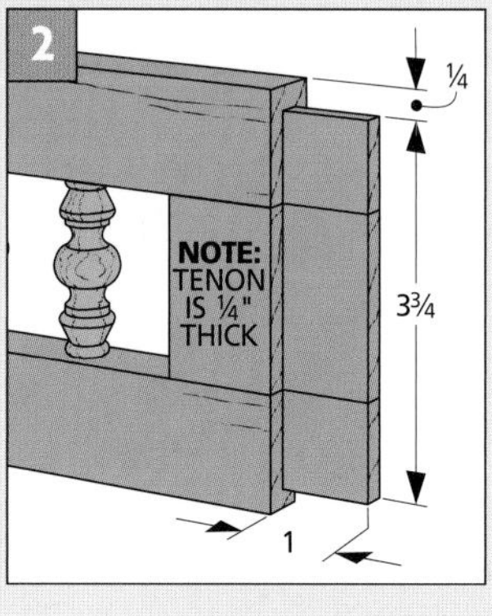
2
¼
NOTE: TENON IS ¼" THICK
3¾
1

MATERIALS LIST

NEW PARTS

G	Upr./Lwr. Top Rails (2)	$^3/_4$ x $1^3/_{16}$ - $32^1/_2$
H	Spacers (2)	$^3/_4$ x $1^7/_8$ - $2^1/_4$

HARDWARE SUPPLIES

(18) $^3/_4$" -dia. gallery spindles, $1^7/_8$" long
(1) $^1/_8$" mirror, $18^3/_8$" x $31^1/_8$"
(1) $^1/_8$" cardboard backing, $18^3/_8$" x $31^1/_8$"

Note: Do not need parts A, B, C.

opening, I created the jig by gluing five separate pieces together.

Once the jig is built, creating the squares is a simple three-step process, as shown in the Shop Jig article below.

TOP RAIL BACK AND FILLER. With the accent squares completed, I set the face piece aside and worked on the top rail back (B). This piece is cut from 1/2"-thick stock, and it's the same size as the face piece (41/4" x 321/2") *(Fig. 1)*.

Next, I cut a wide, 1/4"-deep groove in the front face of the back (B) *(Fig. 1a)*. This groove is filled by the 1/4"-thick cherry top rail filler (C).

TOP RAIL GLUE-UP. After the filler strip is glued in place, the face and back pieces can be glued together *(Fig. 2)*.

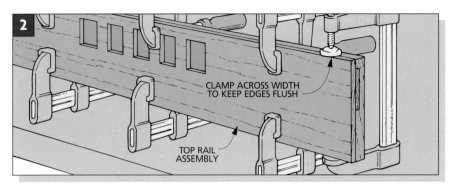

The trick here is making sure the two pieces end up flush as you're gluing them together — especially since the pieces have already been cut to finished size. To help with this, I placed a clamp across the width of the rail at each end.

At this point, the top rail still needs tenons. But I prefer to cut tenons *after* the mortises are complete. (It's easier to trim a tenon to fit than to work inside a mortise.) So I set the top rail aside to work on the other three frame pieces.

SHOP JIG .... *Layout & Chisel Guide*

Creating the square accents in the top rail of the mirror is easy with this simple jig. The jig does two things. It helps when initially laying out the squares on the rail, and then it guides the chisel as you cut the opening to its final shape *(Steps 1 and 3 below)*.

The jig is simply a board with a square opening in it. A lip glued to one edge helps to position the jig on the workpiece so the squares align (see detail 'a' in drawing).

To create this jig, I decided it would be easier to glue four scrap pieces together to create a perfect 11/2"-square opening (see drawing). Then I glued the lip to the top edge.

Before using the jig, you'll need to mark the center of the opening. This mark helps you align the jig on the top face rail *(Step 1)*. To do this, mark the center of the opening on the face of the jig, then transfer the mark to the edge.

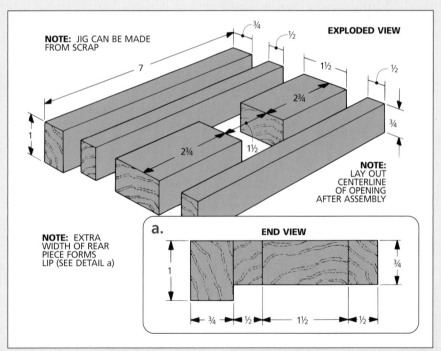

NOTE: JIG CAN BE MADE FROM SCRAP

EXPLODED VIEW

NOTE: EXTRA WIDTH OF REAR PIECE FORMS LIP (SEE DETAIL a)

NOTE: LAY OUT CENTERLINE OF OPENING AFTER ASSEMBLY

a. END VIEW

1 First, mark the centers of the squares (refer to Fig. 1 on page 22). Then using the jig, lay out the squares.

2 Now remove most of the waste for each square by drilling overlapping holes with a Forstner bit.

3 Clamp the layout jig back over the squares and carefully remove the rest of the waste with a sharp chisel.

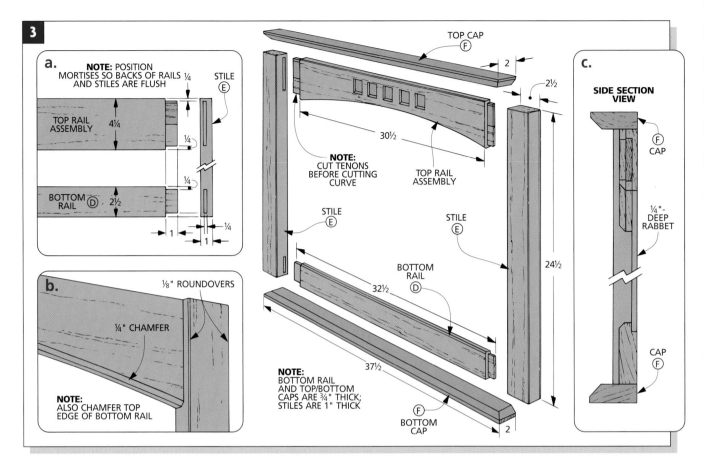

3

a. NOTE: POSITION MORTISES SO BACKS OF RAILS AND STILES ARE FLUSH

STILE (E)

TOP RAIL ASSEMBLY — 4¼

¼

¼

BOTTOM RAIL (D) — 2½

1   ¼   1

b. ⅛" ROUNDOVERS

¼" CHAMFER

NOTE: ALSO CHAMFER TOP EDGE OF BOTTOM RAIL

TOP CAP (F)

2

2½

2½

30½

NOTE: CUT TENONS BEFORE CUTTING CURVE

TOP RAIL ASSEMBLY

STILE (E)

STILE (E)

BOTTOM RAIL (D)

32½

24½

37½

NOTE: BOTTOM RAIL AND TOP/BOTTOM CAPS ARE ¾" THICK; STILES ARE 1" THICK

BOTTOM CAP (F)

2

c. SIDE SECTION VIEW

F CAP

¼"- DEEP RABBET

CAP F

BOTTOM RAIL AND STILES. The bottom rail (D) is cut from ³⁄₄"-thick stock and is quite a bit narrower than the top rail (2¹⁄₂" x 32¹⁄₂"). The stiles (E), on the other hand, are cut from 1"-thick stock (2¹⁄₂" x 24¹⁄₂"). This creates a shoulder between the front faces of the stiles and the rails *(Fig. 3b)*.

MORTISES AND TENONS. With the pieces cut to size, I cut the mortises in the stiles and the tenons on the rails *(Fig. 3a)*. The thing to keep in mind

here is that because the stiles are thicker than the rails, the mortises are offset slightly. And because they aren't centered, you need to lay them out so the pieces "mirror" each other. (For more on mortise and tenon joints, see the Joinery article on page 47.)

TOP RAIL RABBET. After the mortise and tenon joints have been cut, I set the bottom rail and the stiles aside for a moment and turned my attention to creating a rabbet on the back inside edge of

the top rail. This rabbet will hold the mirror, and it's quite wide (1⁷⁄₈") so that after the curve is cut next, the rabbet will still be ³⁄₈" wide at the top of the curve. (To complete the rabbet, the other three pieces will be routed after the frame is assembled later.)

To cut this rabbet, I stood the piece on edge and made a couple of passes over the table saw blade, moving the fence between passes *(Fig. 4)*. What you want is a rabbet that will match the

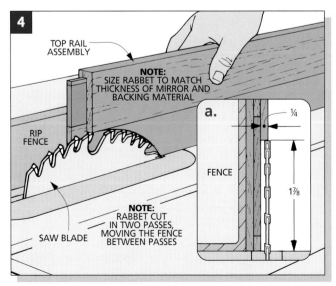

4

TOP RAIL ASSEMBLY

NOTE: SIZE RABBET TO MATCH THICKNESS OF MIRROR AND BACKING MATERIAL

RIP FENCE

a.

¼

FENCE

1⁷⁄₈

NOTE: RABBET CUT IN TWO PASSES, MOVING THE FENCE BETWEEN PASSES

SAW BLADE

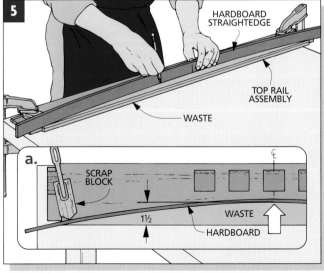

5

HARDBOARD STRAIGHTEDGE

TOP RAIL ASSEMBLY

WASTE

a.

SCRAP BLOCK

1½

WASTE

HARDBOARD

of a $1/8$"-thick mirror plus a piece of backing material (a piece of $1/8$"-thick cardboard). So in my case, the rabbet was $1/4$" deep.

TOP RAIL CURVE. The next thing to do is to cut the gentle curve along the bottom edge of the top rail *(Fig. 3)*. To lay out this curve, I clamped a scrap block at each end of the rail so I could push a strip of hardboard against them and draw the curve *(Fig. 5)*. Then I cut it out on the band saw, staying about $1/16$" from the layout line. And finally, I sanded up to the line with a drum sander chucked up in the drill press.

EDGE TREATMENT. After the curve is cut in the top rail, there are two more things to do before the frame can be assembled. First, I routed $1/4$" chamfers along the inside edges of the top and bottom rails *(Fig. 3b)*. Then I routed $1/8$" roundovers along the front edges of the stiles to soften the corners.

MIRROR FRAME ASSEMBLY. Now that all the pieces are complete, the frame can be glued together.

CAP MOLDING & MIRROR

After the frame was assembled, the next thing I worked on was completing the rabbet on the back. This rabbet will hold the mirror and backing.

COMPLETE RABBET. The rabbet on the top rail has already been cut with the table saw. But to complete the $3/8$"-wide rabbet on the bottom rail and the two stiles, I used a hand-held router and a rabbet bit *(Fig. 6)*. Set the bit to match the depth of the rabbet on the top rail — $1/4$" in my case (refer to *Fig. 4*).

Safety Note: When routing a rabbet with a hand-held router on the inside

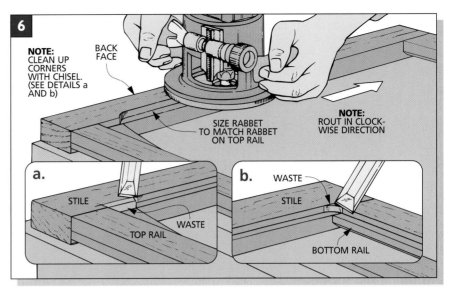

6

NOTE: CLEAN UP CORNERS WITH CHISEL. (SEE DETAILS a AND b)

BACK FACE

NOTE: ROUT IN CLOCK-WISE DIRECTION

SIZE RABBET TO MATCH RABBET ON TOP RAIL

a.

STILE

TOP RAIL

WASTE

b.

WASTE

STILE

BOTTOM RAIL

edge of a frame, be sure to move the router clockwise and take light passes to reduce chipout *(Fig. 6)*.

The rabbet bit will remove most of the material, but the four corners will need to be cleaned up. First of all, at the top corners the rabbet has to be "extended" so it's flush with the rabbets on the sides *(Fig. 6a)*. To do this, I laid out the final corner of the rabbet with a straightedge and scored it with a utility knife. Then I pared away the waste carefully with a sharp chisel.

The rabbet bit can't cut a square corner at the bottom either. So when the top corners are complete, the bottom corners need to be squared up in the same fashion *(Fig. 6b)*.

ADD CAP MOLDING. The last step before installing the mirror is to add a piece of cap molding to the top and bottom of the frame *(Fig. 3)*.

The chamfered molding on the top and bottom is easy to make since the

pieces are identical. And there's a trick you can use to minimize chipout on the ends. Instead of cutting these pieces to final size and then routing the chamfer, start with a single oversized blank ($4^{1}/_{2}$" x $37^{1}/_{2}$"). Then rout a chamfer on each edge of the blank *(Fig. 7)*.

Note: I didn't attempt the chamfer in one pass — that would just be asking for chipout. Instead, I routed it in multiple passes, raising the bit between passes until there was a $1/4$" shoulder left above the chamfer *(Fig. 7a)*. And when routing, it's best to start with the ends. This way, any chipout on the ends will be removed when you rout the long edges of the blank.

Once the chamfers are routed, the top and bottom caps (F) can be ripped from the blank to final width *(Figs. 8 and 8a)*. Then they can be glued to the frame. These caps are centered side-to-side. And they're flush with the back of the frame *(Fig. 3c)*.

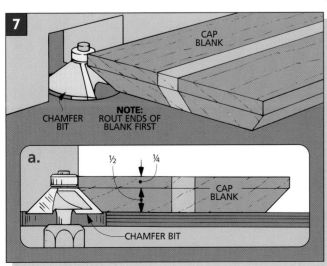

7

CAP BLANK

CHAMFER BIT

NOTE: ROUT ENDS OF BLANK FIRST

a.

$1/2$ $1/4$

CAP BLANK

CHAMFER BIT

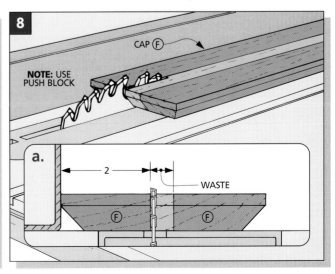

8

CAP (F)

NOTE: USE PUSH BLOCK

a.

2

WASTE

(F)   (F)

APPLYING A FINISH. At this point, the mirror is complete. But before adding the mirror and the hardware for hanging the mirror, I carefully sanded the frame and applied a finish.

This is a perfect project for a wipe-on finish. Getting the finish into the accent squares — and wiping it out — is easy. To reach into the corners of the squares, just use the tip of a rolled-up rag. (You can either use three or more coats of an oil finish or a couple of coats of a thinned-down varnish.)

INSTALLATION. Once the finish has dried, all that's left is to install the mirror and hang it on the wall *(Fig. 9)*. I used a $\frac{1}{8}$"-thick mirror. To make sure it went into the frame easily, I had it cut $\frac{1}{8}$" smaller than the height and width of the rabbeted opening in the back. (My mirror ended up $19\frac{7}{8}$" x $31\frac{1}{8}$".)

Note: It's a good idea to wait to order the mirror until after the frame and rabbet are complete.

With the mirror cut to size, I used it as a pattern to lay out and cut a backing from a piece of cardboard *(Fig. 9)*. (Mine was about $\frac{1}{8}$" thick.) The cardboard provides a "pad" for the back of the mirror and protects the silver coating on the back from scratches.

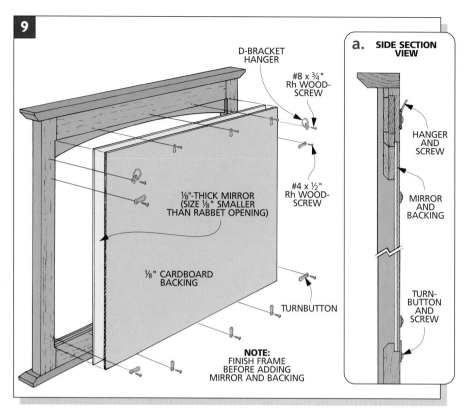

9

D-BRACKET HANGER

#8 x $\frac{3}{4}$" Rh WOOD-SCREW

$\frac{1}{8}$"-THICK MIRROR (SIZE $\frac{1}{8}$" SMALLER THAN RABBET OPENING)

#4 x $\frac{1}{2}$" Rh WOOD-SCREW

$\frac{1}{8}$" CARDBOARD BACKING

TURNBUTTON

NOTE:
FINISH FRAME BEFORE ADDING MIRROR AND BACKING

a. SIDE SECTION VIEW

HANGER AND SCREW

MIRROR AND BACKING

TURN-BUTTON AND SCREW

Then I placed the mirror and the cardboard backing in the frame. Ten turnbuttons around the back of the frame keep everything secure *(Fig. 9)*.

All that remains now is to hang the mirror. Since it's heavy, I took extra care to make sure it was hung securely (see the Technique box below).

TECHNIQUE . . . . *Hanging a Frame*

When the frame is assembled and the mirror is installed, you'll find out that a mirror this size is not light. So when hanging it on a wall, you want to make sure it has plenty of support. The place to start is with the hangers.

HANGERS. I screwed a "D-bracket" hanger to the back of each stile *(Fig. 1)*. (These hangers can be found at most hardware stores.) Then a length of wire is added between the hangers.

Note: You'll want the wire at least a foot longer than the distance between the hangers. You can cut off any extra after it's in place.

KNOT. To add the wire, I used a special knot I learned from a friend of mine who had worked in a framing shop.

To create this knot, I feed the wire through the bracket and back around behind itself *(Fig. 1)*. Then it is fed through the bracket again and out

through the loop. The remaining wire can be wrapped around itself *(Fig. 2)*.

Another tip I learned was to wrap some masking tape around the ends of the wire so it won't scratch the wall.

HANGING. After the wire has been attached to the brackets, the frame can be hung on the wall. Here, I would caution you to hang the mirror on two points — preferably with screws driven into studs (see photo below).

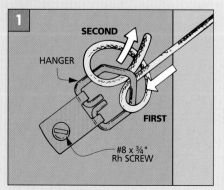

1

SECOND

HANGER

FIRST

#8 x $\frac{3}{4}$" Rh SCREW

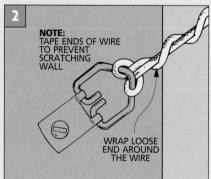

2

NOTE:
TAPE ENDS OF WIRE TO PREVENT SCRATCHING WALL

WRAP LOOSE END AROUND THE WIRE

Picture Frame Moldings

With just a handful of regular router bits, you can create these eye-catching moldings for your frames. Customize them by mixing different types of wood, or adding painted highlights or inlays.

Making a picture frame ought to be one of the easiest projects in woodworking. It's just four strips of wood joined with miters. But if something is worth framing, it deserves something a little more attractive than just four strips of wood.

An easy way to dress up a frame is by routing profiles on the pieces. And using just eight standard router bits, I quickly came up with the ten molding profiles on the following pages. (A few are shown in the photo above.)

CUTTING THE PROFILES. For each of the moldings, the first step is to cut the stock to initial size. This step is critical.

The strips must be straight and of uniform width and thickness. If not, when the profiles are routed there will be uneven contours, and the profiles won't match at the mitered corners.

As for length, I usually add a few inches to allow for the snipe that can occur at the beginning and end of a cut.

RABBETS. All of the profiles include a rabbet on the back side to hold the picture. This rabbet should be at least ¼" deep to allow for a piece of glass (usually ³⁄₃₂" thick), a mat (if needed), the photo or print itself, and the backing material. (If you need a deeper rabbet for an oil painting or a piece of needle-

point that's mounted to a stretcher frame, see the Shop Tip on page 29.)

GROOVES AND INLAYS. One more tip. Some of the profiles have inlay strips set into grooves. To get a tight fit, cut the groove as normal, but cut the strip just a tiny bit wider than the groove. Then very gently taper the sides of the strip with one or two passes with a block plane or a hand scraper.

The tapered sides of the strip will wedge tight against the edges of the groove. Just don't make it too tight or it will split the molding. And, you want it to "bottom out" in the groove so it doesn't have "waves."

BASIC FRAME

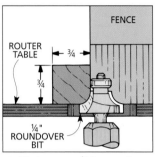

This frame has a simple, uncluttered look. The molding begins as a strip of stock $3/4$" square.

The profile is made by rounding over two edges with a $1/4$" roundover bit *(Steps 1 and 2)*. Then a rabbet is cut to hold the picture and glass. To prevent chipout, cut the rabbet in two passes. First, make a backwards cut only $1/16$" wide *(Step 3)*. Then make a full cut $1/4$" wide to complete the rabbet *(Step 4)*.

INLAY FRAME. I also made a wider version with two grooves *(Steps 5 and 6)* to hold contrasting wood inlays.

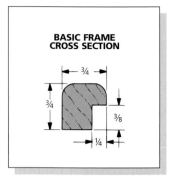

BASIC FRAME CROSS SECTION

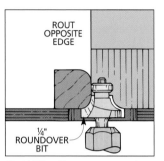

1 First, use a $1/4$" roundover bit to round over one edge on the front face of each frame piece.

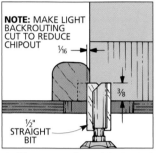

2 With the same setup, rotate each piece 90° and rout a $1/4$" roundover on the other front corner.

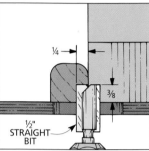

3 To create the rabbet, start by making a light pass from left to right. This will help reduce chipout.

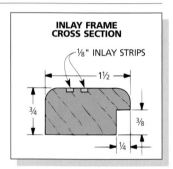

4 To complete the rabbet, reposition the fence, then rout from right to left as with a normal cut.

INLAY FRAME

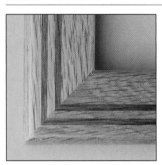

This wider frame is shaped as in Steps 1-4 above. Then two shallow grooves are cut for contrasting inlay strips.

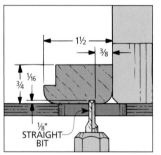

5 After rounding the edges and cutting the rabbet, set a $1/8$" straight bit $1/16$" above the table. Rout the first groove.

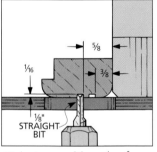

6 Just reposition the fence farther from the bit to cut the second groove. Then add the inlay strips.

INLAY FRAME CROSS SECTION

SHOP TIP .... Grout Trowel Push Block

Even the largest frame piece in this article is less than 2" wide. Trying to guide a piece this narrow past a spinning router bit puts my fingers too close to the bit for comfort. So what I do is use a grout trowel as a push block (see drawing).

The trowel has a rubber bottom and is usually used to smooth grout when installing ceramic tile. The rubber allows you to get a good grip on the curves of the moldings. (You can find trowels at hardware stores and home centers.)

Besides keeping your fingers safely away from the bit, there's another reason using a trowel is a good idea. It helps you keep uniform pressure on the strips so the profiles are consistent. And that's key to having the profile match at each corner.

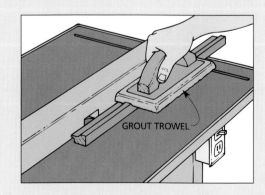

The thickness of the stock used on the frames limits the depth of the rabbets you can cut for the glass, photos, and mats. The 3/4"-thick stock I used is fine for photos with a mat, but if you plan on framing a painting or needlework, you'll need a deeper rabbet.

To accommodate these thicker items, you can create a deeper rabbet by building a second frame (without a rabbet) and screwing it to the back of the main frame. I use the same type of wood for both the front and back frames so the back frame blends in better.

When building the back frame, I cut the pieces to width and length so the back frame is inset 1/4" from all the edges of the main frame. I also taper the outside edges of the back frame in towards the center. This dresses the frame up, plus it looks better if someone should look at the frame from the side.

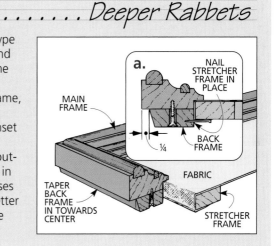

RAISED FIELD FRAME

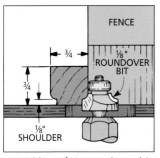

This frame starts out as a square strip. First, round over both edges leaving a shoulder *(Step 1)*. Then round over the shoulders with another pass on both edges *(Steps 2 and 3)*. Finally, rout the rabbet for the photo *(Step 4)*.

VENEER. You can dress up the raised field by adding a veneer to one edge of the strip. Then round the edges leaving a 1/16" shoulder *(Step 1 at bottom of page)*. You don't need to make the second roundover pass on this version.

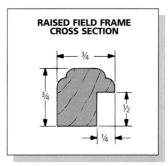

RAISED FIELD FRAME CROSS SECTION

1 With an 1/8" roundover bit, rout a profile on two edges, leaving a 1/8" shoulder. This "raises" the field.

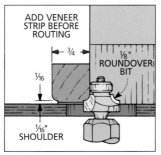

2 Now with the bearing of the bit against the raised field, round over a shoulder with the same setup.

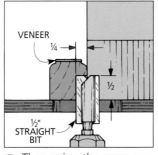

3 Next, flip the workpiece end for end and repeat the procedure to round over the remaining shoulder.

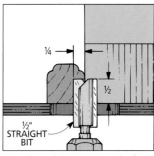

4 The rabbet is cut as before, by making a light back-routing cut first, then making a full depth pass.

VENEERED RAISED FIELD FRAME

Accent the raised field by veneering before routing. (This is a walnut burl veneer.) Note the shallower shoulder.

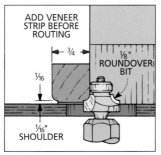

1 After applying the veneer, just round over the edges as before, but this time just leave a 1/16" shoulder.

2 Then using the same procedure as before, rout the rabbet in the back edge to accept the glass and photo.

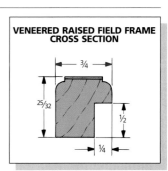

VENEERED RAISED FIELD FRAME CROSS SECTION

CONTEMPORARY FRAME

By gluing several strips together, you can create all types of variations. The round edges of this frame create a smooth, contemporary look. A coved piece widens the frame. This makes it nicer for larger prints or artwork.

First, round over two edges of the first strip (A) *(Step 1)*. Then cut a rabbet to accept the second strip (B) *(Step 2)*.

To make the wide cove in the second strip, take a series of cuts with a core box bit *(Step 3)*. Then rout a rabbet *(Step 4)*.

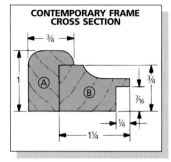

CONTEMPORARY FRAME
CROSS SECTION

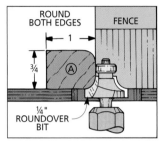 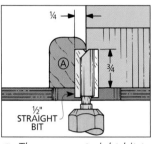 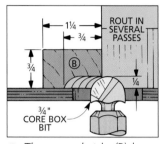 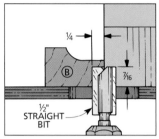

1 *The first step is to rout ¼" roundovers on the top edge of the first strip (A).*

2 *Then use a straight bit to cut a ¾" rabbet that will accept the second strip.*

3 *The second strip (B) has a wide cove cut in several passes with a core box bit.*

4 *Complete the second strip by cutting the rabbet to accept the artwork.*

MULTIPLE MOLDING FRAME

The outside piece (A) of this frame starts with the same profile shown at the top of this page. The edges are rounded and a rabbet is cut to accept a second piece (B) *(Step 1)*.

To make the second piece, round over the front corner *(Step 2)*. Then cut a groove to accept a third strip *(Step 3)*.

The third strip (C) is cut extra wide so it's easier to handle *(Step 4)*. For variations, try a contrasting wood or paint it.

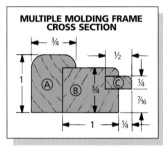

MULTIPLE MOLDING FRAME
CROSS SECTION

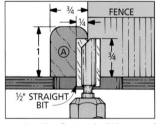 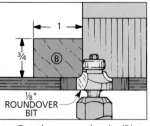 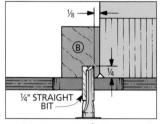 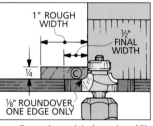

1 *On the first strip (A), round the edges as in Step 1 above and cut rabbet.*

2 *Cut the second strip (B) to fit the depth of the rabbet. Round over one edge.*

3 *Next, rout a ¼" groove in the second strip to accept the third strip.*

4 *Cut the third strip (C), round over one edge, and then trim to width.*

SHOP TIP .... *Installing Brads*

One way to mount the glass, picture, and mat in a frame is to use ½" brads behind the backing. If you make a lot of frames, you might consider buying a special tool called a brad point nailer to press the brads in place. (See page 126 for sources.)

Another (cheaper) method is to use a pair of adjustable pliers (see drawing). Just set the opening width of the pliers to fit around the frame and brad, and squeeze the brad into place. (You may need to adjust the pliers so the jaws stay parallel as the brad is driven into the frame.) To prevent marring the frame, place a piece of cardboard on the outside edge of the frame.

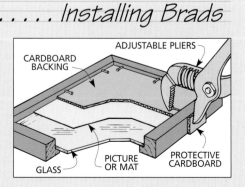

STEPPED PROFILE FRAME

Most frame profiles taper down to the picture on the inside. This one steps up from the outside edge, like a shadow box.

Both strips have an ogee profile cut with a core box bit and a roundover bit *(Steps 1, 2, 5, and 6)*. To accept the second piece (B), a groove is cut in the first piece (A) *(Step 3)*, then its outside edge is cut off to create a rabbet *(Step 4)*.

To complete the second piece, round over the top edge *(Step 7)*. Finally, trim the strip to width *(Step 8)*.

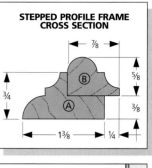
STEPPED PROFILE FRAME CROSS SECTION

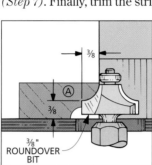

1 First, cut a $1/2$" flute along the outside edge of the first strip (A).

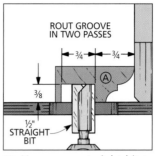

2 Then use a $3/8$" roundover bit to create an ogee profile. Note the shoulder.

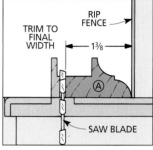

3 Now use a straight bit to rout a groove to hold the second strip (B).

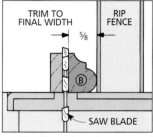

4 Cutting off the edge of the groove creates a rabbet on the inside edge.

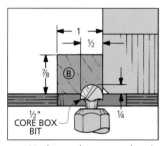

5 Work on the second strip (B) is similar to that on the first strip. However, the cuts are somewhat smaller.

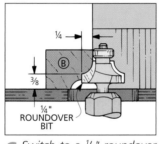

6 Switch to a $1/4$" roundover bit $3/8$" above the table. Routing the roundover creates an ogee profile.

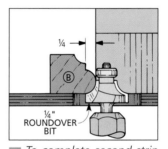

7 To complete second strip (B), lower the bit so it's flush with the table and round over the top edge of the strip.

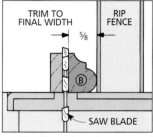

8 Finally, trim the second strip to width and glue it into the rabbet (refer to Cross Section above).

COVE INLAY FRAME

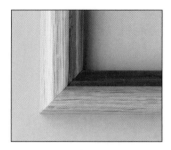

Even on small frames you can add a second strip that's painted or is made from a contrasting wood. In this case, the first strip (A) is only $1/2$" wide *(Step 1)*. To add the second strip (B), a groove is routed with a $1/4$" straight bit *(Step 2)*.

The second strip starts out $1/4$" thick by about 1" wide. Then after routing a cove *(Step 3)*, you can trim this strip to width *(Step 4)*, and glue it into the groove in the first strip.

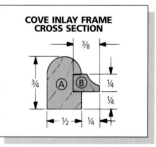
COVE INLAY FRAME CROSS SECTION

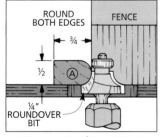

1 First, cut a $1/2$"-wide strip (A) and rout $1/4$" roundovers on both top edges.

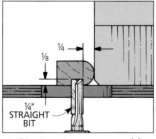

2 Next, cut a groove with a $1/4$" straight bit to hold the cove inlay strip.

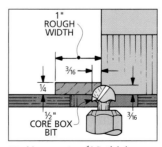

3 Now cut a $1/4$"-thick cove inlay strip (B) and cut a cove with a $1/16$" shoulder.

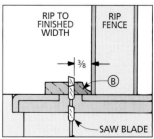

4 Rip the cove inlay strip $3/8$" wide and glue it in the groove to create a rabbet.

BEADED INLAY FRAME

This molding is relatively easy to make and yields a dramatic frame. It starts out as a strip of cherry (A). Then two grooves are routed for inlay strips (B, C) *(Steps 1 and 2)*. After the grooves are routed, two core box bits of different sizes are used to complete the profile *(Steps 3 and 4)*.

Next, cut a rabbet to hold the artwork and glass *(Step 5)*. Then cut two strips (I used walnut), round the edges, and cut them off to form the half-round inlay strips *(Steps 6, 7, and 8)*.

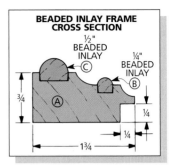

BEADED INLAY FRAME CROSS SECTION

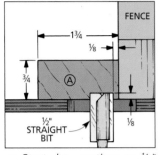

1 *Start by routing a ¹/₂" groove in the cherry strip (A) for a half-round inlay.*

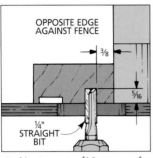

2 *Next, rout a ¹/₄" groove for the second inlay. Note that this groove is deeper.*

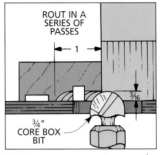

3 *Now you can cut a cove by making several passes with a core box bit.*

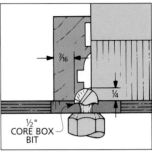

4 *To complete the profile, turn it on edge and rout a ¹/₂" cove ¹/₄" deep on the edge.*

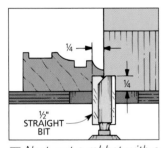

5 *Next, cut a rabbet with a straight bit to accept the picture and the glass.*

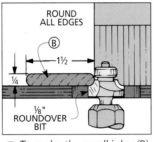

6 *To make the small inlay (B), cut a strip 1¹/₂" wide and round over the edges.*

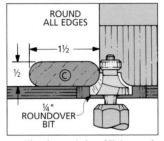

7 *The large inlay (C) is made the same way using a ¹/₂"-thick blank and ¹/₄" bit.*

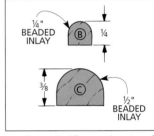

8 *Cut a half-round strip off each edge of blank. Then glue the strips in place.*

EDGE HIGHLIGHT FRAME

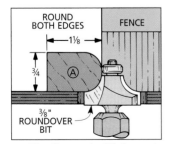

On this frame, I painted the inside strip (B) with gold leaf paint to highlight the inside edge.

The outside strip (A) is walnut. The edges are rounded over *(Step 1)*, and a rabbet holds the second strip *(Step 2)*.

For the second strip I used poplar (which accepts paint well). This strip is cut square to fit the rabbet on the first strip. Then a cove is cut on one corner *(Step 3)*. Finally, a rabbet is cut in it to hold the picture and glass *(Step 4)*.

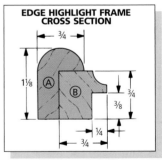

EDGE HIGHLIGHT FRAME CROSS SECTION

1 *The first strip (A) is made from walnut. Round over both edges with a ³/₈" bit.*

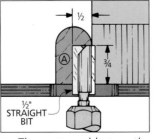

2 *Then cut a rabbet on the first strip to accept the second strip.*

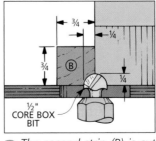

3 *The second strip (B) is cut from poplar. It's ³/₄" square and has a ¹/₄" cove on a corner.*

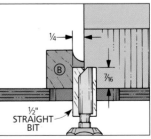

4 *A rabbet is cut in the second piece to hold the picture. Then paint the strip.*

SHOP JIG . . . . Frame Clamp

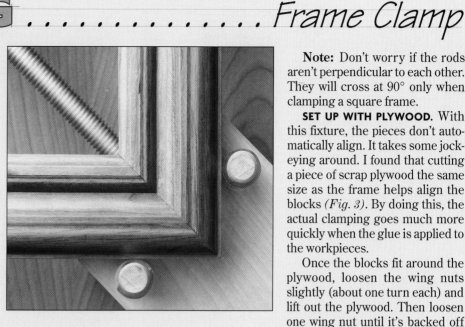

Frames are fun to build — until it's time to clamp them up. It's always a struggle to keep all four corners tight and the pieces properly aligned. That's why I made this clamp. It's adjustable to fit frames of various sizes. And the clamp closes up all four corners.

It's made from four blocks connected with threaded rod. A couple of dowels in each block capture the corner of the frame.

Note: This clamp works best for frames that are square or close to square (5x7 and 8x10).

CONSTRUCTION

The blocks are each built up from three pieces of ³⁄₄"-thick stock.

CUT BLANKS. To make the four corner blocks, start by cutting three blanks to a width of 3¹⁄₂" and 17" long. Next, cut a ¹⁄₂" groove, ¹⁄₂" deep down the center of one of the blanks. Then cut off four 4"-long pieces from each blank.

BUILD BLOCKS. Since the threaded rods have to cross in the center when holding a frame (refer to *Fig. 4*), the grooves on two of the blocks need to be above the grooves on the other two blocks. So when I built up the corner blocks, I assembled the pieces in different order *(Fig. 1)*.

For the two blocks labeled "A," the grooved piece is in the center facing up *(Fig. 1)*. For the two blocks labeled "B," the grooved piece is on top with the groove facing down.

DRILL HOLES. The corners of a frame are held in place between two dowel pegs on top of each block. To allow the clamp to hold large and small frames, drill two holes close together and two more holes farther apart *(Fig. 2)*.

TUBING. After gluing the dowels in place, I cut 1"-long pieces of plastic tubing and slipped them over the dowels *(Fig. 2)*. The tubing protects the frame pieces when pressure is applied. If the tubing is moved high on the peg, it presses against the top of the frame to offset the pressure applied below the frame by the threaded rod.

ASSEMBLY. Now assemble the fixture by slipping a 36"-long piece of ¹⁄₂" threaded rod through the grooves. Then add wing nuts on both ends.

USING THE CLAMP

Now that the clamp is built, you're ready to clamp up a frame. Before setting the frame pieces in place, there are a couple of steps to set up the clamp.

I always start by applying a coat of wax to the top of the blocks. That way, the frame won't stick to the blocks if any glue oozes out of the miter.

Once that's done, lay the blocks down on a flat surface so the threaded rods cross each other in an "X."

Note: Don't worry if the rods aren't perpendicular to each other. They will cross at 90° only when clamping a square frame.

SET UP WITH PLYWOOD. With this fixture, the pieces don't automatically align. It takes some jockeying around. I found that cutting a piece of scrap plywood the same size as the frame helps align the blocks *(Fig. 3)*. By doing this, the actual clamping goes much more quickly when the glue is applied to the workpieces.

Once the blocks fit around the plywood, loosen the wing nuts slightly (about one turn each) and lift out the plywood. Then loosen one wing nut until it's backed off ¹⁄₂" from the block *(Fig. 4)*.

GLUE UP FRAME. Now apply glue to the miters on two of the frame pieces. Set this corner in place so it's *opposite* the loosened block and rests on three of the blocks *(Fig. 4)*. Next glue the remaining three corners and set the pieces in place. Now slide the "loose" block in and tighten all the wing nuts.

After everything is in place, check each corner of the frame to be sure the joints have closed tightly. Apply just enough pressure so the joint closes up.

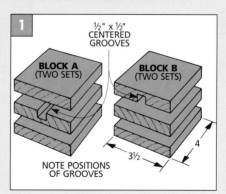

1 ¹⁄₂" x ¹⁄₂" CENTERED GROOVES
BLOCK A (TWO SETS) BLOCK B (TWO SETS)
3¹⁄₂   4
NOTE POSITIONS OF GROOVES

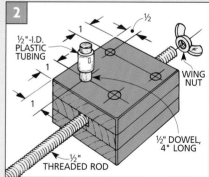

2 ¹⁄₂ 1 1 1 ¹⁄₂"-I.D. PLASTIC TUBING
WING NUT
¹⁄₂" DOWEL, 4" LONG
¹⁄₂" THREADED ROD

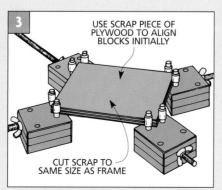

3 USE SCRAP PIECE OF PLYWOOD TO ALIGN BLOCKS INITIALLY
CUT SCRAP TO SAME SIZE AS FRAME

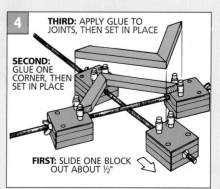

4 **THIRD:** APPLY GLUE TO JOINTS, THEN SET IN PLACE
SECOND: GLUE ONE CORNER, THEN SET IN PLACE
FIRST: SLIDE ONE BLOCK OUT ABOUT ¹⁄₂"

Picture Frame Clock

Combine a frame and a timepiece within a figured veneer case with solid brass hardware. It's sure to become a timeless heirloom. And there are plenty of ways to customize it to suit your tastes.

Walk through almost any office, and you're sure to notice that just about everyone has a photograph sitting on his or her desk.

Visiting a friend's office, I saw that some people have a photo of their spouse or kids; others have pictures of their pets. There were even a few who had a picture of their vehicle. That got me to thinking how a desktop picture frame might make a good project. So I started to think about a design.

CHANGES. By the time I finished building a couple of prototypes, the project had expanded to work in several features that make it as functional as it

is attractive. What I ended up with is a photo frame combined with a desk clock in a folding case. (Clock movements are available from several mail order sources. See page 126.) And during the design process, I came up with several ways to customize the case (more about that in a moment).

FOLD-UP. While some people will want to keep the clock on their desk, the hinges and a catch were added so the clock could be taken along on a trip (see photo on opposite page).

VENEER. The body of the clock is actually a core of MDF that's covered with veneer. This gives you plenty of

opportunities to customize the case. To see some other veneering ideas, refer to the Designer's Notebook on page 38. And if you're new to veneering, this is a perfectly-sized project. Some tips for getting started are included on page 37.

INLAY. The outside of the case has small rabbets around its edges. Then hardwood edging is added to create a shadow line (see photo on facing page).

But you could customize the case by adding an inlay instead of shadow lines. (Inlays can be found in woodworking catalogs and hobby shops.) Another Designer's Notebook on page 41 shows how easy it is to do this.

EXPLODED VIEW

OVERALL DIMENSIONS:
4¼"W x 2½"D x 4¼"H

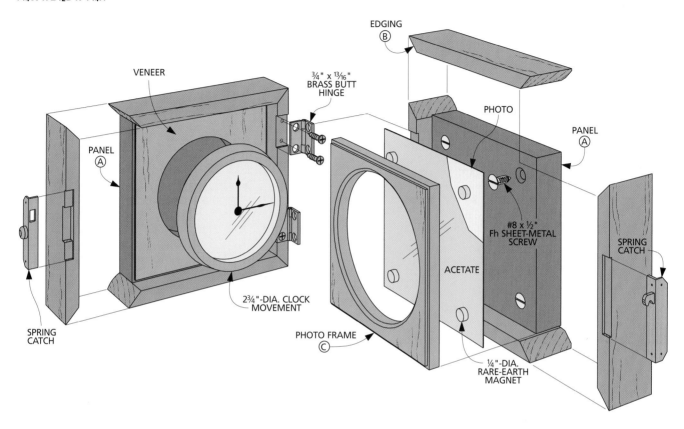

VENEER

EDGING
Ⓑ

¾" x ¹³/₁₆"
BRASS BUTT
HINGE

PHOTO

PANEL
Ⓐ

PANEL
Ⓐ

#8 x ½"
Fh SHEET-METAL
SCREW

SPRING
CATCH

ACETATE

2¾"-DIA. CLOCK
MOVEMENT

SPRING
CATCH

PHOTO FRAME
Ⓒ

¼"-DIA.
RARE-EARTH
MAGNET

A highly figured veneer dresses up the outside of the case. Veneering offers plenty of options for customizing the case. See page 38 for some ideas.

MATERIALS LIST

WOOD
A	Panels (2)	¾ MDF - 3⅝ x 3⅝
B	Edging (8)	⁵/₁₆ x 1¼ - 4¼
C	Photo Frame (1)	¼ x 3⅝ - 3⅝

HARDWARE SUPPLIES
(4) No. 8 x ½" Fh sheet-metal screws
(2) ¾" x ¹³/₁₆" brass butt hinges w/ screws
(4) ¼"-dia. rare-earth magnets
(1) Brass spring catch w/ escutcheon pins
(1) Veneer (approximately 1¼ sq. ft.)
(1) 2¾"-dia. fit-up clock movement
(1) Sheet of acetate, 4" x 4" rough

The clock is made up of two halves that are hinged to open and close like a book. Each half consists of a veneered panel of medium density fiberboard (MDF) with a solid wood frame around the edges. The panel that will hold the clock is veneered on both sides. The other panel is veneered on only one side since it will be covered by a photo and a frame added later *(Fig. 1)*.

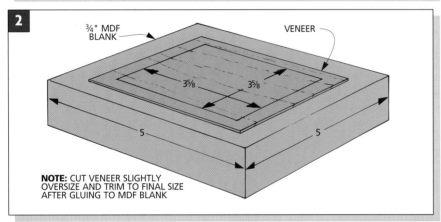

1

DRILL 2⅜"-DIA. HOLE IN CENTER OF CLOCK PANEL

CLOCK PANEL Ⓐ

VENEER

1¾₆"R

NOTE: ROUT SHADOW LINES ON VENEERED EDGES ONLY

a.

⅝

CLOCK PANEL

1/16

1/16

SIDE VIEW

Ⓐ PHOTO PANEL (VENEER OUTSIDE FACE ONLY)

b.

PHOTO PANEL

1/16

1/16

SIDE VIEW

NOTE: ¾" MDF PANELS ARE CUT TO FINAL SIZE AFTER VENEER IS APPLIED

2

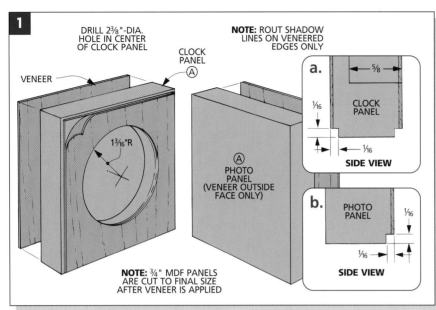

¾" MDF BLANK

VENEER

3⅝

3⅝

5

5

NOTE: CUT VENEER SLIGHTLY OVERSIZE AND TRIM TO FINAL SIZE AFTER GLUING TO MDF BLANK

3

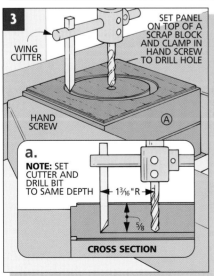

SET PANEL ON TOP OF A SCRAP BLOCK AND CLAMP IN HAND SCREW TO DRILL HOLE

WING CUTTER

HAND SCREW

Ⓐ

a.

NOTE: SET CUTTER AND DRILL BIT TO SAME DEPTH

1¾₆"R

⅝

CROSS SECTION

4

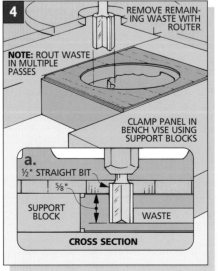

REMOVE REMAINING WASTE WITH ROUTER

NOTE: ROUT WASTE IN MULTIPLE PASSES

CLAMP PANEL IN BENCH VISE USING SUPPORT BLOCKS

a.

½" STRAIGHT BIT

⅝"

SUPPORT BLOCK

WASTE

CROSS SECTION

To make the two halves, I started with the veneered panels (A). If you've never done any veneering, don't worry. The small size of these pieces makes the process pretty simple. To walk you through it, there's a Technique article on the opposite page.

Instead of cutting the MDF panels to size and then veneering them, I started with oversized panels. This way, I could trim the panels to the exact size *after* they were veneered. So I began by cutting two oversized blanks out of ¾"-thick MDF. (I made mine 5" x 5".) Then I cut three pieces of veneer approximately 4" x 4" square *(Fig. 2)*.

When veneering the clock panel, check to make sure that the grain of the veneer runs in the same direction on both sides of the panel. Then, once the glue is dry, the panels can be cut to final size (3⅝" x 3⅝") *(Fig. 2)*.

SHADOW LINES. To set the panels apart from the edging that is added later, I decided to create a shadow line.

Note: Instead of a shadow line, you could add an inlay strip. This option offers a wide variety of ways to customize the look of the clock. See the Designer's Notebook on page 41.

To create the shadow lines, I routed a small (1/16" x 1/16") rabbet around the veneered edges of each panel *(Figs. 1a and 1b)*. This exposes the MDF on the bottom of the rabbet, but you won't notice it once the edging is added and the clock is stained.

CLOCK HOLE. The quartz clock movement simply press fits into a 2⅜"-dia. flat-bottomed hole in the center of the clock panel. (Sources of clock movements are listed on page 126.) You can buy a bit to cut this hole, but they can be pricey. And unless you plan on making a lot of clocks, it may not be worth it. So I tried an alternate method.

Using a sharp wing cutter, I cut the outer edge of the hole first *(Fig. 3)*. To prevent the drill bit of the cutter from drilling through the panel, make sure it's set flush with the end of the cutter bit before you start *(Fig. 3a)*.

Then with a router and a ½" straight bit, I nibbled away the waste in the center of the hole *(Fig. 4)*. This can be done with a hand-held router, but don't try to rout the waste away in one pass. Instead, remove the waste in stages, lowering the bit ¼" or so each time *(Fig. 4a)*. This way, the router will be much easier to control.

Veneering may seem mysterious or complicated if you've never done it before. But really, it's a simple process. And this clock is a good project to start with. It's small, so you don't have to worry about matching or piecing sheets of veneer together. Essentially, there are three steps: cutting the veneer, gluing it down, and clamping it in place.

CUTTING

Because veneer is so thin, it splits easily. This can make cutting it a bit of a challenge. Even with a sharp blade, it's possible to tear the veneer, especially when cutting across the grain. To avoid this problem when making the clock, I decided to veneer an oversized panel. Then when the glue is dry, you can cut the veneered panel to size on the table saw without any trouble.

For the clock, I started with an MDF panel about 5" square. Then I cut my veneer pieces slightly smaller (about 4" square). Since the panel will be trimmed to final size after the veneer is applied, the veneer doesn't have to be cut perfectly square, just close.

If you are cutting the veneer from a larger sheet, pay attention to the grain and figure pattern. You'll want to select the nicest areas of the veneer to use, but you also want to make sure that the color and grain direction match for each piece on both panels of the clock.

To get a better sense of what the veneer will look like when it is finished, try wiping it down with mineral spirits. Then simply move your MDF block around on the veneer and mark off the sections you want to use.

GLUING

With the veneer cut to rough size, it can be glued to the MDF. You have several choices when it comes to an adhesive. Traditionally, furniture makers have used hide glue for veneering. Today, contact cement has become popular. But I didn't want to deal with either one of these for such a small project. So I decided to use yellow glue.

No matter what kind of glue you use, there's one thing to watch out for. Because veneer is so thin, the glue may actually bleed through the surface of the veneer, especially with porous veneers (like mahogany). This can create a problem when it comes time to apply a stain or finish to the project.

To minimize this problem I try not to use an excessive amount of glue. This way, if any glue does ooze through the veneer, it can usually be scraped off cleanly with a cabinet scraper.

Note: Before applying a finish, you might want to wipe the clock down with mineral spirits to make sure there are no glue stains.

CLAMPING

When clamping veneers, the goal is to apply even pressure across the entire surface. With large projects, this can be quite a challenge; one that may require specialized clamps and presses. But it's not difficult at all with the Picture Frame Clock. To even out the clamping pressure, I just sandwiched the blank between two scraps of MDF *(Fig. 1)*.

In order to prevent the workpiece from sticking to the scraps, I placed a couple of pieces of waxed paper in between *(Fig. 1)*. Then I used C-clamps to hold the "sandwich" together.

After the glue is dry, the panels can be squared up and cut to final size on the table saw *(Fig. 2)*. A zero-clearance insert will reduce chipout on the bottom face of the panel.

One final note on finishing. Try to keep any final sanding to a minimum. It's very easy to sand right through the thin veneer layer.

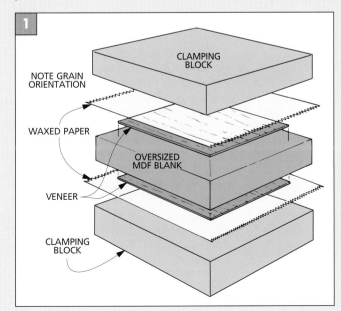

1
CLAMPING BLOCK
NOTE GRAIN ORIENTATION
WAXED PAPER
OVERSIZED MDF BLANK
VENEER
CLAMPING BLOCK

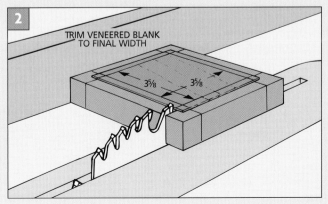

2
TRIM VENEERED BLANK TO FINAL WIDTH
3⅝   3⅝

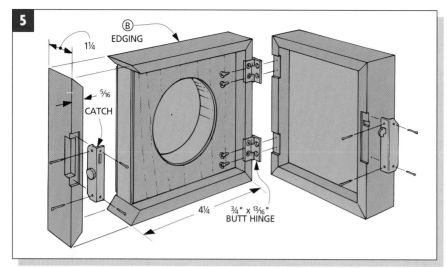

5

EDGING ⓑ

1¼

⁵⁄₁₆

CATCH

4¼

¾" x ¹³⁄₁₆"
BUTT HINGE

6

PLACE WORKPIECE
ON FLAT SURFACE
FOR ASSEMBLY

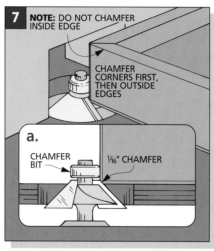

7

NOTE: DO NOT CHAMFER
INSIDE EDGE

CHAMFER
CORNERS FIRST,
THEN OUTSIDE
EDGES

a.

CHAMFER
BIT

¹⁄₁₆" CHAMFER

EDGING & FRAME

Both the clock panel and the photo panel are framed with hardwood edging *(Fig. 5)*. This edging is wider than the thickness of the panels in order to create a recess inside the case for the clock movement and the photo frame.

EDGING. I used two blanks to make the edging (B), each one about 20" long. First, I ripped the blanks to a width of 1¼". Then I resawed each blank so it ended up ⁵⁄₁₆" thick.

With the width and thickness of the blanks correctly sized, I mitered the individual edging pieces to fit around the two panels *(Fig. 5)*.

The edging is glued flush with the *outside* face of each panel. To do this, I placed the panels and edging on a smooth, flat surface while gluing and clamping the pieces *(Fig. 6)*.

With the glue dry and the two halves essentially complete, the next step is to relieve some of the sharp edges. I started by routing a small chamfer across each mitered corner of the edging. Then I chamfered the *outside* edges of each half of the clock *(Fig. 7)*.

HARDWARE. Since I had selected a fancy veneer to use on this project, I wanted to pick some nice hardware to match. A couple of solid brass hinges connect the two halves of the clock. And

DESIGNER'S NOTEBOOK

Veneers let you work with rare or highly-figured woods that might be too expensive otherwise.

VENEERING OPTIONS

■ Since the Picture Frame Clock is veneered, you can give it the appearance of almost any type of wood. The small amount of veneer required for the

project means you can experiment with a variety of looks at minimal cost.
■ You can create a totally different look for the clock by combining a veneer

with a contrasting wood for the edging. For example, the case in the far left photo is veneered with cherry. Walnut was used for the edging.
■ Another alternative is to use a figured veneer with an edging of the same species (near photo). Here, birds-eye maple is trimmed with maple edging.
■ For even more options, see the Designer's Notebook about adding inlays on page 41. Then consider mixing veneers, inlays, and edging to give your clock a unique appearance.
■ If you can't find what you want locally, a broad selection of veneers, inlays, and exotic woods is available through mail order sources. See page 126 for information on some of these sources.

a spring-loaded brass catch holds them closed. (Sources of this hardware are listed on page 126.)

Attaching this hardware is pretty straightforward. The first thing to do is rout the shallow hinge mortises on each half *(Fig. 8)*. The depth of the mortise equals the thickness of one of the hinge leaves *(Fig. 8a)*. This way the two halves of the case will close against each other tightly.

Once the hinges are installed, the next step is to add the catch. The catch I used is a two-piece affair designed to be surface mounted with small escutcheon pins. However, you'll still need to cut a mortise for the mechanism of the catch. And in order for the two halves of the clock to close tightly, you'll need to mortise the inside face of the catch and strike plate flush with the edging of the clock *(Fig. 9)*. (For details about mortising the catch into the case, see the Technique box below.)

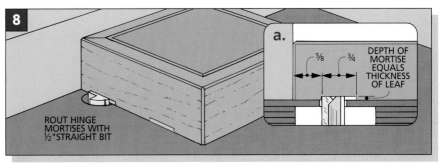

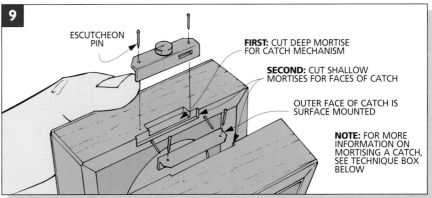

TECHNIQUE .... *Mortising a Catch*

Installing the spring-loaded catch on the Picture Frame Clock isn't difficult, but it does require a little patience and some sharp chisels.

The catch I used has two parts — a spring-loaded catch and a strike plate. (For sources, refer to page 126.) All you need to do is cut a few shallow mortises to accept each of these parts. I started with the catch.

CATCH. There are actually two mortises that you'll need to cut to accept the catch mechanism. One is inside the other. First, I chiseled out a short, deep mortise for the body of the catch *(Figs. 1 and 1a)*. The depth and width of this mortise is sized to match the mechanism, but the length is a bit more tricky.

The mortise has to be long enough to allow for the throw of the catch mechanism — but no longer. If you make the mortise too long, there won't be any material left for fastening the escutcheon pins *(Fig. 1)*. So after marking the locations of the edges of the catch, I carefully measured to locate the mortise for the body.

The second step is to cut a shallow mortise on the adjacent face so the inside face of the catch is flush with the edging *(Fig. 1a)*. Once this is done, the

catch can be secured in place with the escutcheon pins provided.

STRIKE PLATE. The strike plate only requires a shallow mortise. The first thing to do is to locate the position of the strike plate. The easiest way to do this is to insert the strike into the catch. Then close the clock to locate and lay out the mortise *(Fig. 2)*.

To mortise the strike plate, just make a small dimple in the edging to allow for the rivet on the back of the plate. Then chisel out a mortise so the plate sits flush with the edging.

Once both parts of the catch are installed, the edging pieces should meet without a gap when the clock is closed (see photo above).

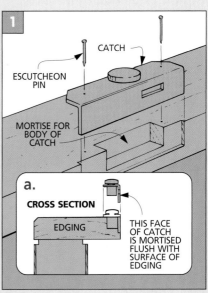

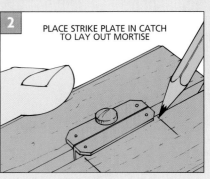

PHOTO FRAME. When it came to making the frame for the photo half of the clock, I was looking for a way to hold the photograph securely, but still allow it to be changed easily. The solution I came up with was a simple one — magnets. Four small magnets are used to hold both the frame and the photo in place. But more on this later.

VENEER. The photo frame (C) starts off as a slightly oversized blank made from ¼"-thick stock. And since I wanted the frame to match the panels of the clock, I glued the same figured veneer to both sides of the frame blank. (Veneering both sides helps prevent the thin stock from cupping.)

Once the blank is veneered, you can cut the frame to size. It should fit into the recessed opening of the clock with enough clearance so it can be easily removed to change the photo.

DRILL HOLE. The photo frame has a large hole in the center to reveal a photograph. The edge of this hole is chamfered to match the rest of the clock. I wasn't too concerned about drilling the hole, but I was a little nervous about routing the chamfer inside the hole on a piece this thin and small.

The solution I came up with was to use double-sided tape to attach the frame temporarily to a larger blank made out of ¾"-thick MDF. Using a wing cutter again, I made a hole in the center of the frame, drilling all the way through both the workpiece and the MDF blank (*Figs. 11 and 11a*).

Next, with the frame still attached to the MDF, I chamfered the edge of the photo opening (*Figs. 12 and 12a*). (This is the side of the photo frame that will face out.) Then I carefully removed the frame from the MDF.

Use the photo frame as a pattern to trim the photo and a piece of acetate that will fit over the photo.

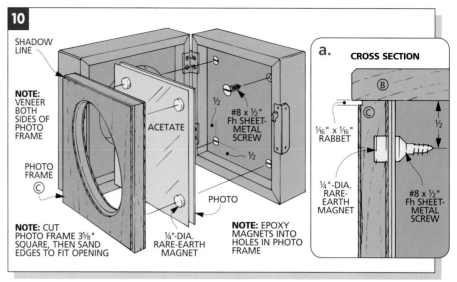

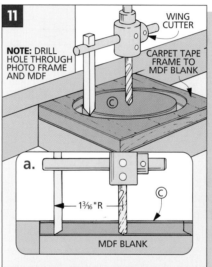

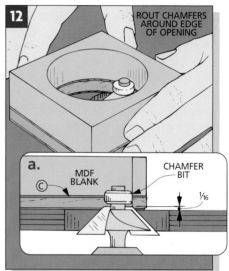

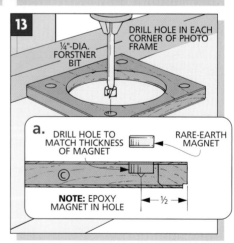

SHADOW LINES. To complete the frame, rout rabbets on the outer edges to create shadow lines identical to those on the panels of the clock (*Fig. 10a*).

MAGNETS. The photo frame is held in place with four small rare-earth magnets. A little dab of epoxy secures these magnets into holes drilled in the back of the photo frame (*Figs. 13 and 13a*). Then four small sheet-metal screws are countersunk into the photo panel of the clock to give the magnets something to grab onto (*Fig. 10a*).

FINISHING. When it came time to finish this project, I decided to give it a coat of stain for a couple of reasons. First, I wanted to even out the color of the solid wood edging and the veneered panels. And second, the stain helps to darken and conceal the exposed MDF edges of the shadow lines.

After applying the stain, I wiped on three coats of an oil finish. Then once the finish is dry, you can add the clock movement and figure out which photograph to put in the frame. To help protect the photo from dust and fingerprints, I cut a piece of clear acetate to place between the frame and the photograph (*Fig. 10* and photo at left). ∎

DESIGNER'S NOTEBOOK

Inlay strips come in dozens of sizes and designs. That gives you plenty of options for customizing the look of the Picture Frame Clock. And installing inlay is as simple as rout, miter, and glue.

INLAYS

■ Instead of shadow lines, another way to dress up the Picture Frame Clock is to add a decorative inlay strip. Inlay strips are made up of many tiny pieces of wood of varying shades (or even minerals and metal), usually organized into a geometric pattern. (See the photo at right for a few samples and refer to page 126 for sources of inlays.)

■ To apply the inlay, start by routing a shallow rabbet around the edge of the panel *(Fig. 1)*. The width and depth of the rabbet will be determined by the inlay strip you're using *(Fig. 1a)*.

■ Then miter the inlay strips to length and carefully glue them into the rabbets *(Fig. 2)*. (See the Shop Tip below for a mitering tip.) Try not to use too much glue to avoid squeeze-out around the edges of the inlay.

■ To hold the inlay strips in place, I just wrapped a few rubber bands around the panel. Then after the glue is dry, you can use a cabinet scraper to shave the inlay flush with the surface of the case *(Fig. 3)*.

■ Finally, apply a finish right over the inlay as you finish the clock case.

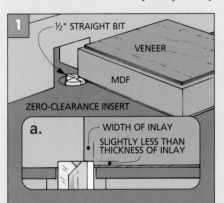

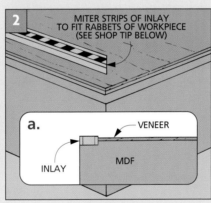

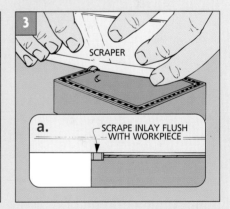

SHOP TIP . . . . *Fitting Inlay*

Getting a tight fit on a mitered corner is tough enough with large work-pieces. And when the workpiece is a small piece like an inlay strip, it's likely to get even closer inspection, so tight miters are especially important.

That's where this mitering jig can help. It guides a sharp chisel to give you a clean, precise miter cut.

The jig is just a scrap of wood with a groove cut in it the same width as the inlay. Then one end is mitered at 45° *(Fig. 1)*.

Note: It's important that this angle be exact.

To use the jig, put a piece of inlay strip in the jig (face up) and miter one end with a chisel *(Fig. 1)*. Then position this piece on the clock case and mark the other end with a knife *(Fig. 2)*. Then put the piece back in the jig to miter it to length.

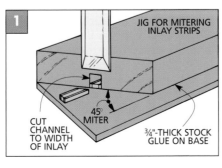

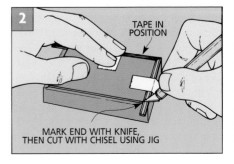

Hall Mirror

Perfect as the last stop before you dash out the door and as the first stop when arriving home, this handsome mirror provides a place for your coat, keys, and a check on your appearance.

Before I started designing this mirror, I knew exactly where I wanted it to hang — in the hallway right inside my front door. But I also knew it should be more than just something nice to look at. It should be useful, too. So I added a few features that let people "unload" a bit when they walk through the door.

PEGS. First, there are some Shaker pegs at the bottom of the frame. (I found mine at a craft store.) These can hold a hat, a coat, a backpack, or a purse that hasn't quite made it to the hall closet.

SHELF. Another design improvement was the addition of a shelf. It runs almost the full width of the frame. A bead molding creates a lip around its edges to help keep things from sliding off. This makes the shelf a great place to display small collectible items, or to store car keys or letters to be mailed.

MOLDINGS. The top and bottom of the mirror are dressed up with shop-made cove moldings. The top also has a simple cap molding. And a bead molding (similar to the one around the shelf) provides a finishing touch inside the opening for the mirror.

MORTISE AND TENON. Of course, all these features don't amount to much if the frame isn't strong. After all, a mirror by itself is plenty heavy. And when you add a few coats on the pegs, you'll need a frame that will hold up.

So I built the frame for the mirror with mortise and tenon joints. This makes it plenty strong but still easy to build. (For more on mortise and tenon joinery, see the article on page 47.)

HANGERS. But strong construction isn't the only consideration. You still have to hang it on the wall. To make sure this mirror is secure, I used keyhole hangers. These metal hangers are mortised into the back of the frame for extra strength, and they "lock" over screws driven into the wall.

EXPLODED VIEW

OVERALL DIMENSIONS:
$31\frac{3}{8}$W x $4\frac{3}{4}$D x $29\frac{1}{8}$H

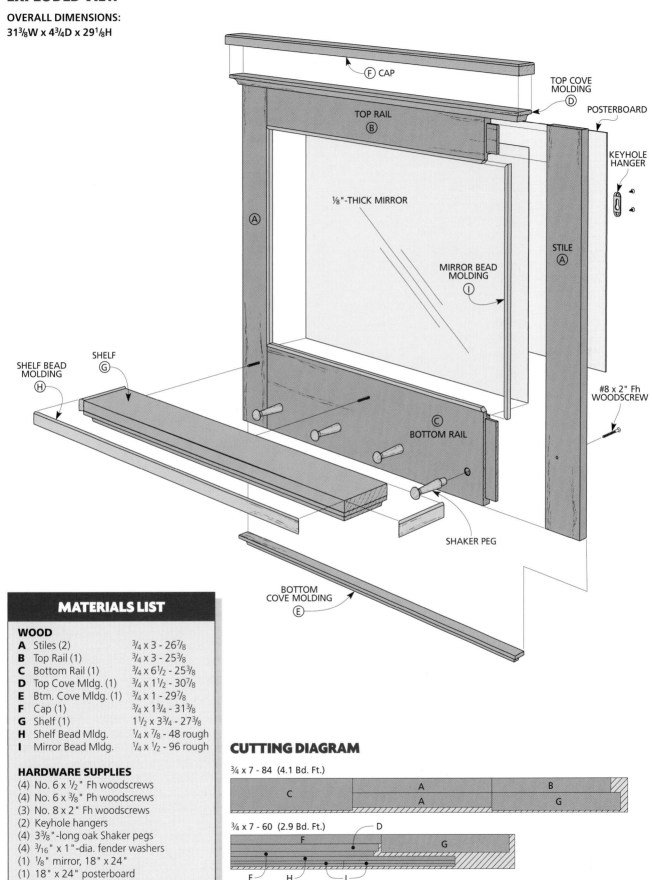

F CAP
TOP COVE MOLDING
TOP RAIL B
D
POSTERBOARD
KEYHOLE HANGER
$\frac{1}{8}$"-THICK MIRROR
A
MIRROR BEAD MOLDING I
STILE A
#8 x 2" Fh WOODSCREW
SHELF BEAD MOLDING H
SHELF G
BOTTOM RAIL C
SHAKER PEG
BOTTOM COVE MOLDING E

MATERIALS LIST

WOOD

A	Stiles (2)	$\frac{3}{4}$ x 3 - $26\frac{7}{8}$
B	Top Rail (1)	$\frac{3}{4}$ x 3 - $25\frac{3}{8}$
C	Bottom Rail (1)	$\frac{3}{4}$ x $6\frac{1}{2}$ - $25\frac{3}{8}$
D	Top Cove Mldg. (1)	$\frac{3}{4}$ x $1\frac{1}{2}$ - $30\frac{7}{8}$
E	Btm. Cove Mldg. (1)	$\frac{3}{4}$ x 1 - $29\frac{7}{8}$
F	Cap (1)	$\frac{3}{4}$ x $1\frac{3}{4}$ - $31\frac{3}{8}$
G	Shelf (1)	$1\frac{1}{2}$ x $3\frac{3}{4}$ - $27\frac{3}{8}$
H	Shelf Bead Mldg.	$\frac{1}{4}$ x $\frac{7}{8}$ - 48 rough
I	Mirror Bead Mldg.	$\frac{1}{4}$ x $\frac{1}{2}$ - 96 rough

HARDWARE SUPPLIES

(4) No. 6 x $\frac{1}{2}$" Fh woodscrews
(4) No. 6 x $\frac{3}{8}$" Ph woodscrews
(3) No. 8 x 2" Fh woodscrews
(2) Keyhole hangers
(4) $3\frac{3}{8}$"-long oak Shaker pegs
(4) $\frac{3}{16}$" x 1"-dia. fender washers
(1) $\frac{1}{8}$" mirror, 18" x 24"
(1) 18" x 24" posterboard

CUTTING DIAGRAM

$\frac{3}{4}$ x 7 - 84 (4.1 Bd. Ft.)

C	A	B
	A	G

$\frac{3}{4}$ x 7 - 60 (2.9 Bd. Ft.)

D
F
G
E   H   I

The Hall Mirror is basically a rectangular frame held together with mortise and tenon joinery. And to dress up the frame, decorative molding is added to the top and bottom *(Fig. 1)*.

STILES AND RAILS. I started work on the frame by making the stiles (A) from $3/4$"-thick stock *(Fig. 1)*.

With the stiles cut to size, work can begin on the rails. The top rail (B) and bottom rail (C) are the same overall length. However, their widths are different. The top rail (B) is the same width as the stiles. But to allow room for the shelf and pegs (installed later), the bottom rail (C) is $6\frac{1}{2}$" wide *(Fig. 1)*.

MORTISE AND TENON. At this point, you cut the mortise and tenon joints *(Figs. 1a and 1b)*. (For a step-by-step article on this, refer to page 47.) When the joints are complete, glue and clamp the frame together.

RABBET. After the glue has dried, the next step is to rout a rabbet in the back of the frame for the mirror to sit in. To do this, I used a $3/8$" rabbet bit in a hand-held router *(Fig. 2)*.

Note: The rabbet is $3/8$" deep. To prevent chipout, make several passes to get the rabbet to its final depth.

Although a rabbet bit does a good job of routing the rabbet, it leaves a radius in each corner. So you'll have to square up the corners with a chisel.

COVE MOLDING. Once the rabbet is complete, the next step is to add cove molding to the top and bottom of the frame. To make the molding, first cut the top cove molding (D) and bottom cove molding (E) to size *(Fig. 1)*.

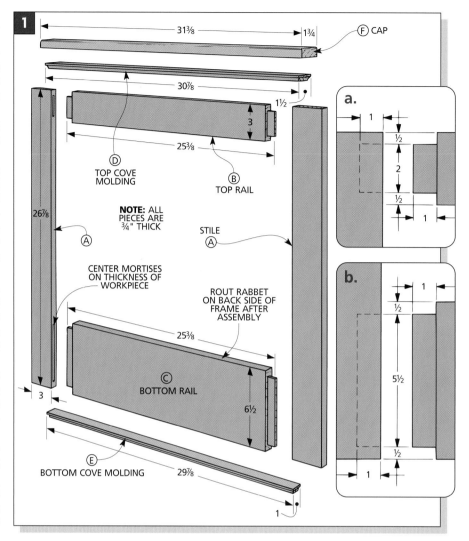

Now the profile can be routed on each piece of molding. To do this, I used a $1/2$" cove bit in the router table.

Note: It works best to start on the ends first. That way, any chipout will be cleaned up when you cut the cove along the front edge. And just like cutting the rabbet on the back of the frame, it's a good idea to cut the cove by making a couple of shallow passes.

After routing the coves, both pieces of molding can be glued and clamped to the frame assembly.

Note: The molding is centered from side to side on the frame and is flush with the back. A quick way to center the molding is to mark the center on both the top and bottom of the frame and on each piece of cove molding. Then just align your marks when clamping the molding in place.

CAP. To complete the frame, a $3/4$"-thick cap (F) is glued on the top cove molding *(Fig. 3)*. The cap has $1/8$" roundovers routed along the top front edge and both ends *(Figs. 1 and 3)*.

With the roundover complete, the cap can be glued to the top cove molding. Here again, position the cap so it's centered from side to side and flush with the back.

SHELF

After the cap has been installed, you can begin work on the shelf. The $1\frac{1}{2}$"-thick shelf is glued up from two pieces of $\frac{3}{4}$"-thick stock. Keeping the edges of these pieces aligned while they're being glued together can be difficult. So I glued up two oversized pieces. Then after the glue dried, I cut the shelf (G) to finished size *(Figs. 4 and 4a)*.

Next, rout a cove on the shelf to match the cove molding on the top and bottom of the frame *(Fig. 4a)*.

INSTALLATION. Now the shelf can be attached to the frame. What can be a little tricky here is mounting the shelf on the front side of the frame with screws installed from the back.

To help get the shelf in position, first draw a line on the front side of the frame where you want the shelf to be located (1" below the frame opening) *(Fig. 5)*. Then align the shelf with the line and clamp it in place.

Now mark the location of the screws on the back side of the frame *(Fig. 6)*. Then drill the $\frac{3}{16}$"-dia. counterbored shank holes through the frame only.

With the shelf still clamped to the frame, the shank holes can be used as guides for drilling pilot holes into the shelf. Then remove the clamps and glue and screw the shelf to the frame.

BEAD MOLDING. Now bead molding can be added to the front and sides of the shelf to form a lip around the edge.

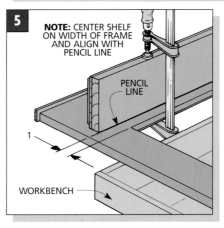

4
FIRST: GLUE UP OVERSIZED SHELF BLANK
SHELF G
28
4
SECOND: CUT SHELF TO FINISHED DIMENSIONS ($3\frac{3}{4}$" x $27\frac{3}{8}$")
THIRD: ROUT COVE ON FRONT AND ENDS (SEE DETAIL a)

a. $3\frac{3}{4}$
END VIEW
$1\frac{1}{2}$
ROUT $\frac{1}{2}$" COVE ON FRONT EDGE AND ENDS

5 **NOTE:** CENTER SHELF ON WIDTH OF FRAME AND ALIGN WITH PENCIL LINE
PENCIL LINE
1
WORKBENCH

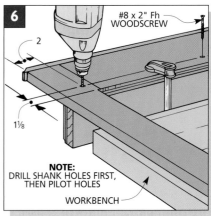

6 #8 x 2" Fh WOODSCREW
2
$1\frac{1}{8}$
NOTE: DRILL SHANK HOLES FIRST, THEN PILOT HOLES
WORKBENCH

The molding is a decorative detail that keeps things from sliding off (refer to *Fig. 8*). At the same time, bead molding can be added to the inside of the frame next to the mirror.

The shelf bead molding (H) and the mirror bead molding (I) are made the same way. But they're different widths. The shelf molding is $\frac{7}{8}$" wide while the mirror molding is $\frac{1}{2}$" *(Figs. 8a and 8b)*. To create the molding, I used a $\frac{1}{8}$" roundover bit in the router table to round the edges of a wide blank. Then I ripped the moldings from the blank.

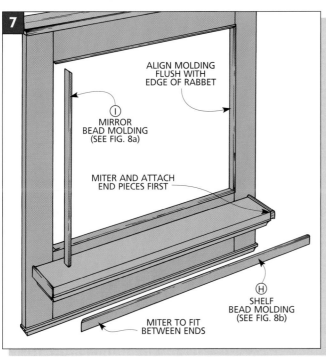

7
ALIGN MOLDING FLUSH WITH EDGE OF RABBET
MIRROR BEAD MOLDING (SEE FIG. 8a)
MITER AND ATTACH END PIECES FIRST
SHELF BEAD MOLDING (SEE FIG. 8b)
MITER TO FIT BETWEEN ENDS

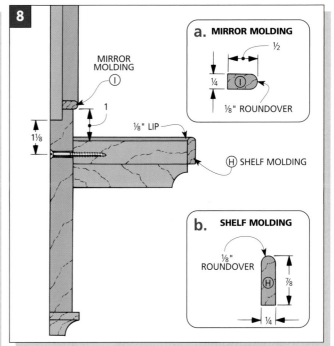

8
MIRROR MOLDING (I)
$1\frac{1}{8}$
1
$\frac{1}{8}$" LIP

a. MIRROR MOLDING
$\frac{1}{2}$
$\frac{1}{4}$
(I)
$\frac{1}{8}$" ROUNDOVER

(H) SHELF MOLDING

b. SHELF MOLDING
$\frac{1}{8}$" ROUNDOVER
(H)
$\frac{7}{8}$
$\frac{1}{4}$

At this point, there are just a few finishing touches to add to the mirror.

PEGS. With the molding installed, the next step is to add Shaker pegs to the frame (for sources, see page 126). The easiest way to do this is to lay the frame on its back and mark the location for the four pegs under the shelf *(Fig. 9)*.

Then using a Forstner bit in a hand drill, the $\frac{5}{8}$"-deep holes can be drilled to accept the tenon on each peg *(Fig. 9a)*.

As I was dry-assembling the Shaker pegs in the holes, there was a small problem. The shoulders on the pegs wouldn't sit flush against the frame. That's because there was a small radius under the shoulder *(Fig. 9a)*. To solve the problem, I drilled a small countersink around the face of each hole. This

provides just enough clearance for the radius so the pegs sit flush. Then glue and install the pegs.

HANGERS. When you combine the weight of the frame, the mirror, and several coats on the pegs, you'll want a secure way to mount the mirror on the wall. That's why metal keyhole hangers were added to the back side of the frame. These hangers are designed to be mortised and screwed to the frame. And the keyhole slot in each hanger "locks" the frame to a screw in the wall. (Refer to the Shop Tip below for details about installing the hangers.)

MIRROR INSTALLATION. After the hangers are installed, the last step is fitting the mirror to the frame and holding it in place. The frame was designed to hold a standard $\frac{1}{8}$"-thick mirror cut to an even size (18" high x 24" long). But

just to be safe, it's a good idea to take the frame along with you when buying the mirror to make sure it fits.

To hold the mirror in the frame, I drilled shallow 1"-dia. holes for four fender washers 6" in from each side *(Fig. 10)*. The washers will be secured by panhead screws.

But before installing the mirror, you should apply any stain and finish. (I used a coat of a honey maple stain, then two coats of an oil-urethane finish.)

Then place the mirror in the frame and back it up with a piece of posterboard. (The posterboard helps protect the mirror from getting scratched by the washers.) Finally, install the fender washers and screws. ■

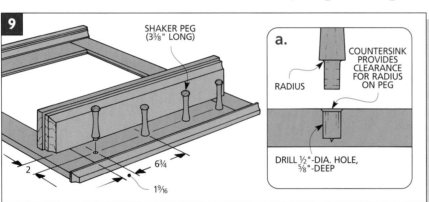

9

SHAKER PEG ($3\frac{3}{8}$" LONG)

2    $6\frac{3}{4}$ $1\frac{9}{16}$

a.

RADIUS

COUNTERSINK PROVIDES CLEARANCE FOR RADIUS ON PEG

DRILL $\frac{1}{2}$"-DIA. HOLE, $\frac{5}{8}$"-DEEP

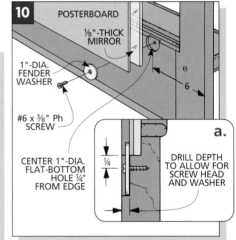

10

POSTERBOARD

$\frac{1}{8}$"-THICK MIRROR

1"-DIA. FENDER WASHER

#6 x $\frac{3}{8}$" Ph SCREW

CENTER 1"-DIA. FLAT-BOTTOM HOLE $\frac{1}{4}$" FROM EDGE

6

a.

$\frac{1}{4}$

DRILL DEPTH TO ALLOW FOR SCREW HEAD AND WASHER

SHOP TIP . . . . *Keyhole Hangers*

The trick to installing keyhole hangers is creating room for a screw head. This is done by drilling one mortise inside another.

First, draw a centerline on the back of the frame

and trace the position of the hanger *(Fig. 1)*. Then drill two $\frac{1}{8}$"-deep holes at the outside of the outline. These holes create the mortise that holds the hanger plate.

Next, drill overlapping $\frac{3}{8}$"-deep holes between the first two mortise holes *(Fig. 2)*. These overlapping holes create clearance for the roundhead screw. But before you can actually set

the plate into the shallow mortise, you'll need to clean up the sides of the mortise with a chisel.

Finally, drill the pilot holes and screw the hanger in place *(Fig. 3)*.

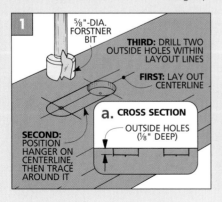

1

$\frac{5}{8}$"-DIA. FORSTNER BIT

THIRD: DRILL TWO OUTSIDE HOLES WITHIN LAYOUT LINES

FIRST: LAY OUT CENTERLINE

SECOND: POSITION HANGER ON CENTERLINE, THEN TRACE AROUND IT

a. CROSS SECTION

OUTSIDE HOLES ($\frac{1}{8}$" DEEP)

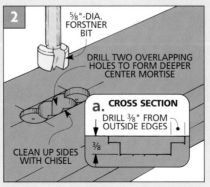

2

$\frac{5}{8}$"-DIA. FORSTNER BIT

DRILL TWO OVERLAPPING HOLES TO FORM DEEPER CENTER MORTISE

CLEAN UP SIDES WITH CHISEL

a. CROSS SECTION

DRILL $\frac{3}{8}$" FROM OUTSIDE EDGES

$\frac{3}{8}$

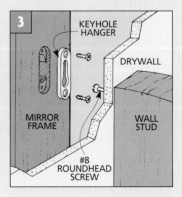

3

KEYHOLE HANGER

DRYWALL

MIRROR FRAME

WALL STUD

#8 ROUNDHEAD SCREW

JOINERY . . . . *Mortise & Tenon*

Mortises and tenons could be called the "bread and butter" of woodworking joints. They're not as flashy as dovetails or box joints, but a mortise and tenon joint is often the backbone of a woodworking project. And the main reason for this is its strength.

The close fit between the mortise and the tenon provides a strong mechanical joint. In addition, there's a large glue surface where the tenon cheeks meet the sides of the mortise.

Making the joint isn't difficult. The instructions below walk you through the process step by step.

MORTISE

Anytime I'm getting ready to make a mortise, I'm concerned with a couple of things — speed and accuracy.

I like to remove the waste from the mortise quickly (especially if I have a lot of them to make). But I also want to make sure the ends of the mortise are square with the sides, and the sides are square with the face of the workpiece. This is essential to getting a good fit with the tenon.

To accomplish this, I like to use a drill press *(Fig. 1)*. Using a Forstner or brad point bit, I drill a series of overlapping holes to create a rough opening. Then I square up the ends and sides with a chisel *(Fig. 2)*.

Note: If your workpiece is too long or heavy to place on a drill press, try

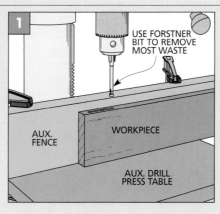

USE FORSTNER BIT TO REMOVE MOST WASTE

AUX. FENCE

WORKPIECE

AUX. DRILL PRESS TABLE

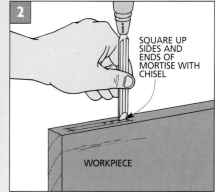

SQUARE UP SIDES AND ENDS OF MORTISE WITH CHISEL

WORKPIECE

using a portable drill with a dowel jig or a Portalign to guide the drill bit.

I like this method because it doesn't require any lengthy setups. The width of the mortise is determined by the

diameter of the drill bit. The depth is set by the depth stop on the drill press. All you need is a simple fence clamped to the drill press table to establish the position of the mortise in the workpiece.

TENON

To cut tenons, I install a dado blade in my table saw and remove the waste from the cheeks of the tenon by making multiple passes. The rip fence serves as a stop to determine the length of the tenon. An auxiliary fence attached to the miter gauge steadies the workpiece and backs up the cut *(Figs. 3 and 3a)*.

Then I slide the workpiece back and forth over the blade to clean up any saw marks left behind *(Fig. 4)*.

At first glance, you might think this method violates one of the cardinal rules of woodworking — never use the miter gauge and rip fence together. (The reason for this is that the cutoff piece can get trapped between the blade and the fence and kick back.)

But when you're cutting a tenon with a dado blade, you're not making a through cut. So there isn't any cutoff piece to worry about.

One reason I like this method is that you can cut a tenon quickly. The dado blade removes a wide swath of material with each pass.

But more importantly, I find it easy to "fine tune" the fit of the tenon by making some quick adjustments. If the tenon is too thick, I simply raise the dado blade a hair. If the tenon is too short, I just move my rip fence away from the blade.

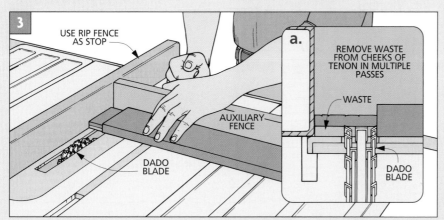

USE RIP FENCE AS STOP

AUXILIARY FENCE

DADO BLADE

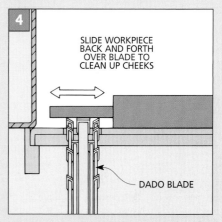

a.

REMOVE WASTE FROM CHEEKS OF TENON IN MULTIPLE PASSES

WASTE

DADO BLADE

SLIDE WORKPIECE BACK AND FORTH OVER BLADE TO CLEAN UP CHEEKS

DADO BLADE

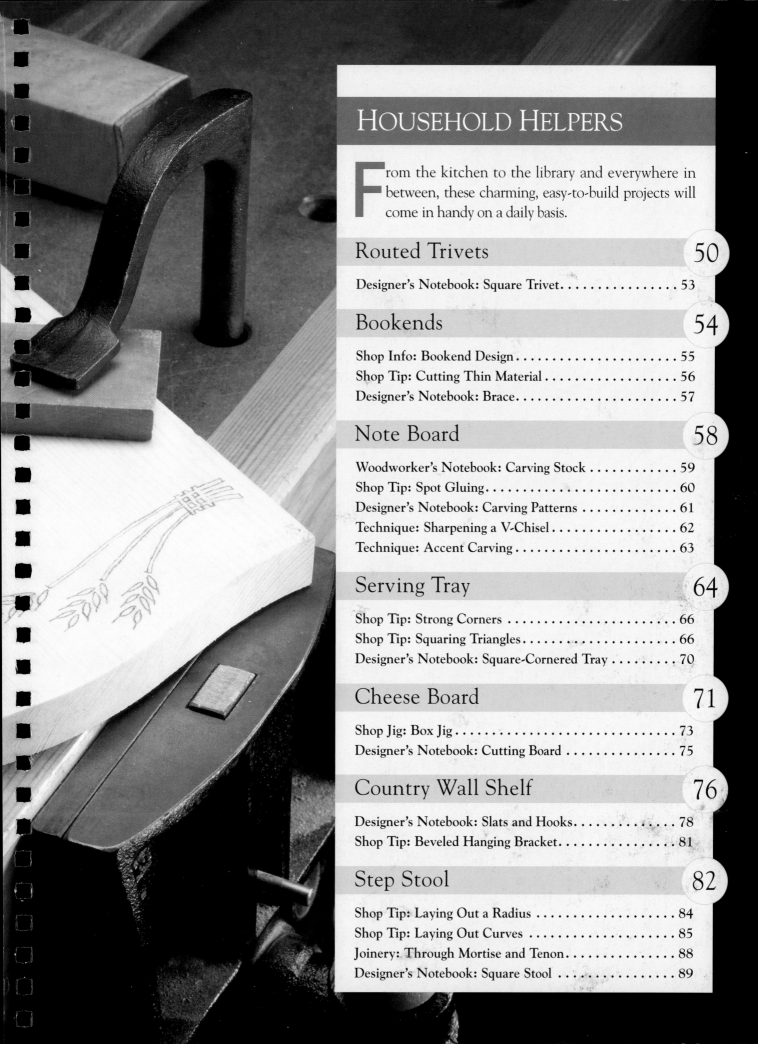

HOUSEHOLD HELPERS

From the kitchen to the library and everywhere in between, these charming, easy-to-build projects will come in handy on a daily basis.

Routed Trivets

A special criss-cross pattern of grooves gives this easy-to-make trivet a unique, classy look.
In round or square (or even one of each), it's sure to add to your kitchen's atmosphere.

Making a round trivet like the one beneath the teapot is an interesting challenge. This trivet has grooves routed at right angles on opposite sides of the workpiece to create a unique lattice pattern.

When I first saw one of these trivets, I couldn't help wondering how to hold a round workpiece in place to rout parallel grooves. Then it dawned on me — rout the grooves while the workpiece is square, then cut it to the round shape.

ROUTING. The series of grooves that create the lattice pattern may look complicated, but don't worry. It's all just a matter of setting up the router table cor-

rectly, using custom spacers, and following the proper sequence.

ROUNDING JIG. In woodworking, straight lines are always easier than curved ones. But I like the look of this project when it's round, so I had to find an easy way to turn the square blank into a round trivet.

As it turns out, all I needed was a simple shop-made jig to hold it steady. Then I could use the trammel attachment on my router to create the perfect circle (refer to page 52).

SQUARE TRIVETS. After making a few round trivets, I felt like I had a pretty good handle on the process. So I

decided to make some square ones too. A square trivet offers a different look, either by itself or as a companion to a round one (see photo above).

In many ways, the square trivets are easier to make than the round ones. For more on the square version, see the Designer's Notebook on page 53.

STOCK THICKNESS. As I began experimenting with making trivets, I found that the thickness of the stock played a big part in the overall appearance of the lattice pattern. Using stock that's $3/8$" to $1/2$" thick seems to look best, and that required doing some initial preparation (construction begins on the next page).

PREPARATION

To start, I resawed (ripped on edge) some stock to a thickness of $1/2''$. (There's a tip on resawing on page 114.) Then to make an 8''-dia. round trivet, I glued up enough of this $1/2''$ stock to form a 9'' x 9'' square *(Fig. 1)*.

Note: If you're going to make the square version of the trivet, it's actually a 7'' square. The routing setup and sequence are also different (refer to the Designer's Notebook on page 53).

ROUTER TABLE SETUP

The lattice pattern is formed by routing double-stopped grooves on both faces of this square. To set up the router table to cut the grooves, mount a $1/2''$ carbide-tipped core box bit *(Fig. 1b)*.

I decided to use a core box bit because it cuts a round bottom in each groove. This complements the round shape of the trivet.

POSITION FENCE. Once the bit is in place, set up the router table to cut a groove centered on the workpiece. Since I was working with a 9'' square, I positioned the fence $4^{1}/2''$ from the *center* of the core box bit *(Fig. 1)*.

STOP BLOCKS. This center groove is routed on both faces so the ends stop 1'' from both edges of the workpiece. To do this, clamp plywood stop blocks to the table so the inside edges are $7^{3}/4''$ from the center of the bit *(Fig. 1)*.

SPACERS

At this point, the router table is set up to rout the center grooves. But, before you begin routing, you have to make three sets of spacer blocks for the additional grooves. The idea is to use the spacers to rout progressively shorter grooves that will fit the final round shape of the trivet *(Fig. 1a)*.

GROOVES #2 AND #3. The spacers used to cut grooves #2 and #3 on either side of the center groove consist of two strips of $1/8''$ hardboard and a 1''-wide strip of $3/4''$ wood.

When these spacers are mounted, one hardboard strip is placed against each stop block. This way the second and third grooves will stop slightly shorter than the center groove (refer to *Fig. 4* on page 52).

The 1''-wide spacer is placed against the fence to shift the grooves 1'' to each

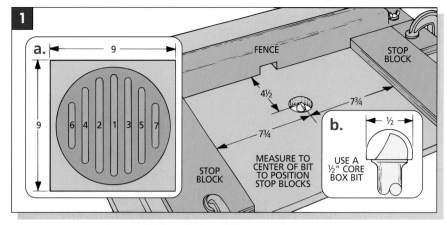

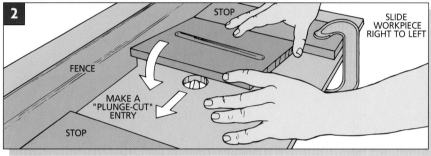

side of the center groove. Cut this spacer long enough to fit snugly between the $1/8''$ spacers so it holds them up against the stops and keeps them from tipping (refer to *Fig. 4*).

Note: I found that labeling each of the spacers with fraction-style numbers made it easier to keep the sets together during all the routing steps. For example, I marked the first set of spacers for grooves #2 and #3 with 2/3.

GROOVES #4 AND #5. The second set of spacers used for grooves #4 and #5 consist of two strips $7/8''$ wide that go against the stops and a strip 2'' wide that goes against the fence (refer to *Fig. 5* on page 52). I labeled these with 4/5.

GROOVES #6 AND #7. The spacers used for grooves #6 and #7 consist of two strips $1^{7}/8''$ wide that go against the stops and a strip 3'' wide that goes against the fence (refer to *Fig. 6* on page 52). I labeled this set with 6/7.

ROUTING SEQUENCE

When all the spacers have been cut to size, the grooves can be routed. The depth of cut must be a little more than half the thickness of the stock to produce the lattice pattern. On $1/2''$-thick stock I found the best depth for the grooves was $5/16''$.

For a smooth cut, it's best to make two passes. On the first pass, all the

grooves are routed to half depth (about $3/16''$). Then the entire sequence is repeated to deepen the grooves to the full depth of $5/16''$.

FIRST PASS. Now the routing can begin. The routing sequence starts with a pass on each side of the workpiece to create the center grooves.

To do this, first position the workpiece in the upper right-hand corner created by the fence and the right stop block. Then make a "plunge-cut" by tipping the workpiece down onto the bit *(Fig. 2)*.

To rout the stopped groove, just slide the workpiece from right to left keeping the top edge tight against the fence.

Next, simply flip the workpiece over to rout a center groove on the other side. However, be sure to position the workpiece so the groove you just cut is perpendicular to (pointing toward) the fence *(Fig. 2 and Fig. 3 on next page)*.

Note: I found that the grooves are a very strong image on the top of the workpiece. The image was so strong, in fact, that I kept wanting to turn the workpiece so the groove on the top side (the side I was looking at) ran parallel to the fence — the same way I was moving the workpiece.

The trick, though, is to concentrate on keeping the visible grooves always pointing *toward* the fence, even though the workpiece is moved *parallel* to the fence.

SECOND PASS. The second set of cuts creates the two grooves on both sides of the center groove (grooves #2 and #3). The position of these grooves is controlled by the 2/3 spacer set *(Fig. 4)*. With the three spacers in position, place the stock in the upper right-hand corner and rout groove #2. Then keep the same face up but rotate the workpiece 180° and cut groove #3 on the other side of the center groove *(Fig. 4)*.

After these two grooves are routed, flip the workpiece over and repeat the process on the opposite side.

THIRD PASS. The third set of cuts requires the 4/5 spacers to rout grooves #4 and #5 *(Fig. 5)*. It's repetitive, but just make sure the visible grooves (on the top side of the workpiece) are pointing toward the fence when the cuts are made.

FOURTH PASS. Finally, the fourth set of cuts uses the 6/7 spacer set, and follows the same procedure as before.

FULL DEPTH. After all seven grooves have been routed on each side to approximately half depth, adjust the height of the bit so it cuts to full depth ($^5/_{16}$"). Then repeat the entire sequence of passes on both sides of the workpiece.

MAKING IT ROUND

After the grooves are routed, the trivet can be cut to the round shape using a router with a $^1/_4$" straight bit and a trammel attachment.

JIG. To hold the workpiece in place while routing, it's mounted to a jig. The jig consists of a piece of $^3/_4$" plywood with a 2x4 scrap fastened to the bottom so it can be held in a vise *(Fig. 7)*.

Next, three $^1/_2$"-dia. holes are drilled in the plywood for the dowel pins that hold the workpiece steady during the routing operation. First drill a $^1/_2$" hole at the center of the plywood and glue a dowel in the hole so it projects just less than the thickness of the workpiece.

Place the workpiece on the plywood so the dowel goes through the hole created by the center grooves. Now mark the locations of the end holes.

Remove the workpiece and drill these two holes to accept $^1/_2$"-dia. dowels. Finally, drill a small hole in the end of the center dowel to accept the trammel point.

SET UP TRAMMEL. The pattern of the routed grooves is designed for an 8"-dia. trivet. To rout to this diameter, set the distance between the trammel point and the inner edge of the router bit to 4" *(Fig. 8)*.

Note: If you don't have a plunge router, you'll need to drill a $^1/_4$" starting hole to get the bit in position before turning on the router. Make sure the edge of the hole just touches the outside of the trivet circumference.

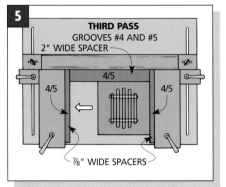

3 FIRST PASS — NO SPACERS — FENCE — ROUT RIGHT TO LEFT — STOP — STOP — C-CLAMP — NOTE: SHADED GROOVE BEING ROUTED ON "DOWN" SIDE

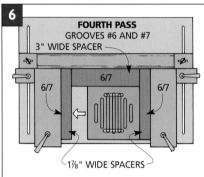

4 SECOND PASS — GROOVES #2 AND #3 — 1" WIDE SPACER — 2/3 — 2/3 — $^1/_8$" WIDE SPACERS

5 THIRD PASS — GROOVES #4 AND #5 — 2" WIDE SPACER — 4/5 — 4/5 — 4/5 — $^7/_8$" WIDE SPACERS

6 FOURTH PASS — GROOVES #6 AND #7 — 3" WIDE SPACER — 6/7 — 6/7 — 6/7 — $1^7/_8$" WIDE SPACERS

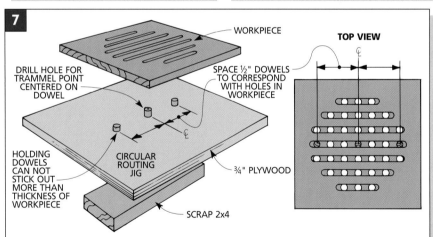

7 WORKPIECE — TOP VIEW — DRILL HOLE FOR TRAMMEL POINT CENTERED ON DOWEL — SPACE $^1/_2$" DOWELS TO CORRESPOND WITH HOLES IN WORKPIECE — HOLDING DOWELS CAN NOT STICK OUT MORE THAN THICKNESS OF WORKPIECE — CIRCULAR ROUTING JIG — $^3/_4$" PLYWOOD — SCRAP 2x4

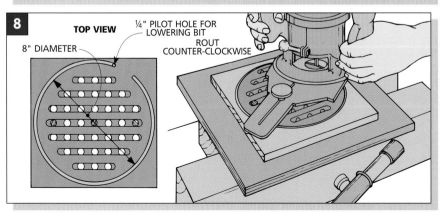

8 TOP VIEW — 8" DIAMETER — $^1/_4$" PILOT HOLE FOR LOWERING BIT — ROUT COUNTER-CLOCKWISE

Now rout the circumference in three passes, setting the bit deeper after each complete pass.

ROUND EDGES

When the trivet is routed free, remove it from the jig and rout a bullnose profile on the edge (*Fig. 9*).

Although the roundover bit I used has a ball-bearing pilot, I didn't feel it gave enough control when rounding the edge. So, I added a stabilizing brace (*Fig. 10*).

To position this brace, place the trivet so the edge is firmly against the fence and almost touching the bit.

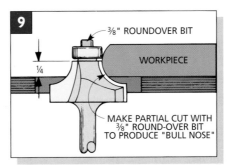

Then clamp the brace so it's perpendicular to the fence with one edge touching the trivet. Now just round over the edge of the trivet by rotating it counterclockwise.

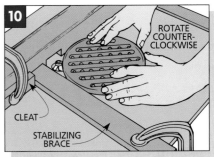

FINISH. After the edges are rounded, all that's left is to sand the trivet smooth and finish it. I used a tung oil and urethane combination finish. (For sources of finishes, see page 126.) ∎

DESIGNER'S NOTEBOOK

It's easy to make a square trivet, if the table is set up correctly and you follow the right sequence.

CONSTRUCTION NOTES:

■ The square trivet doesn't have a center groove. Instead, set up the router table to rout wide grooves that straddle the centerline. For the 7" square trivet, position the fence 2¾" from the bit (*Fig. 1*).

Note: I used a ½" straight bit to produce flat-bottomed grooves.

■ All six grooves stop ¾" from the edge of the trivet. To control these cuts, clamp plywood stop blocks to the router table so the inside edges are 5¾" from the outside edge of the bit

(*Fig. 1*). This setup is used to rout the inner grooves (*Fig. 2*).

■ To rout the next pair of grooves, cut a spacer 1" wide and long enough to fit between the stops (*Fig. 3*).

■ Finally, cut another spacer 2" wide for the third pair of grooves (*Fig. 4*).

Note: If you get burn marks at the ends of the cut, sand them with sandpaper mounted in a slotted dowel.

■ Now round all the corners and round over the edges.

SQUARE TRIVET

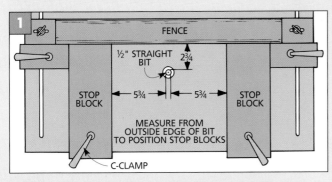

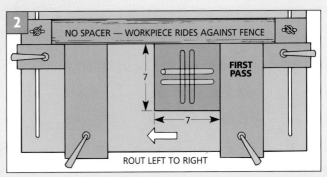

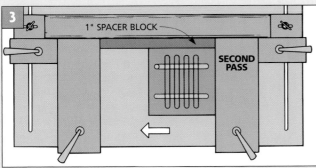

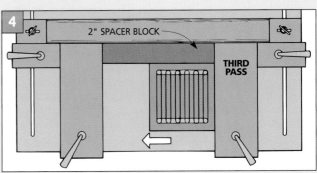

Bookends

It's easy to make good-looking bookends, but making them do their job right takes some know-how. This impressive pair combines classic styling with the ability to hold even the heaviest set of books.

When I started stocking my new bookcase with books on woodworking, I realized I needed some bookends to maintain order. That's when it dawned on me how scarce really good bookends are.

I've seen lots of good-looking bookends. But, there's more to a good bookend than good looks. It has a heavy responsibility and has to be designed to hold up. After all, if they don't keep your books from falling down, what's the point of even using them?

NOT A MATTER OF MASS. No matter how big the books are, a bookend doesn't have to be massive to do its job.

Design, not bulk, is the key. The trick is to let the books supply the weight to hold themselves up.

DESIGN. The easiest way to make a bookend that works is to evaluate why typical bookends — both heavyweights and lightweights — fall down on the job.

The Shop Info box on the next page highlights some of the things you have to take into consideration when designing bookends.

After reading it, you'll understand exactly why the Bookends here look the way they do (and why some different-looking bookends might not work so well under pressure).

OPTIONS. The version shown above has clean, classic lines that will add something to most any home library. However, depending on what type of statement you'd like to make, there is a different style available. For more on this option, see the Designer's Notebook on page 57.

MATERIALS. The main part of the Bookends (the L-shape) is made from solid 4/4 oak, for looks and strength.

The base plate that slides under the books is actually made of brass. But don't worry about cutting this thin metal — it's made easy with a simple hardboard backing (see page 56).

EXPLODED VIEW

OVERALL DIMENSIONS:
7½"W x 5D x 8¾H

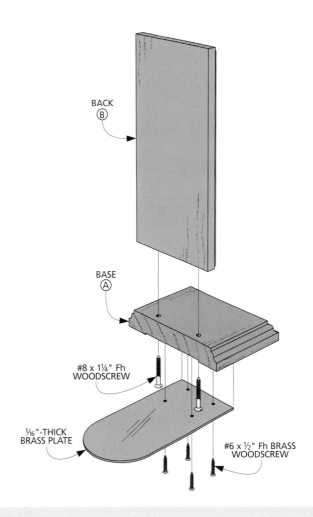

BACK
Ⓑ

BASE
Ⓐ

#8 x 1¼" Fh
WOODSCREW

1/16"-THICK
BRASS PLATE

#6 x ½" Fh BRASS
WOODSCREW

MATERIALS LIST

WOOD
A Base (2)   ³/₄ x 5 - 3½
B Back (2)   ³/₄ x 4 - 8
Note: Quantities listed are for a
set of bookends.

HARDWARE SUPPLIES
(4) No. 8 x 1¼" Fh woodscrews
(8) No. 6 x ½" Fh brass screws
(2) 1/16"-thick brass (3" x 6")

SHOP INFO .... Bookend Design

Bookends that rely solely on weight to get the job done have to be *huge* to work. If you take just one book out, even the heaviest bookends will slide when the library leans. So naturally, it makes sense to sacrifice some weight and use a better design.

LIGHTWEIGHT. The most common lightweight bookends are L-shaped *(Fig. 1)*. They can be scaled to look great and have surfaces that invite decoration. But essentially, L-shaped book-

ends are nothing more than a block with most of the mass removed. So they slide under pressure too.

One common solution to make up for the missing mass is to add a non-slip surface to the bottom of the bookend. But this doesn't help. Since friction is directly related to weight, no matter how much "grab" the bottom of a bookend has, the L-shape still slides or tilts because it's not heavy enough to bear down for a good grip.

T-SHAPED BOOKENDS. The bookend design I've found that really does the trick is a modified version of the L-shape. If you extend the base with a base plate to give the bookend the profile of an upside-down "T," you have the ideal shape *(Fig. 2)*.

The T-shape works because part of the base plate is *under* the books. This turns the bookends into one solid mass, so the books rest on the plate and actually support themselves.

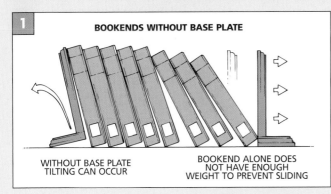

1 BOOKENDS WITHOUT BASE PLATE

WITHOUT BASE PLATE
TILTING CAN OCCUR

BOOKEND ALONE DOES
NOT HAVE ENOUGH
WEIGHT TO PREVENT SLIDING

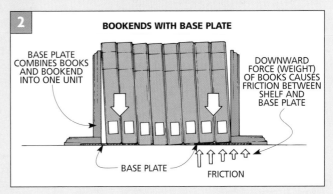

2 BOOKENDS WITH BASE PLATE

BASE PLATE
COMBINES BOOKS
AND BOOKEND
INTO ONE UNIT

DOWNWARD
FORCE (WEIGHT)
OF BOOKS CAUSES
FRICTION BETWEEN
SHELF AND
BASE PLATE

BASE PLATE   FRICTION

BASIC BOOKENDS

Start by cutting the base (A) and back (B) to size *(Fig. 1)*. These pieces come together to form the "L" shape.

Then to dress them up a little, I used a $5/32$" Roman ogee bit on the router table to profile the edges *(Fig. 1a)*. Finally, I glued and screwed the two pieces together.

Note: To provide clearance when routing a base plate recess later, counterbore the screw holes $3/8$" *(Fig. 1b)*.

BASE PLATE. To make the bookend functional, add a plate to the bottom of the base to make a "T" shape. One end of this plate is recessed into the base.

MATERIAL. The trick is to make the plate thin enough to slip under the books. I settled on two: plastic laminate

and 14-gauge sheet brass (see Sources on page 126).

RECESS BASE. It's best to cut the recess first and then cut the plate to fit snug in the recess. To do this, use a $1/2$" straight bit in the router table. Adjust the router so the bit sticks up above the table the thickness of the plate *(Fig. 2a)*. (Use the plate material itself as a gauge.)

SET FENCE. To establish the size of the recess, set up the router table using the fence and two stop blocks. To set the length of the recess, position the fence 2" from the far side of the bit *(Fig. 3)*.

SET STOPS. Then stops are used to control the width. I clamped plywood scraps to the router table so their edges were 4" from either side of the bit *(Fig. 3)*. Then, I routed the recess, using the fence and stops to control the limits of the cuts *(Fig. 4)*.

CLEAN UP CORNERS. After the recess has been routed in the base, square the corners with a chisel.

MAKE THE PLATE

Now the plate can be installed. This takes two steps: cutting the plate to size and fastening it in position.

CUTTING THIN MATERIAL. Cutting thin material on a table saw is tricky. The problem is the edge that overhangs the slot in the table insert vibrates as the blade cuts and the edge ends up

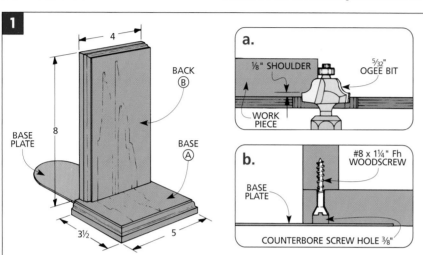

1
4
BACK (B)
BASE PLATE
8
BASE (A)
3½
5

a.
$1/8$" SHOULDER
$5/32$" OGEE BIT
WORK PIECE

b.
#8 x 1¼" Fh WOODSCREW
BASE PLATE
COUNTERBORE SCREW HOLE $3/8$"

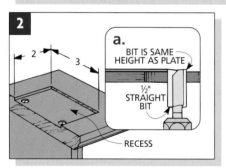

2
2
3
a. BIT IS SAME HEIGHT AS PLATE
$1/2$" STRAIGHT BIT
RECESS

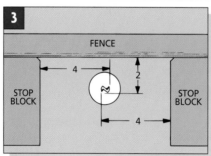

3
FENCE
4
2
STOP BLOCK
STOP BLOCK
4

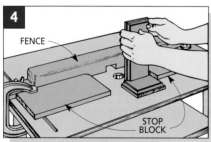

4
FENCE
STOP BLOCK

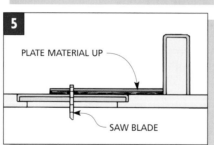

5
PLATE MATERIAL UP
SAW BLADE

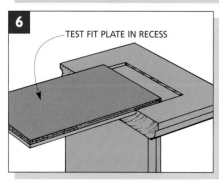

6
TEST FIT PLATE IN RECESS

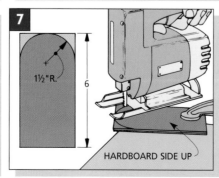

7
1½" R.
6
HARDBOARD SIDE UP

SHOP TIP
Cutting Thin Material

To support the plate all the way to the edge during sawing, I backed it with $1/8$" hardboard (I used a couple strips of carpet tape to stick the plate to the hardboard).

PLATE MATERIAL
CARPET TAPE
$1/8$" HARDBOARD BACKING

ragged. To help prevent these problems, I backed the base plate with hardboard (see the Shop Tip at the bottom of the opposite page).

CUT TO SIZE. Now cut the plate and hardboard to size on the table saw. Begin by sawing off one side to make sure one edge of the plate and hardboard is even *(Fig. 5)*.

Note: Brass is very soft and is easy to cut with a carbide-tipped saw blade.

Next, set the fence to the width of the recess in the base. With the freshly-cut edge against the fence, rip the plate to width and test the fit in the base *(Fig. 6)*. Then cut it to a length of 6".

END PROFILE. After the plate is cut to size, cut a semicircle, on the end that will slip under the books. To do this, first draw the arc on the backing. Then, clamp the piece with the hardboard side up, cut the curve to shape with a jig saw, and file it smooth *(Fig. 7)*.

CHAMFER EDGES. Before installing the plate, chamfer its edges on the router table. To do this, set the height of the chamfer bit so it takes just a tiny cut off the edge *(Fig. 8)*. Then, with the plate facing down, guide it past the bit with the hardboard riding on the bearing.

Finally, smooth the chamfer with 220-grit silicon carbide paper. Then

carefully separate the plate from the hardboard and knock off the other sharp edges with the sandpaper.

MOUNT THE PLATE

After the edges are smooth, the plate can be mounted to the base. This is where the method will differ slightly, depending on whether the plate is plastic laminate or brass.

PLASTIC LAMINATE. A plastic laminate plate can be glued to the base with epoxy. Begin by roughing up the surface that will be mounted in the recess with 60-grit sandpaper. Then glue the plate in place.

BRASS. To mount the brass plate, I used a trick that dates back to the days when gunmakers would inlay decorative brass patchboxes on the stocks of their flintlock rifles. The trick involves fastening the plate with brass screws, then filing off the screw heads flush with the plate.

INSTALL SCREWS. To install the screws, position the plate in the base recess. Then, drill pilot holes through the plate and into the base.

COUNTERSINK. After drilling the pilot holes, countersink just deep enough so the screw head is just part way into the

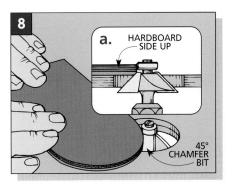
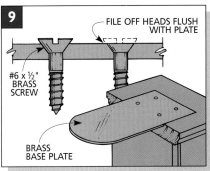

plate *(Fig. 9)*. (The screw slot should be a little higher than the plate surface.)

FILE FLUSH. After the screws are tightened, file the heads off flush with the plate. This gets rid of the screw slot, leaving a solid brass "rivet" holding the plate to the base. Then sand and polish the bottom of the plate smooth. ∎

DESIGNER'S NOTEBOOK

Add extra weight and style to the bookends with these braces.

CONSTRUCTION NOTES:

▪ Braces add weight and stability to the Bookends, as well as a touch of style.
▪ To make each brace, first cut two ³⁄₄"-thick pieces to rough size and laminate them together (see bottom view).

▪ Then cut two radii (one ³⁄₄" and the other 1¹⁄₈") connected with a tangent line (see drawing).
▪ Finally, add ogee profiles to match the ones you cut on the base and back earlier. And profile both sides of the braces.
▪ Each brace is then centered and screwed to a Bookend from underneath. Just be sure to drill pilot holes first. Also, glue it to the face of the Bookend back piece.

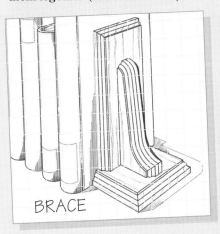

BRACE

MATERIALS LIST

NEW PARTS
C Braces (2)   1½ x 2¼ - 6

HARDWARE SUPPLIES
(4) No. 8 x 1¼" Fh woodscrews

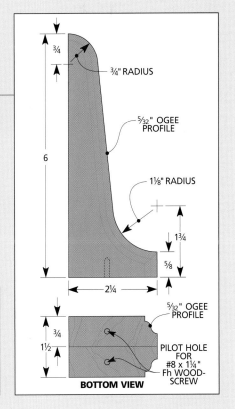

Note Board

*Just a few pieces of wood and a weekend are all you need to organize the things you can never find.
Try your hand at one of two accent carving patterns to give this project that personal touch.*

You know how it goes. When the phone call is really important, you can never find anything to write with (or write on). This Note Board solves that problem. Besides holding a standard office calendar (8½" x 11"), it also has a shelf to keep a note pad and pen close at hand.

The Note Board is a simple project. There are only five different wood parts, and the joinery is quite simple. You might even have all the stock you need on hand in your shop already. So, if you choose to build only the Note Board as shown, you can easily be finished in a couple of days.

CARVING. On the other hand, if you decide to include a carving pattern for some extra pizazz (see inset photo), there are some things to consider before you begin.

The first consideration is the stock you choose. Without the carving pattern, this Note Board could be made out of just about any ¾" stock. But if you want to add the pattern, you'll want to choose stock that is appropriate for carving (see the Woodworker's Notebook on the opposite page).

The second thing to consider is the carving itself. Just because it's an artistic pattern with curved lines

doesn't mean you have to wing it. There's a step-by-step procedure that will make accent carving a lot easier, especially if you haven't had a lot of experience with it (see the Technique article on page 63).

PATTERNS. Speaking of carving, you also have a choice of *what* to carve. Two different patterns are shown in the Designer's Notebook on page 61.

EXPLODED VIEW

OVERALL DIMENSIONS:
12³/₄W x 3¹/₂D x 17¹/₂H

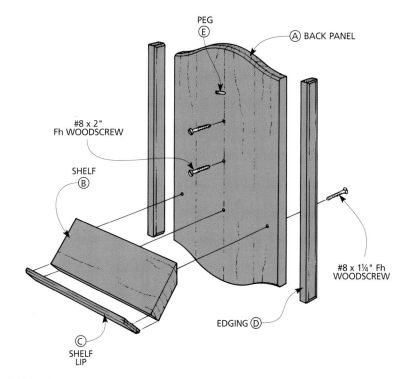

PEG
Ⓔ

Ⓐ BACK PANEL

#8 x 2"
Fh WOODSCREW

SHELF
Ⓑ

#8 x 1¹/₄" Fh
WOODSCREW

EDGING Ⓓ

Ⓒ

SHELF
LIP

MATERIALS LIST

WOOD

A	Back Panel (1)	³/₄ x 11¹/₄ x 17¹/₂
B	Shelf (1)	³/₄ x 3¹/₄ x 11
C	Shelf Lip (1)	¹/₄ x 1¹/₄ x 11
D	Edging (2)	³/₄ x 1 x 15¹/₂
E	Peg (1)	¹/₈ dowel x 1

HARDWARE SUPPLIES
(3) No. 8 x 1¹/₄" Fh woodscrews
(2) No. 8 x 2" Fh woodscrews

CUTTING DIAGRAM

³/₄ x 7¹/₂ - 48 (2.5 Bd. Ft.)

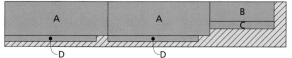

WOODWORKER'S NOTEBOOK

If you decide to add the carving pattern to the Note Board, take a moment to choose the right wood.

CARVING STOCK

Before you get started on the Note Board, I should mention something about the kind of wood to use. If you're planning to do one of the carving patterns, remember that choosing the right type of wood is just as important as choosing the right tool.

SOFT. The perfect wood for this type of carving has two qualities. First of all, it should be soft. This will make it easier for you to control the chisel and make the necessary cuts.

The second quality to look for when choosing wood for carving is a tight, straight grain pattern. (Or better yet, no visible grain pattern at all.)

In fact, woods traditionally used for carving, like basswood, have barely noticeable grain patterns.

PINE. For the Note Board, I decided to use pine. It's not as well-known for carving as basswood, but pine can also be a good carving wood. Keep in mind, though, that the type of wood is only one half of the equation. You also have to choose the *right* boards.

To look at the Note Board on page 58, you might think it was a good project to use some scraps of pine that were lying around the shop. But that's not necessarily the case.

Pine is generally considered a soft wood, but some pieces of pine are a lot harder than others. The harder boards can be readily identified by their dark grain patterns. This darker grain (called latewood) contains resins that make it much harder than the lighter

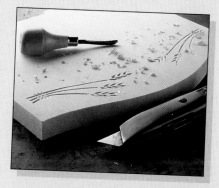

(and normally softer) earlywood. Carving through latewood is difficult.

So when you pick out your pieces for the Note Board, pick out the softest boards with the lightest grain patterns that you can find. The result will be a crisp and clean carving, and a project that was more fun to build.

BACK PANEL

I began by gluing up a blank for the back panel (A) *(Fig. 1)*. Ripping the blank to width is easy. Cutting the curves is a little more involved.

To lay out the curves, I used a half pattern *(Fig. 1)*. (Making a full pattern requires cutting two identical curves.) By flipping the half pattern over, the curves mirror each other exactly.

Note: To make the pattern, enlarge *Fig. 1a* on a photocopy machine until the squares are 1". Then glue it to a piece of cardboard (or hardboard), cut the curve, and sand it smooth.

Next, trace the pattern onto the blank and cut the curves staying 1/16" outside the line. Then sand up to the line.

Note: If you plan to carve a pattern, it's best to do it now (pages 61 and 63).

Now to complete the panel, rout a 1/8" chamfer along the front edge of each end of the back panel *(Fig. 2)*.

SHELF

A shelf is the first piece to be added to the back panel. It's attached at an angle and has a lip for a pen and a note pad.

Start by cutting the shelf (B) to rough size *(Fig. 3)*. (Later, one edge will be beveled, but it's easier to clamp the lip to the shelf while it still has square edges.)

Now, glue a shelf lip (C) to the edge of the shelf *(Fig. 3)*. Once it's dry, the lip can be chamfered *(Fig. 3a)*. Routing this tiny piece is much safer now that it's been glued to the shelf.

Next, tilt the table saw blade to 45° and rip the shelf to final width *(Fig. 3b)*.

You can't just glue the shelf in place. Its grain runs *across* the panel's. The panel expands and contracts across its width, and this movement would eventually cause the joint to come apart.

The solution is to attach the shelf with screws *(Fig. 4)*. To do this, first drill oversized shank holes. Then spot glue the shelf to the panel to hold it in place while the pilot holes are drilled and the shelf is attached (see Shop Tip above).

SHOP TIP
Spot Gluing

To position the shelf on the panel, all you need are two drops of glue and some hand pressure. Later, it can be secured with screws.

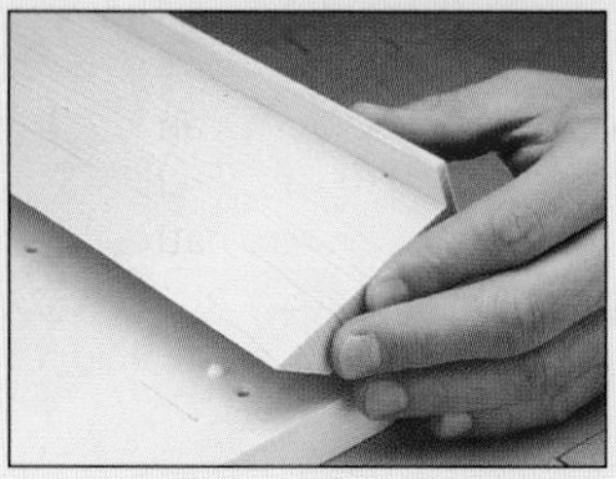

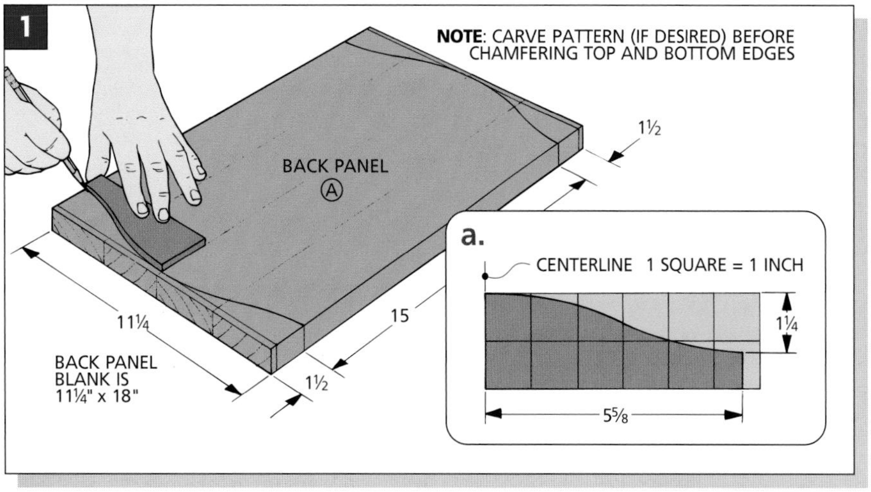

1
NOTE: CARVE PATTERN (IF DESIRED) BEFORE CHAMFERING TOP AND BOTTOM EDGES
BACK PANEL
A
1½
11¼
15
1½
BACK PANEL BLANK IS 11¼" x 18"
a.
CENTERLINE 1 SQUARE = 1 INCH
1¼
5⅝

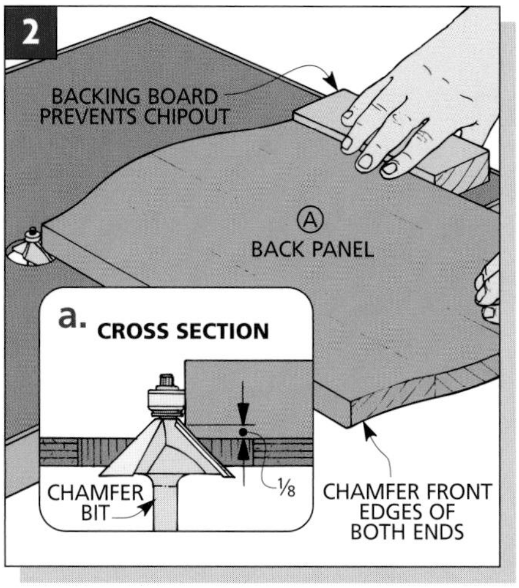

2
BACKING BOARD PREVENTS CHIPOUT
A
BACK PANEL
a. CROSS SECTION
CHAMFER BIT
⅛
CHAMFER FRONT EDGES OF BOTH ENDS

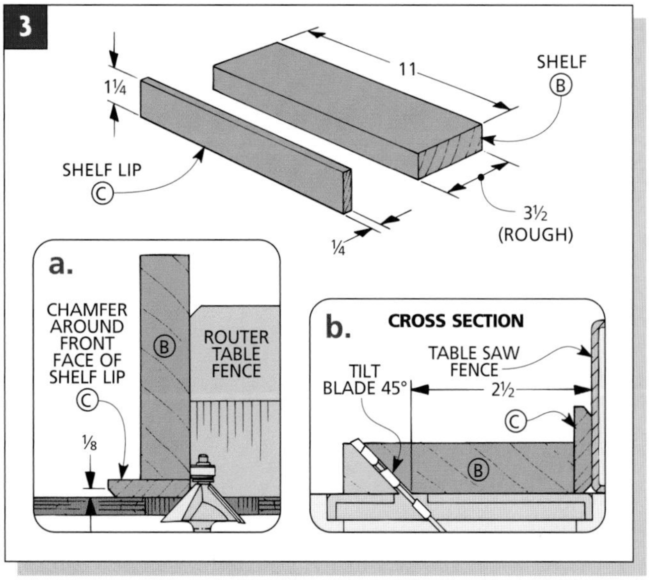

3
1¼
11
SHELF
B
SHELF LIP
C
3½ (ROUGH)
¼
a.
CHAMFER AROUND FRONT FACE OF SHELF LIP
C
B
ROUTER TABLE FENCE
⅛
b. CROSS SECTION
TABLE SAW FENCE
TILT BLADE 45°
2½
C
B

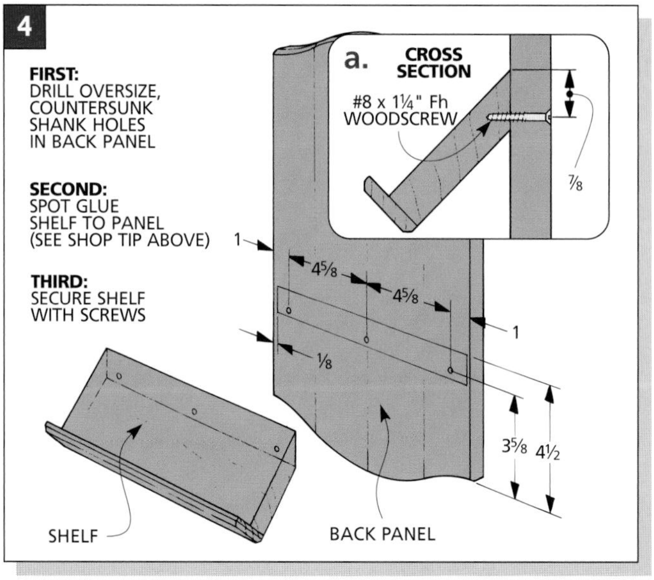

4
FIRST: DRILL OVERSIZE, COUNTERSUNK SHANK HOLES IN BACK PANEL
SECOND: SPOT GLUE SHELF TO PANEL (SEE SHOP TIP ABOVE)
THIRD: SECURE SHELF WITH SCREWS
a. CROSS SECTION
#8 x 1¼" Fh WOODSCREW
⅞
1
4⅝
4⅝
1
⅛
3⅝
4½
SHELF
BACK PANEL

DESIGNER'S NOTEBOOK

Adding a hand-carved pattern to the top of the Note Board really makes the project one of a kind. Choose either pattern below, and transfer it easily with a photocopier and some transfer paper.

CARVING PATTERNS

■ These simple patterns are perfect for trying your hand at carving. In no time at all, you'll be able to master a few simple techniques so you can add a decorative accent to a project.

■ Carving these patterns doesn't require a large initial investment either. You'll need one inexpensive carving chisel, a sharp utility knife, and some scrap pieces for practice.

■ If you're artistic, you might not need a pattern. But just in case, you can use one of the reduced-size patterns below.

Note: You'll need to enlarge the pattern on a photocopier or scanner until it's 11¼" wide (roughly 195%).

■ I used transfer paper to get the pattern on the wood (see page 126 for sources). Transfer paper leaves "dry" lines you can erase easily after carving.

■ To transfer the pattern, tape it to the panel (image up) so the curves line up. Then slip transfer paper between the pattern and the wood (dark side down). Now trace the pattern with a pencil.

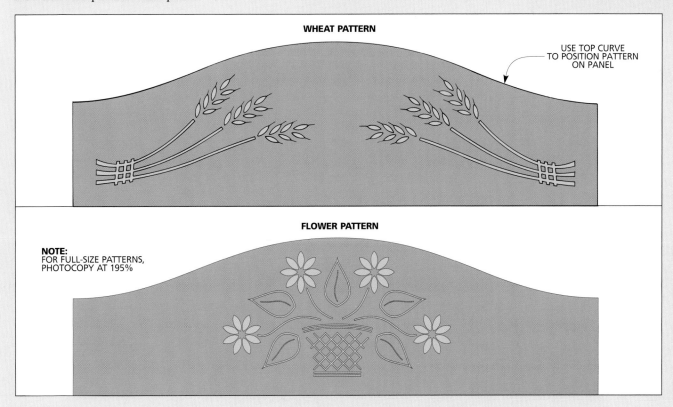

WHEAT PATTERN

USE TOP CURVE
TO POSITION PATTERN
ON PANEL

FLOWER PATTERN

NOTE:
FOR FULL-SIZE PATTERNS,
PHOTOCOPY AT 195%

EDGING & PEG

All that's left are some decorative edging pieces and a peg to hang the calendar.

First cut two pieces of edging (D) and chamfer three edges *(Figs. 5 and 5a)*.

Now simply glue and clamp the edging to the panel *(Fig. 5b)*. (Let the glue set a bit before you attach each edging piece. This way, the edging won't slide around.)

Then drill a hole angled at 10° to accept the ⅛"-dia. peg (E) that holds the calendar *(Fig. 6)*.

For the finish, I applied a coat of wood conditioner, then two coats of a maple stain. For a top coat, I used a tung oil and urethane combination. ■

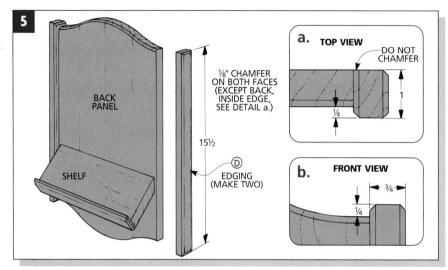

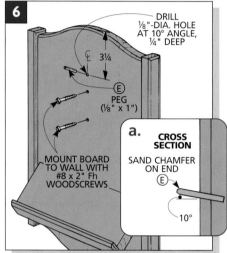

TECHNIQUE . . . . *Sharpening a V-Chisel*

Compared to a regular chisel, sharpening a carving tool is a bit more involved — especially one like the V-parting chisel used to carve the patterns on the Note Board.

For a V-parting tool, you begin like you're sharpening a regular chisel (with the beveled face down). But because a V-parting tool has two sides that come together at an angle, both outside faces must be sharpened *(Fig. 1)*. (I use a medium-grit oil or water stone.)

To do this, hold the chisel at a 20°-25° angle and move it along the stone.

To keep the angle consistent, use short strokes. (Sharpen both sides evenly.)

BURR. What you're looking for is a small burr that runs completely across the inside face on each side. To keep this burr from breaking off and forming a ragged edge, I remove it by dragging the face against the corner of a leather strop.

HOOK. With the burr removed, there's still a small "hook" left on the outside corner *(Fig. 2a)*. If you don't remove it, the tool will be hard to control. To remove it, gently roll the tip of the chisel across a medium stone *(Fig. 2)*.

But be careful not to remove too much metal. Instead of just grinding away the hook, you'll create a divot that prevents a clean cut. (If this happens, square up the edges and start again.)

POLISH. Finally, polish the chisel with a leather strop or buffing wheel. Polishing sharpens the tool by removing tiny nicks in the edge where the outside and inside faces come together.

To do this, add jeweler's rouge to the leather and repeat the steps to polish the edge *(Fig. 3)*. Don't overdo it though. You can change the angle of the bevel.

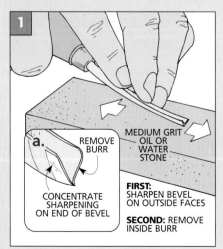

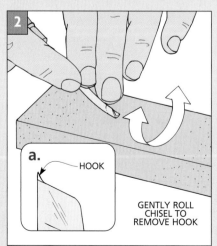

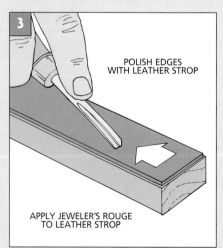

The best tool I found for carving accents on the Note Board was a V-parting chisel. Its palm-handle grip is comfortable and easy to control.

Note: The steps shown here are for the wheat pattern shown on page 61. But the same types of cuts are used to carve the flower pattern.

There are two basic cuts needed to carve the pattern. The first is a long shallow cut for the stalks *(Fig. 1)*. I found it easiest to hold the chisel at a low angle with one hand and guide it with the other. But don't try to make the entire cut at once (it's hard to stop cleanly). Carve most of the stalk in one direction, then finish it from the other.

For the stalks, it's important to keep the lines smooth and even. If you want the line to widen, just raise the handle a little. Then the chisel will dig in deeper and make a wider cut.

The second cut shapes the kernels of wheat. This is also a two-step process *(Fig. 2)*. Start by pushing the tool into the wood about half the length of the kernel.

Then repeat this cut from the opposite direction. An oval-shaped chip will pop out where the cuts meet. Keep the angle of the tool the same for each cut to get a cleaner carving *(Fig. 2a)*.

For one last detail, use a utility knife to score a line through each kernel to make the "beard" (refer to *Step 5*).

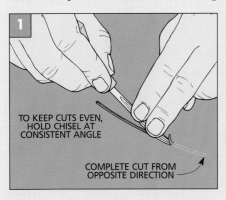

1 TO KEEP CUTS EVEN, HOLD CHISEL AT CONSISTENT ANGLE

COMPLETE CUT FROM OPPOSITE DIRECTION

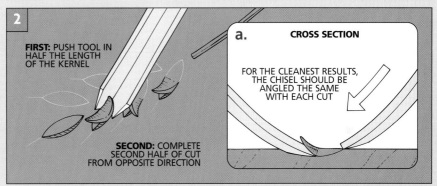

2 FIRST: PUSH TOOL IN HALF THE LENGTH OF THE KERNEL

SECOND: COMPLETE SECOND HALF OF CUT FROM OPPOSITE DIRECTION

a. CROSS SECTION

FOR THE CLEANEST RESULTS, THE CHISEL SHOULD BE ANGLED THE SAME WITH EACH CUT

STEP-BY-STEP

You might be tempted just to "jump in" and start carving this wheat pattern. But in order to avoid chipout, it's important to follow a certain sequence.

I started with the stalks. This curved cut is the hardest to control. And if you carve the ties before the stalks, there's a good chance the wood will chip out.

The ties are also a two-step process. It's easy to "overshoot" the cut.

Finally, I cut the kernels of wheat. There isn't any particular sequence here. But make sure you don't cut the kernels too close together. Any closer than $1/8$", and the pine may chip out.

1 *To carve the wheat, first transfer the pattern to the panel. Then begin by cutting the stalks. But don't cut the whole stalk at once. Stop about 1" short.*

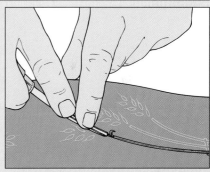

2 *Complete the stalk by starting from the opposite end and connecting with the first cut. For an even line, hold the chisel at the same angle as before.*

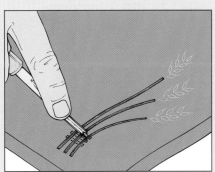

3 *Next carve the ties. Again, cut these from both directions (for better control of the depth and length of the cut).*

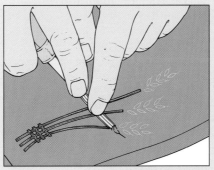

4 *For a kernel, you want a single, oval-shaped chip. This is done in two steps, with the angle of the chisel consistent.*

5 *To add "beards," simply take a sharp utility knife and make a scoring cut through the center of each kernel.*

Serving Tray

The smallest pieces in this project draw the most attention — the contrasting splines at every joint line.
But the most intriguing feature is the way the rounded corners are made so they're strong and durable.

Sometimes the best reason for building a project is to test out a new woodworking technique. That was my approach as I started to work on this Serving Tray. The tray itself didn't seem as important as having the chance to try out a corner joint I'd never used before.

The technique I chose involves cutting a radius (or rounded) corner, without bending it. That in itself isn't too difficult (just cut it from an oversized piece). But the challenge is to join this corner piece to the other frame pieces. You can't simply glue the corner blocks in place, because you'd be gluing end grain to end grain (which doesn't make for a very strong joint).

Therefore, it's necessary to do a little planning ahead on how the corner pieces are laid out and cut.

GROOVE AND SPLINE. The best solution I found was to use a set of three groove and spline joints in each place where the frame pieces came together. Not only does this make for strong joints (the grain of the splines runs perpendicular to the joint line), but it also gives each corner of the Serving Tray an interesting visual accent.

The splines are resawn from thicker stock, so you can choose just about any hardwood you like. (You can try to match the shade of the rest of the project, or choose a darker wood to add even more contrast.)

Note: You might be tempted to substitute hardboard for the splines, since it's readily available in $1/8$"-thick sheets. However, you would be losing much of the strength of the joint, since hardboard has no grain.

SQUARE CORNERS. There's also an option for a simpler version of the tray using miters. The corners are still reinforced with splines, but you won't need to cut as many parts. See the Designer's Notebook on page 70.

EXPLODED VIEW

OVERALL DIMENSIONS:
15W x 9¼D x 3½H

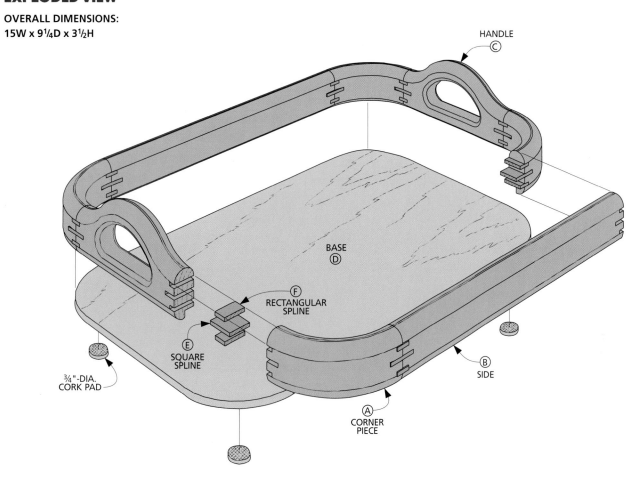

HANDLE Ⓒ

BASE Ⓓ

Ⓕ RECTANGULAR SPLINE

Ⓔ SQUARE SPLINE

¾"-DIA. CORK PAD

Ⓑ SIDE

Ⓐ CORNER PIECE

MATERIALS LIST

WOOD
A Corner Pieces (4)   1⅝ x 3⅛ - 3⅛
B Sides (2)   ¾ x 1⅝ - 11¾
C Handles (2)   ¾ x 3½ - 6
D Base (1)   ¼ ply - 12 x 17¾
E Square Splines (8)   ⅛ x 1 - 1
F Rect. Splines (16)   ⅛ x ½ - 1

HARDWARE SUPPLIES
(12) ½" wire brads
(4) ¾"-dia. cork pads

CUTTING DIAGRAM

¾ x 3½ - 60 (1.5 Bd. Ft.)

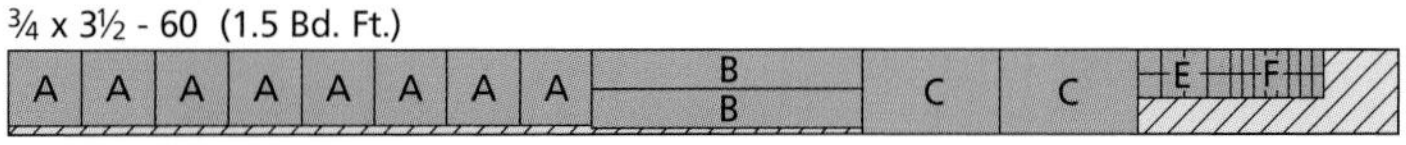

| A | A | A | A | A | A | A | A | B / B | C | C | E | F | |

¼" PLYWOOD - 12 x 24

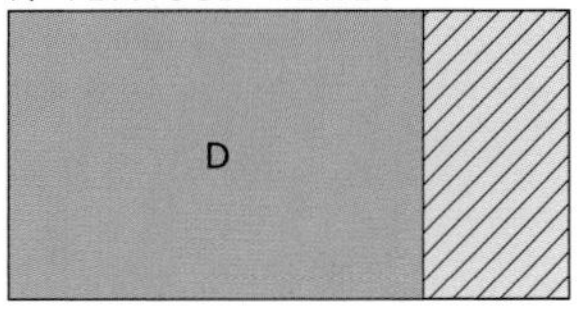

| D | |

CORNER PIECES

To make the corners (A) for the Serving Tray, I started by laminating two pieces of 4/4 stock ($3/4$" to $13/16$" actual thickness) which will produce a blank $1^1/2$" to $1^5/8$" thick *(Fig. 1)*. (Or, you can use a piece of 8/4 stock.)

CUT BLOCKS. To cut the four blocks needed for the corner pieces, begin by cutting off the end of the blank at a 45° angle. Then cut off four triangular-shaped blocks *(Fig. 1)*. To make the blocks square, see the Shop Tip below.

LAY OUT CORNERS. Now the curved corners can be laid out on the blocks. The easiest way to do this is to tape the four blocks together. Then use a compass to draw two circles *(Fig. 2)*. (The Shop Tip at right explains why.)

The outside circle has a radius of 3". The inside circle is drawn so the corner pieces have a thickness equal to the stock thickness for the tray sides. (I used stock that was $13/16$" thick so the radius of the inside circle is $2^3/16$".)

SIDES & HANDLES

After drawing these circles, I cut the stock for the tray's sides and handles. Each side (B) is $11^3/4$" long *(Fig. 5)*. These side pieces are cut to width so they equal the thickness (height) of the corner block ($1^5/8$" in my case).

SHOP TIP
Squaring Triangles

To make a square block, cut the triangular "ears" off with a band saw. Clamp the stop block so each side equals the desired radius.

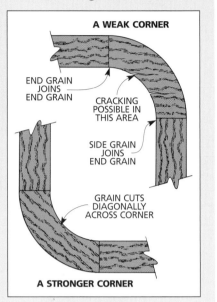

CUT OFF EARS

OUTSIDE CORNER RADIUS PLUS $1/8$"

STOP BLOCK

SHOP TIP . . . . . . *Strong Corners*

The easy, cheap way to make the rounded corners for the Serving Tray is to lay out the radii on a piece of stock and cut out the corner on the band saw. But I don't think it's the best way to cut corners.

The problems have to do with grain direction. The corner makes a 90° turn, so the grain cuts directly across the narrow width, which could lead to cracking. In addition, the joints are weak. You're either joining end grain to end grain or end grain to side grain (neither combination is particularly strong).

Cutting the corners from square blocks produces diagonal grain, solving both problems.

A WEAK CORNER

END GRAIN JOINS END GRAIN

CRACKING POSSIBLE IN THIS AREA

SIDE GRAIN JOINS END GRAIN

GRAIN CUTS DIAGONALLY ACROSS CORNER

A STRONGER CORNER

The pieces for the handles (C) are cut to a length of 6" *(Fig. 5)*. Since the handles rise above the level of the corners and the sides, these pieces are cut extra wide (tall), to a height of $3^1/2$".

GROOVE & SPLINE JOINTS

Now the joints can be cut to connect all the pieces. I used a spline and groove joint. This requires cutting grooves in

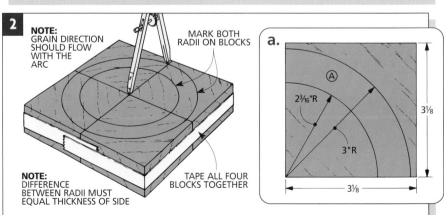

1

29

$4^7/16$

WASTE AREA

LAMINATE TWO PIECES OF 4/4 STOCK TOGETHER $1^1/2$" TO $1^5/8$" THICK

CUT FOUR IDENTICAL CORNERS

CUT OFF "EARS" (SEE SHOP TIP AT LEFT)

$3^1/8$ $3^1/8$

CUT TRIANGLES AT 45° ANGLE

(A)

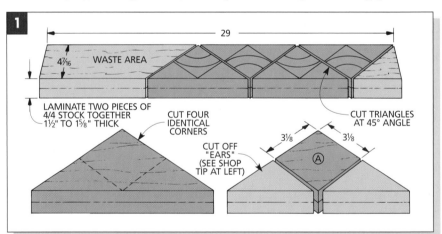

2

NOTE: GRAIN DIRECTION SHOULD FLOW WITH THE ARC

MARK BOTH RADII ON BLOCKS

a.

$2^3/16$"R

3"R

(A)

$3^1/8$

$3^1/8$

NOTE: DIFFERENCE BETWEEN RADII MUST EQUAL THICKNESS OF SIDE

TAPE ALL FOUR BLOCKS TOGETHER

the mating ends of each piece, and then cutting splines to fit the grooves.

GROOVES. To show off the joint, I cut grooves in each piece — two shallow grooves and a deep groove in between.

To cut the shallow grooves, set the blade to a height of 1/4". Then position the rip fence so it's 3/8" from the inside of the blade *(Fig. 5a)*.

Note: I used a rip blade here, because all its teeth are ground flat across the top, producing a flat-bottom groove.

CORNER GROOVES. When the saw is set up, hold the corner block firmly against the fence and cut a shallow groove in one edge *(Fig. 3)*. (Make sure the groove is cut on an edge where the ends of the curve are drawn.) Then rotate the block and make a second cut in the other edge at the other end of the curve.

SIDE GROOVES. Next, matching grooves are cut in the ends of the side pieces (B). Here, I used a 2x4 block to support the piece while it's pushed through the blade *(Fig. 4)*. Make this cut on both ends of the side pieces, with the same edge against the fence.

Note: Since this entire procedure requires working with the same edge against the fence for all three cuts in each piece, I marked the outside (top) edge of all the pieces with an "X" *(Fig. 5)*.

HANDLE GROOVES. With the saw still in the same setup, make this same cut in both ends of the two handle pieces (C). Again, I used a 2x4 block to support the handle as the groove is cut.

To cut the other shallow groove, it would seem easiest to simply turn the pieces around (so the opposite edge is against the fence) and make the cut.

This would work fine on the corner pieces and the sides, but not on the handle (it's wider). Instead, you have to adjust the rip fence so the measurement from the *outside* of the corner block to the *outside* of the blade is 3/8" *(Fig. 6a)*.

Once the fence is adjusted, go ahead and make the second set of shallow grooves in the ends of all the pieces (corner blocks, sides, and handles). When you're done, all of the pieces should have two shallow grooves that align between the pieces *(Fig. 6)*.

CENTER GROOVE. The last step is to cut the deeper center groove. Raise the blade to a height of 1/2". Then position the fence so the blade is centered between the first two cuts *(Fig. 7a)*. Make this cut on all the pieces, again keeping the edge with the "X" out.

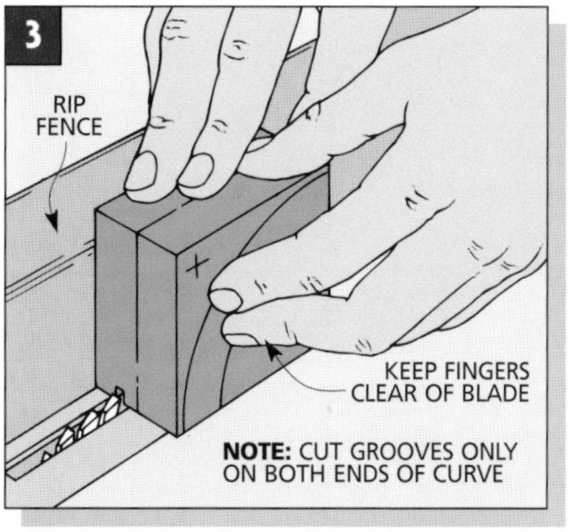
3
RIP FENCE
KEEP FINGERS CLEAR OF BLADE
NOTE: CUT GROOVES ONLY ON BOTH ENDS OF CURVE

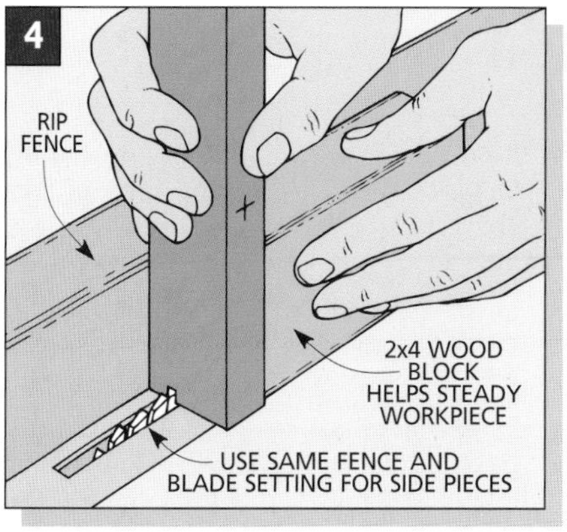
4
RIP FENCE
2x4 WOOD BLOCK HELPS STEADY WORKPIECE
USE SAME FENCE AND BLADE SETTING FOR SIDE PIECES

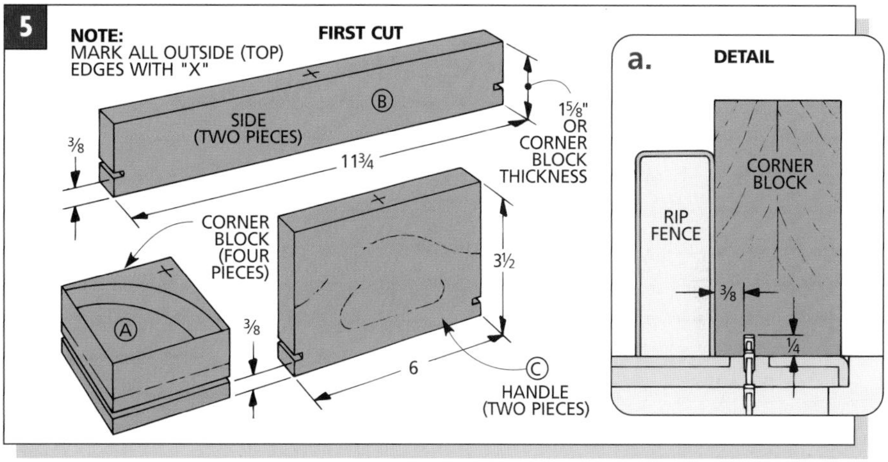
5
NOTE: MARK ALL OUTSIDE (TOP) EDGES WITH "X"
FIRST CUT
SIDE (TWO PIECES)
B
3/8
11 3/4
1 5/8" OR CORNER BLOCK THICKNESS
CORNER BLOCK (FOUR PIECES)
A
3/8
3 1/2
6
C
HANDLE (TWO PIECES)
a. DETAIL
CORNER BLOCK
RIP FENCE
3/8
1/4

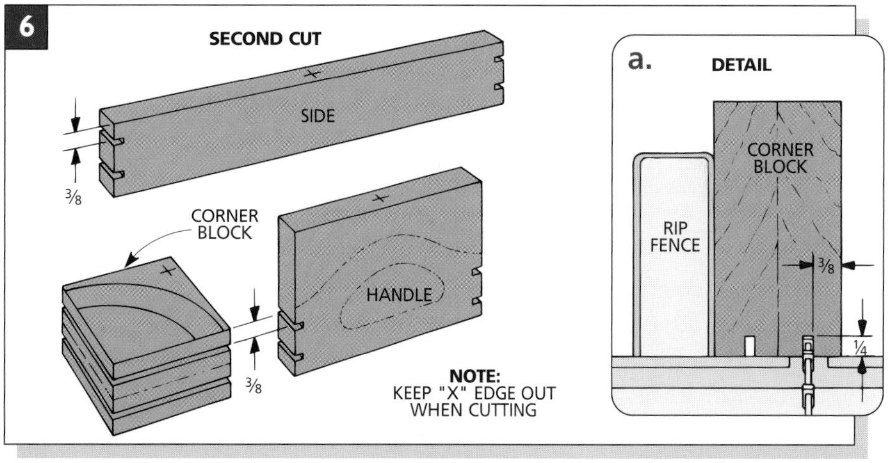
6
SECOND CUT
SIDE
3/8
CORNER BLOCK
HANDLE
3/8
NOTE: KEEP "X" EDGE OUT WHEN CUTTING
a. DETAIL
CORNER BLOCK
RIP FENCE
3/8
1/4

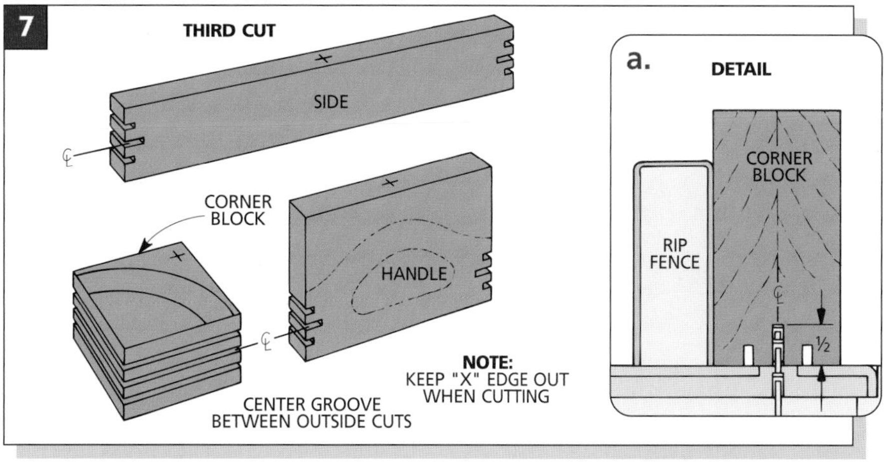
7
THIRD CUT
SIDE
CORNER BLOCK
HANDLE
NOTE: KEEP "X" EDGE OUT WHEN CUTTING
CENTER GROOVE BETWEEN OUTSIDE CUTS
a. DETAIL
CORNER BLOCK
RIP FENCE
1/2

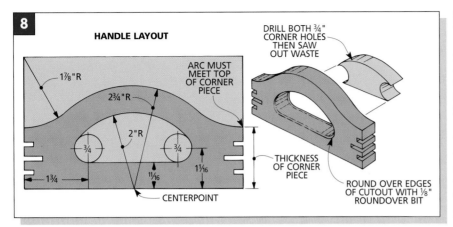

8 HANDLE LAYOUT

1⅞" R

2¾" R

2" R

ARC MUST MEET TOP OF CORNER PIECE

¾

¾

1¾

11/16

11/16

CENTERPOINT

DRILL BOTH ¾" CORNER HOLES THEN SAW OUT WASTE

THICKNESS OF CORNER PIECE

ROUND OVER EDGES OF CUTOUT WITH ⅛" ROUNDOVER BIT

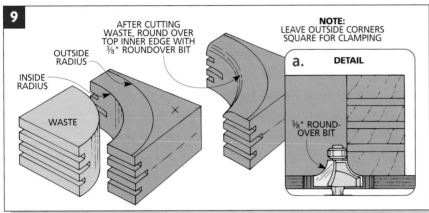

9

OUTSIDE RADIUS

INSIDE RADIUS

WASTE

AFTER CUTTING WASTE, ROUND OVER TOP INNER EDGE WITH ⅜" ROUNDOVER BIT

NOTE: LEAVE OUTSIDE CORNERS SQUARE FOR CLAMPING

a. DETAIL

⅜" ROUND-OVER BIT

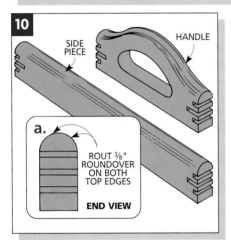

10

SIDE PIECE

HANDLE

a.

ROUT ⅜" ROUNDOVER ON BOTH TOP EDGES

END VIEW

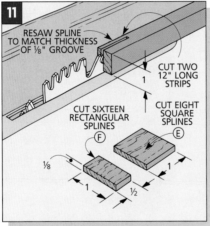

11

RESAW SPLINE TO MATCH THICKNESS OF ⅛" GROOVE

CUT TWO 12" LONG STRIPS

1

CUT SIXTEEN RECTANGULAR SPLINES

CUT EIGHT SQUARE SPLINES

⅛

1

½

F

E

1

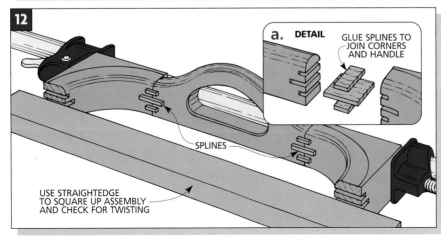

12

a. DETAIL

GLUE SPLINES TO JOIN CORNERS AND HANDLE

SPLINES

USE STRAIGHTEDGE TO SQUARE UP ASSEMBLY AND CHECK FOR TWISTING

HANDLE & CORNERS

After the grooves are cut in all the pieces, I cut the handle to final shape. The inside of the handle is defined by a ¾"-dia. hole at each end *(Fig. 8)*. Then a 2"-radius arc is drawn to connect the holes.

DRAW CURVES. The outside of the tray handle is shaped by two intersecting curves. One is a 2¾" radius drawn from the same center point as the radius for the inside of the handle. This curve intersects with two 1⅞"-radius curves drawn from each top corner of the block *(Fig. 8)*.

CUT OUT HANDLES. After the curves are drawn, drill the ¾"-dia. holes. Then cut out the center of the handle with a scroll saw or jig saw and sand the edge smooth. Next, round over these inside edges with a ⅛" roundover bit *(Fig. 8)*. Also cut the top outside edge of the handle to shape and sand it smooth.

CORNERS. After the handles are shaped, I cut the inside radius of each corner piece on a band saw *(Fig. 9)*. Sand this edge smooth with a drum sander on a drill press. (However, leave the outside corner square. It's used as a clamping surface during assembly.)

ROUND OVER EDGES. Usually I would wait until after assembly to sand and round over the edges. But here, you can't round the top inside edges of the tray because the handles will be in the way.

I rounded over the top edges of the sides and handles with a ⅜" roundover bit in the router table *(Fig. 10)*. Also round over the top inside edges of the corner pieces *(Fig. 9a)*.

ASSEMBLY

To join the pieces, you have to cut three splines for each joint *(Fig. 11)*. The splines can be cut from the same wood to match the tray stock, or from contrasting (darker) wood to highlight the joint.

For strength, the splines are cut so the grain runs perpendicular to the joint line. I cut the splines by resawing ⅛"-thick strips *(Fig. 11)*. The width of these strips should be enough so the splines extend out about ⅛" to allow for some shifting during glue-up *(Fig. 12)*.

GLUING. Once the splines are cut, assembly can begin. First, glue splines to join two corner pieces and one handle. Clamp this unit together *(Fig. 12)*.

As the clamp is tightened, make sure the ends of the corners don't twist. They must be square so they can be joined to the side pieces. I placed a straightedge against the ends of the corner pieces to check for square *(Fig. 12)*.

ADD SIDES. After the end units are glued up, add the sides. Now, it can be tricky to keep the frame from twisting. The best approach is to place the clamps on a smooth level surface *(Fig. 13)*.

Then put the frame in position and push down firmly against the clamps. Tighten each clamp a little at a time, making sure the frame doesn't twist.

COMPLETE CORNER PIECES

When the glue is dry, you can complete the corner pieces. First, use a band saw to cut off the outside corner *(Fig. 14)*.

FILE INSIDE. As these cuts are made, the band saw automatically trims off the spline's excess on the outside of the tray. Use a file to remove the excess on the inside. Then sand the inside and outside edges of the tray frame.

ROUND OVER CORNERS. All the tray's top edges were rounded over before assembly except the outside of the corner pieces. Rounding over these edges is awkward. I held the tray frame vertically on the router table and slid it in an arc into a $\frac{3}{8}$" roundover bit *(Fig. 15)*.

TRAY BOTTOM

The last step is to add the bottom. I made the bottom out of hardwood plywood to match the tray frame stock.

RABBET. Before getting to the tray bottom, a rabbet is cut on the bottom of the frame. To do this, I used a rabbet bit on the router table *(Fig. 16)*. Set the bit to a height of $\frac{1}{4}$" and rout the rabbet around the entire inside perimeter.

Note: The depth of the rabbet (shown as $\frac{1}{4}$" in *Fig. 16*) is actually deeper than the final tray bottom thickness to allow room for the cork pads.

After the rabbet is routed, the tray bottom can be cut to fit. Place the tray frame on the tray bottom. Then mark the outline of the rabbet *(Fig. 17)*.

The plywood bottom is cut to width and length (on the marked lines) on a table saw to get a smooth cut. Then sand the corners round on a disc sander.

DETAILS. Now fasten the tray bottom to the frame with glue and brads. Then sand the tray and glue the cork pads to the bottom *(Fig. 18)*. Finally, I applied two coats of polyurethane varnish. ■

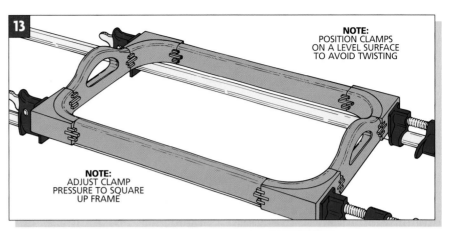

13

NOTE: POSITION CLAMPS ON A LEVEL SURFACE TO AVOID TWISTING

NOTE: ADJUST CLAMP PRESSURE TO SQUARE UP FRAME

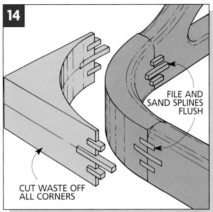

14

CUT WASTE OFF ALL CORNERS

FILE AND SAND SPLINES FLUSH

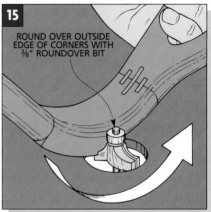

15

ROUND OVER OUTSIDE EDGE OF CORNERS WITH $\frac{3}{8}$" ROUNDOVER BIT

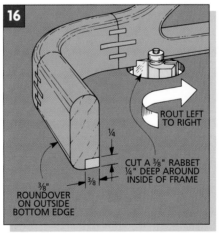

16

ROUT LEFT TO RIGHT

$\frac{1}{4}$

$\frac{3}{8}$

$\frac{3}{8}$" ROUNDOVER ON OUTSIDE BOTTOM EDGE

CUT A $\frac{3}{8}$" RABBET $\frac{1}{4}$" DEEP AROUND INSIDE OF FRAME

17

TRACE AROUND INSIDE EDGE OF RABBET

$\frac{1}{4}$" PLYWOOD BASE

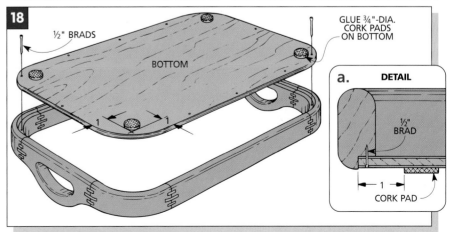

18

$\frac{1}{2}$" BRADS

BOTTOM

GLUE $\frac{3}{4}$"-DIA. CORK PADS ON BOTTOM

1   1

a. **DETAIL**

$\frac{1}{2}$" BRAD

1

CORK PAD

DESIGNER'S NOTEBOOK

Making the tray with mitered corners gives it a different look, and adds a little extra serving space. It's also even simpler to build, since you don't have to worry about the rounded corner pieces.

CONSTRUCTION NOTES:

■ Making the square version of the Serving Tray is really more a matter of what you *don't* have to do, rather than what you do. Specifically, you skip the rounded corner pieces (A) and go straight to the larger parts.

■ Start by cutting the sides (B) and handles (C) to rough size (note the new dimensions in the Materials List below right and *Fig. 1*).

■ Now miter the sides and handles to final length, making sure the opposite pieces are symmetrical to each other. (For tips on cutting accurate miters, refer to the Technique article beginning on page 14.)

■ Cut the handles to shape, adding the handholds as before *(Fig. 1)*.

■ Then rabbet the bottom inside edges of these pieces for the base (to be added later) *(Fig. 1)*.

Note: The rabbet is now ¼" x ¼".

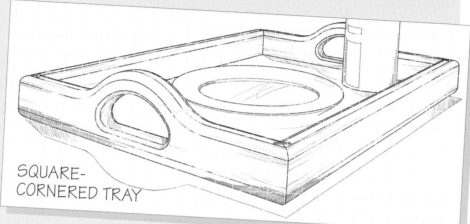

SQUARE-CORNERED TRAY

■ Then round over all the remaining square edges of the sides and handles, including inside the handholds *(Fig. 1)*.

■ Next, cut a pair of saw kerfs in each side and handle *(Fig. 2)*. To do this, tilt the saw blade 45°, lower it to cut a ¼"-deep kerf, and use the rip fence as a stop to position the workpiece.

■ Now resaw four rectangular splines (D) to match the thickness of the kerfs *(Fig. 2)*. Cut each to length to match the combined depth of the two kerfs it will be placed in.

Note: The grain of the splines should run across the joint line *(Fig. 3)*.

■ Leave the splines a hair wide to start (the excess is removed after assembly to create a smooth joint on top of the tray).

■ Finally, assemble the tray. First glue all the splined miter joints, then glue and nail the base in place *(Fig. 4)*. Then you can add the finishing details just like on the round-cornered tray.

MATERIALS LIST

CHANGED PARTS

B	Sides (2)	¾ x 1⅝ - 18
C	Handles (2)	¾ x 3½ rough - 12¼
D	Base (1)	¼ ply - 11¼ x 17
F	Rect. Splines (4)	⅛ x 1⅝ - ½

Note: Do not need parts A and E.

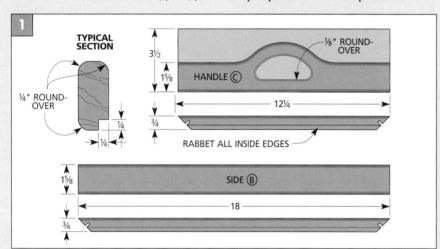

Figure 1 — TYPICAL SECTION; ¼" ROUND-OVER; HANDLE C; ⅛" ROUND-OVER; 3½; 1⅝; 12¼; ¾; RABBET ALL INSIDE EDGES; SIDE B; 1⅝; 18; ¾

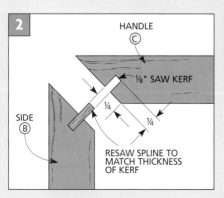

Figure 2 — HANDLE C; ⅛" SAW KERF; ¼; ¼; SIDE B; RESAW SPLINE TO MATCH THICKNESS OF KERF

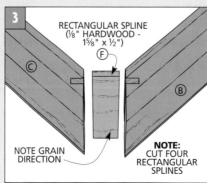

Figure 3 — RECTANGULAR SPLINE (⅛" HARDWOOD - 1⅝" x ½"); C; F; B; B; NOTE GRAIN DIRECTION; **NOTE:** CUT FOUR RECTANGULAR SPLINES

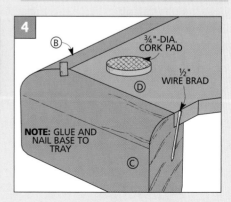

Figure 4 — B; ¾"-DIA. CORK PAD; ½" WIRE BRAD; D; **NOTE:** GLUE AND NAIL BASE TO TRAY; C

Cheese Board

Whether you build it for yourself or as a gift, this cheese board is a useful accessory that doesn't take long to make. Using a simple shop-made box jig, you can rout the decorative grooves quickly and easily.

There is probably more than one method for making the fancy routed design in the top face of this Cheese Board. But the easiest, most efficient way I found was to use a special shop-made box jig along with a hand-held router.

BOX JIG. With a box jig, you don't tie up your router table. And you'll have the freedom of freehand routing with the added confidence provided by the support and accuracy of the jig.

And there's another advantage to building the box jig. Once it's built, it's easy to use again in the future. Just pull it out, fasten it to the bench, and make

another Cheese Board as a gift — a year or two from now.

Sometimes that's the fun of building from a jig — it makes rebuilding an exact duplicate of the project quick and accurate. That's just what I needed for last year's holiday presents.

The box jig is fairly straightforward to make (see the Shop Jig article on page 73 for details).

MATERIALS. You won't need any hardware for the Cheese Board itself — just the wood for the blank. It's glued up from 4/4 stock.

You can make the whole blank out of one type of stock for a clean look (as

shown in the photo above). Or, if you're feeling creative, you could try experimenting with contrasting (alternating) colors of wood.

That's all you'll need to build the Cheese Board. But you should also keep in mind the materials required to build the box jig on page 73. To build the jig, you'll need plenty of ³/₄" plywood for the frame pieces, along with some ordinary drywall screws.

CUTTING BOARD. With a few slight variations, you can build this project as a handsome cutting board instead of a Cheese Board. See the Designer's Notebook on page 75 for instructions.

BLANK

Usually when building a jig, I build the jig first, and then use it to make the project. But for the Cheese Board, I started by building a blank, and then made the jig to fit around it. That way I was sure that the blank would fit tightly into the jig and the jig would be square.

Note: To use the jig to make another Cheese Board, you do have to cut the blank to fit tight in the opening in the jig.

BLANK. To make the blank, I started by ripping four pieces of 4/4 stock ($^{13}/_{16}$" actual thickness) $1^{3}/_{4}$" wide and 12" long. Then edge-glue the four pieces to form a 7"-wide blank *(Fig. 1)*. Once the glue dries, plane the blank flat and sand it smooth.

Note: The blank could be made from one wide piece of stock, but it might warp, and I tend to think of a cheese board like a cutting board — it should be built up instead.

After the blank is flat, cut it to a finished width of $6^{1}/_{2}$" *(Fig. 1a)*. It looks best if the joint line is centered on the blank, so trim a little bit off each side.

Then square up one end and trim the blank to a finished length of 11".

BOX JIG

After the blank was cut to finished size, I built a box jig to fit around it. The box jig is actually a frame with stop fences screwed to the top of it. Once the blank is placed into the frame, the router can work around the inside of the fences and rout the design.

See the opposite page for details on building the box jig.

SET UP ROUTER

After the box jig was built, I set up to rout the border and checkerboard design.

ADJUST BIT. Start by mounting a sharp $^{1}/_{2}$" V-groove bit in the router. Then lower the bit to rout a $^{1}/_{4}$"-wide groove *(Fig. 2a)*. Check the depth and width by making a test cut in a scrap.

CENTER BASE. Once the bit is set to the correct depth, check to be sure the bit is perfectly centered on the plastic router base plate *(Fig. 2)*. If it's not centered, the routed groove won't be a uniform distance from all four fences.

If the bit is off center, loosen the screws and center the base plate on the bit (measuring in at least two directions).

SPACER BLOCKS

Next, I cut five $^{3}/_{4}$"-wide plywood spacer blocks to use when routing the design. Cut two of the spacer blocks 11" long and the other three $7^{1}/_{4}$" long *(Fig. 3)*.

Note: To get a perfectly symmetrical design, the Cheese Board blank should be exactly $6^{1}/_{2}$" wide and the spacer blocks exactly $^{3}/_{4}$" wide. To check the width of the spacer blocks, stack all the blocks with the saw cut edges tightly together and measure the stack. It should be an increment of $^{3}/_{4}$" (5 blocks x $^{3}/_{4}$" = $3^{3}/_{4}$").

FASTENING DOWN THE JIG

After cutting the spacer blocks, I secured the jig down to my bench between dogs *(Fig. 4)*.

Note: If you don't have a bench with dogs, you can always use double-sided carpet tape instead.

Next, insert the Cheese Board blank into the box jig and check that the blank sits flush with or slightly above the surrounding plywood frame pieces *(Fig. 5)*. If the blank is lower, just shim under the blank with several thicknesses of tape.

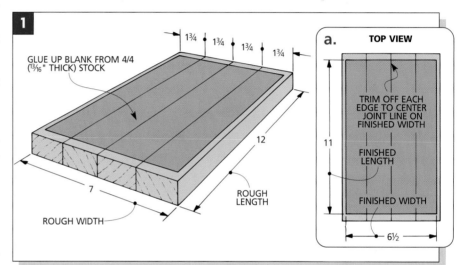

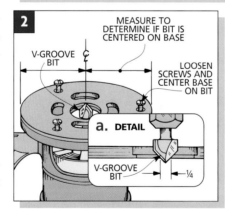

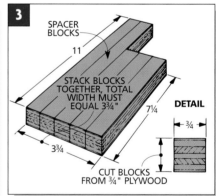

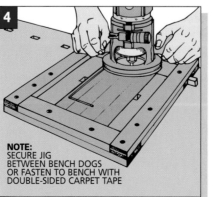

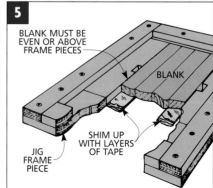

This jig helps you rout a border and checkerboard pattern of V-grooves. The pattern's location is determined by the diameter of your router base and the location of the fences.

MATH. To determine the distance of the fences from the edge of the blank, you have to do some math. First, measure the diameter of your router base (6" in my case) and divide it in half (3").

Now subtract the distance from the outside of the blank to the center of the border. The design calls for the V-groove to be $2\frac{5}{8}$" from the top edge and $\frac{5}{8}$" from the sides and bottom. So in my case: $3" - 2\frac{5}{8}" = \frac{3}{8}"$ and $3" - \frac{5}{8}" = 2\frac{3}{8}"$.

So, the edge of my fence was $\frac{3}{8}$" from the top edge of the blank and $2\frac{3}{8}$" from the sides and bottom edge *(Fig. 1)*.

FRAME PIECES. My fences were 2" wide, mounted flush with the outside of the frame. This meant that the width of the frame pieces had to equal the fences (2") plus the distance from the blank to the fence ($\frac{3}{8}$" and $2\frac{3}{8}$"). So my top piece (A) was $2\frac{3}{8}$" wide and side (B) and bottom (C) pieces are $4\frac{3}{8}$" wide *(Fig. 2)*.

Note: The figures shown here are for a 6"-dia. router base.

FRAME. Start the frame by cutting two side frame pieces (B) to the same length as the blank (11") and to width *(Fig. 2)*.

Then, to make it easier to remove the blank from the jig, I cut notches for finger holes in each piece *(Fig. 2)*.

Next, cut the bottom frame piece (C) and the top frame piece (A) to width.

To determine the length of the top and bottom frame pieces, measure the width of the blank ($6\frac{1}{2}$") and add the combined width of the two side pieces ($8\frac{3}{4}$"). Then cut the top and bottom frame pieces to this length ($15\frac{1}{4}$").

SIDE FENCES. Now cut the side fences (D) 2" wide and $17\frac{3}{4}$" long *(Fig. 2)*. Then screw them to the side frame pieces (B) *(Step 1 in Fig. 3)*.

Clamp the frame pieces together tight around the blank *(Step 2 in Fig. 3)*. Then drive screws through the four corners to hold the frame together.

TOP/BOTTOM FENCES. Next, measure the distance between the side fences and cut top and bottom fences (E) to this length and to width *(Fig. 3)*.

Finally, screw the top and bottom fences down to the top and bottom frame pieces *(Step 3 in Fig. 3)*.

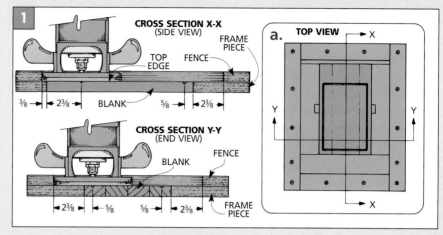

1

CROSS SECTION X-X (SIDE VIEW)

FRAME PIECE — TOP EDGE — FENCE — BLANK

$\frac{3}{8}$ — $2\frac{3}{8}$ — $\frac{5}{8}$ — $2\frac{3}{8}$

CROSS SECTION Y-Y (END VIEW)

BLANK — FENCE — FRAME PIECE

$2\frac{3}{8}$ — $\frac{5}{8}$ — $\frac{5}{8}$ — $2\frac{3}{8}$

a. TOP VIEW — X — Y — Y — X

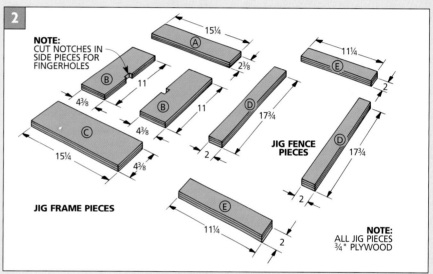

3 JIG ASSEMBLY

1

NOTCH FOR FINGERHOLE — SIDE FRAME PIECES — #6 x $1\frac{1}{4}$" DRYWALL SCREW — SIDE PIECE

CUTTING BOARD BLANK

SIDE FENCE

BOTTOM FRAME PIECE

FENCE HANGS OVER FRAME $2\frac{3}{8}$" ON THIS END

FENCE HANGS OVER FRAME $4\frac{3}{8}$" ON THIS END

2 CLAMP FRAME PIECES IN POSITION AROUND BLANK

3

SCREW FENCES TO FRAME WITH CORNERS FLUSH

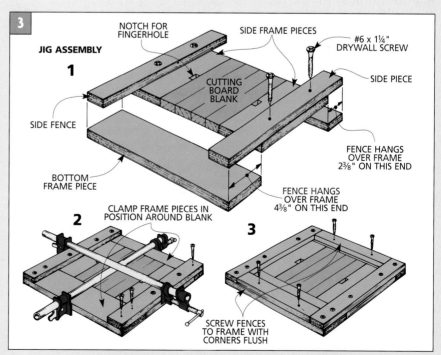

2

NOTE: CUT NOTCHES IN SIDE PIECES FOR FINGERHOLES

JIG FRAME PIECES

(A) $15\frac{1}{4}$ — $2\frac{3}{8}$

(B) 11 — $4\frac{3}{8}$

(B) 11 — $4\frac{3}{8}$

(C) $15\frac{1}{4}$ — $4\frac{3}{8}$

(E) $11\frac{1}{4}$ — 2

(E) $11\frac{1}{4}$ — 2

(D) $17\frac{3}{4}$ — 2

(D) $17\frac{3}{4}$ — 2

JIG FENCE PIECES

NOTE: ALL JIG PIECES $\frac{3}{4}$" PLYWOOD

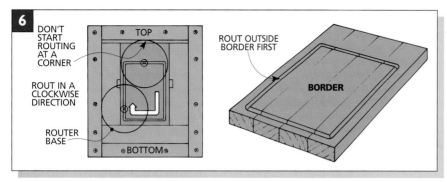

6

DON'T START ROUTING AT A CORNER

TOP

ROUT IN A CLOCKWISE DIRECTION

ROUTER BASE

BOTTOM

ROUT OUTSIDE BORDER FIRST

BORDER

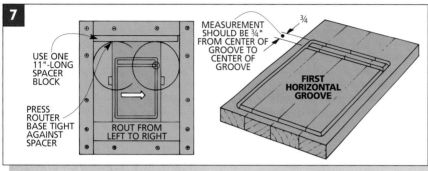

7

USE ONE 11"-LONG SPACER BLOCK

PRESS ROUTER BASE TIGHT AGAINST SPACER

ROUT FROM LEFT TO RIGHT

MEASUREMENT SHOULD BE ¾" FROM CENTER OF GROOVE TO CENTER OF GROOVE

¾

FIRST HORIZONTAL GROOVE

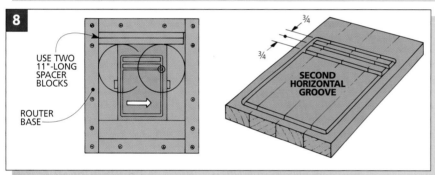

8

USE TWO 11"-LONG SPACER BLOCKS

ROUTER BASE

¾

¾

SECOND HORIZONTAL GROOVE

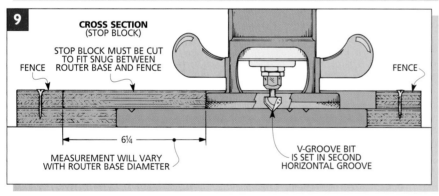

9

CROSS SECTION (STOP BLOCK)

STOP BLOCK MUST BE CUT TO FIT SNUG BETWEEN ROUTER BASE AND FENCE

FENCE

FENCE

6¼

MEASUREMENT WILL VARY WITH ROUTER BASE DIAMETER

V-GROOVE BIT IS SET IN SECOND HORIZONTAL GROOVE

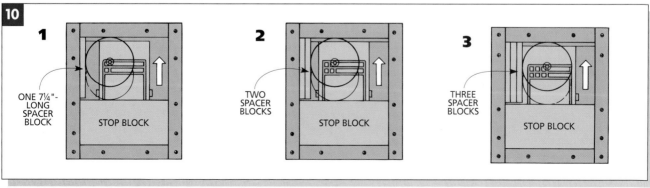

10

1

ONE 7¼"-LONG SPACER BLOCK

STOP BLOCK

2

TWO SPACER BLOCKS

STOP BLOCK

3

THREE SPACER BLOCKS

STOP BLOCK

ROUT DESIGN

Finally, the fun begins — the actual routing. To check that everything is set up correctly, I always rout a test blank first. (I used a piece of scrap plywood.)

BORDER. To rout the border, hold the router base tight against one of the fences. (Don't start at a corner — it tends to burn.) Rout clockwise around the inside of the jig *(Fig. 6)*.

HORIZONTAL GROOVES. Once the border is routed, clean out any dust or chips from the jig. Then place one of the 11"-long spacer blocks inside the jig against the top fence *(Fig. 7)*.

Note: Keep the face of the spacer block up and the sawn edges to the sides.

Now hold the router base tight against the spacer block and make a horizontal pass from left to right *(Fig. 7)*.

Next, add another spacer block and make a second horizontal pass working from left to right *(Fig. 8)*.

STOP BLOCK. Now the short vertical grooves can be routed. These grooves run from the top border groove down to the second horizontal groove. To stop them at the second groove, I cut a stop block from a piece of ¾" plywood.

To determine the width of the stop block, place the V-groove bit in the second horizontal groove and measure the distance from the router base plate to the bottom fence *(Fig. 9)*. Then cut the stop block to this width and to length to fit between the side fences.

VERTICAL GROOVES. Now place the stop block against the bottom fence and one of the 7¼" spacer blocks against the left side fence *(Step 1 in Fig. 10)*. Then, with the router against the spacer block, rout the vertical groove.

Next, insert a second 7¼" spacer block against the first and rout the next vertical groove *(Step 2 in Fig. 10)*. Finally, insert the third spacer block and rout the third vertical groove *(Step 3)*.

After the three grooves are routed on the left side, follow the same routing sequence with the blocks against the right fence. (Rout from top down.)

CHECK SQUARES. Once the grooves are routed, measure the squares between the grooves for uniformity. If the spacer blocks are the correct size and the bit set to the correct depth, the tops of the squares should be uniform.

FINISHING DETAILS

With the routing complete, lay out three ³/₄"-dia. holes near the top of the Cheese Board *(Fig. 11)*. The first is used to hang the board on the wall, and the other two form inside arcs for the handle.

Also lay out a 1" radius for the top end of the handle. Then drill the holes and cut the top to shape *(Fig. 11)*.

RADIUS AND BULLNOSE. Next, form a ³/₈" radius on each corner and rout bull-nose profiles on all the edges and the hanging hole *(Figs. 11a and 12a)*.

FINISH. I finished the Cheese Board with two coats of a non-toxic wood finish (see Sources on page 126). ■

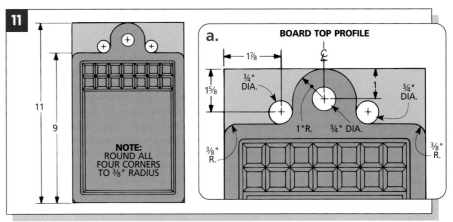

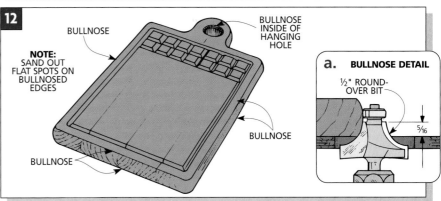

DESIGNER'S NOTEBOOK

Give yourself a larger option by removing the board's handle and mirroring the routed pattern.

CONSTRUCTION NOTES:

■ To make this Cutting Board, first glue up a blank (note the larger dimensions in the drawing below).

■ Then build the box jig to fit the size of this new blank (see drawing). Note that this time the blank is *centered* in the jig. And since the blank is wider, you'll need six spacers to rout the short grooves.

■ Using the same technique as before, rout the pattern on *both* ends of the blank (see drawing and refer to *Figs. 6, 7, 8, and 10* on page 74).

■ Finally, add the radius to each corner and rout a bullnose profile (refer to *Figs. 12 and 12a* above).

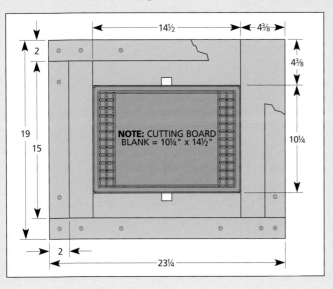

Country Wall Shelf

This shelf is simple enough to build in a day or two, but its versatility makes it a nice piece to keep. Whether it's displaying plates and mugs or storing hats and gloves, you'll be glad you built it.

Sometimes it's nice to find a project that can be built in a day or two, but is useful and versatile enough to hang around the house for years afterward. That's the great thing about this Country Wall Shelf. Whatever purpose you use it for when it's finished, it will be well worth the little time you spent building it.

Depending on your needs and space, you can hang the shelf in your entryway and use it for hats and gloves, or keep it near the kitchen to display plates and mugs. You could even use it as a home for trophies and medals in a child's room. The possibilities are endless.

No matter what goes on the shelf, you want it to stay put. So a rock-solid hanging bracket secures it to the wall.

MATERIALS. There isn't a lot of complicated joinery or hardware to worry about when making the shelf, and all the main parts are made from ¾" stock. (I chose No. 2 common pine to give the project a cozy, country look and feel.) A few Shaker pegs and dowel plugs will round out your supplies (refer to the Materials List on the opposite page).

PROFILE. Part of what makes this shelf so charming is the curved profile that's cut into each of the three support pieces. But don't worry if you haven't

cut a lot of irregular shapes before — instructions and the template pattern are all laid out here.

OPTIONS. The shelf itself is very versatile. And there are options built right into the construction that you can include or modify as you work.

First, the top of the shelf has a groove used to hold plates. If you're not planning to display plates, naturally you can skip this step.

If you'd rather have a shelf in the hallway, the Designer's Notebook on page 78 shows how to replace the Shaker pegs with coat hooks and how to build a slatted top.

EXPLODED VIEW

OVERALL DIMENSIONS:
44½"W x 8D x 7¼H

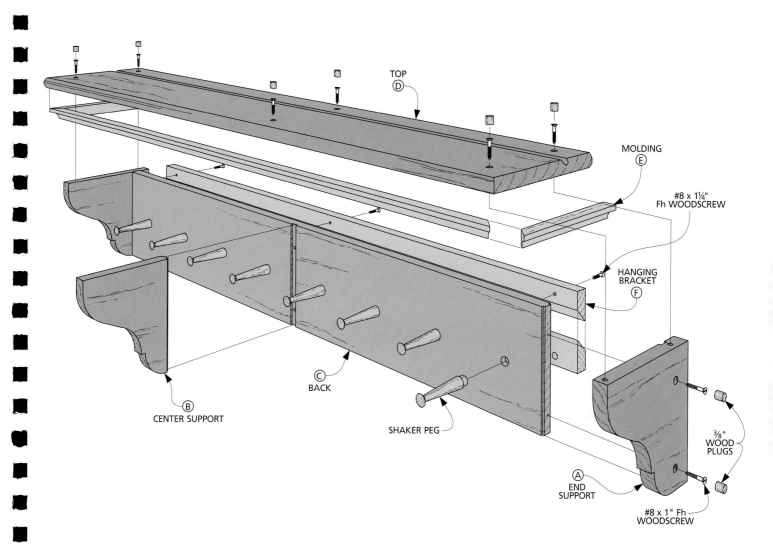

TOP
Ⓓ

MOLDING
Ⓔ

#8 x 1¼"
Fh WOODSCREW

HANGING
BRACKET
Ⓕ

BACK
Ⓒ

CENTER SUPPORT
Ⓑ

SHAKER PEG

⅜"
WOOD
PLUGS

END
SUPPORT
Ⓐ

#8 x 1" Fh
WOODSCREW

MATERIALS LIST

WOOD
A	End Supports (2)	¾ x 6½ - 6⅞
B	Center Support (1)	¾ x 6½ - 5½
C	Back (1)	¾ x 6½ - 41
D	Top (1)	¾ x 8 - 44½
E	Moldings (2)	¾ x ¾ - 44 rough
F	Hanging Bracket (1)	¾ x 3 - 41

HARDWARE SUPPLIES
(8) No. 6 x 1" Fh woodscrews
(12) No. 8 x 1" Fh woodscrews
(3) No. 8 x 1¼" Fh woodscrews
(3) No. 8 x 2" Fh woodscrews
(8) 3½"-long Shaker pegs
(12) ⅜" wood plugs
(9) ¾" wire brads

CUTTING DIAGRAM

1x10 (¾ x 9¼) - 72 (4.75 Bd. Ft.)

1x8 (¾ x 7¼) - 48 (2.5 Bd. Ft.)

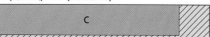

1x8 (¾ x 7¼) - 48 (2.5 Bd. Ft.)

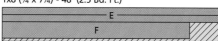

SUPPORTS

I started by cutting to size the three supports that hold up the shelf.

GRAIN DIRECTION. But before you start cutting, there's one thing to note here. The grain direction should run the *length* of all the pieces. This is natural on the long pieces that are cut later, like the back and top. But since the supports are almost square, it's easy to get things turned around *(Fig. 1).*

The first thing I did was to cut a $\frac{3}{4}$"-thick blank to a rough length of 20". Then I ripped it to a width of $6\frac{1}{2}$". That way, all three supports will be exactly the same width. Once that was done, I cut the supports (A, B) to finished length from the blank *(Fig. 1).*

Note: The supports are different lengths because the center support butts against the back, while the end supports extend behind the back to allow for a hanging bracket (refer to *Fig. 2* and the Shop Tip on page 81).

TEMPLATE

After the supports are cut to size, a profile is laid out on each one. It's easy to do this by making a template first *(Fig. 1a).*

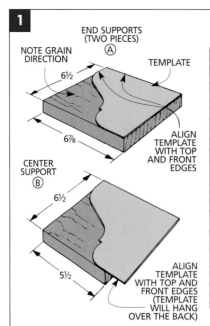
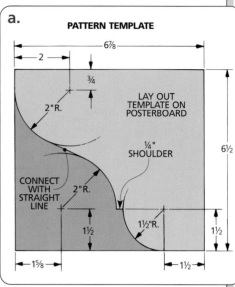

ARCS. The profile is determined by the arcs of three circles *(Fig. 1a).* You'll need to connect the upper and middle arcs with a straight line. Then to create the "notched" shoulder, measure $\frac{1}{4}$" straight out from the small bottom arc to the middle arc. Once that's completed, cut out the pattern carefully.

TRANSFER PATTERN. Before tracing the pattern, make sure the front and top edges of the template and the workpiece are flush *(Fig. 1).*

Note: Don't cut out the profiles yet. It's easier to cut the dadoes and tongues in the next step and to test-fit the parts together while the edges are square.

DESIGNER'S NOTEBOOK

This shelf is perfect for the hallway and easy to build.

CONSTRUCTION NOTES:

■ Construction of the supports and back is mostly the same. However, you won't need to drill holes for the pegs.
■ When it's time to make the top, cut four slats (G) to size (see drawing below). Then rout $\frac{1}{16}$" chamfers on all the edges of the slats.

■ Drill the counter-bored shank holes to secure each slat to the supports (see drawing).
■ The next thing to do is to screw the rear slat flush with the back

SLATS AND HOOKS

edge of the side supports. Then space the remaining slats $\frac{1}{8}$" apart (detail 'a').
■ Finally, plug each of the screw holes and attach the hooks (see drawing).

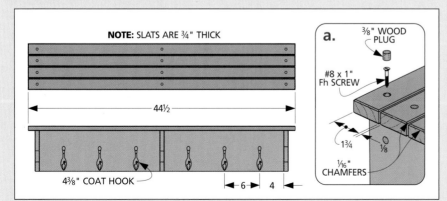

MATERIALS LIST

NEW PARTS
G Slats (4) $\frac{3}{4}$ x $1\frac{3}{4}$ - $44\frac{1}{2}$
Note: Do not need parts D, E.

HARDWARE SUPPLIES
(6) $4\frac{3}{8}$" coat hooks w/ screws
(18) No. 8 x 1" Fh woodscrews
(18) $\frac{3}{8}$" wood plugs

DADOES

The supports are connected to the back with tongue and dado joints (Fig. 2). I started by cutting the dadoes.

The first dado to cut is for the center support. It's centered on the length of the back (Figs. 2 and 2b).

Next, a dado is cut across the inside face of each end support to join them to the back. These dadoes are positioned to allow 3/4" between the back and the wall for the hanging bracket added later (Fig. 2a). To position these dadoes on the end supports, I used the table saw fence as a stop (Fig. 3).

TONGUES

After cutting the dadoes, a tongue is formed on the end of the center support and at each end of the back to fit into the dadoes. I formed these tongues by cutting two rabbets with a combination blade on the table saw.

AUXILIARY FENCE. Since the rip fence has to be locked down next to the blade, I screwed a piece of plywood to the fence to protect the fence. Then raise the blade until it leaves a tongue that fits the dadoes (Fig. 4).

Note: It's a good idea to cut a tongue on a piece of scrap first to help set the blade height correctly.

PEGS

After the joints are finished, the Shaker pegs can be installed (see Sources on page 126). Ordinarily, these pegs are glued into holes. But I've found they usually come loose, so I came up with a way of screwing them to the back.

MODIFY PEGS. The Shaker pegs I used for the shelf have tenons. This tenon is cut off to a length of 3/8". Then drill a pilot hole into the end (Fig. 5a).

MOUNTING HOLES. Next, 1/2"-dia. holes are bored 3/8" deep in the back to accept the pegs (Fig. 5).

Note: Each set of four pegs is centered between the center support and the end support. In my case, this meant the first hole and the fourth hole had to be 2 5/8" from the end of the back and from the shoulder of the center dado respectively (Fig. 5).

SHANK HOLES. After the mounting holes are bored, drill shank holes all the way through. These are for the screws used to hold the pegs to the back.

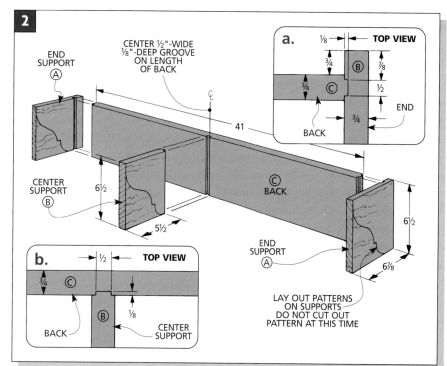

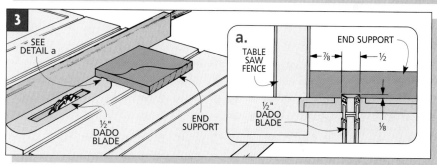

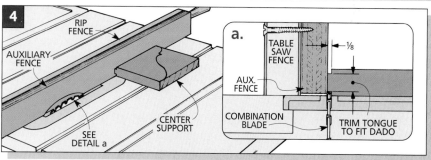

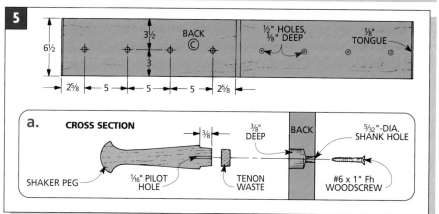

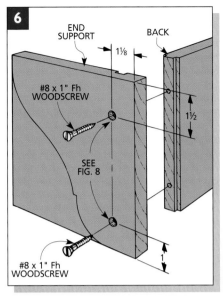

6 END SUPPORT / BACK / $1\frac{1}{8}$ / #8 x 1" Fh WOODSCREW / $1\frac{1}{2}$ / SEE FIG. 8 / #8 x 1" Fh WOODSCREW / 1

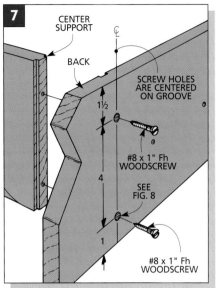

7 CENTER SUPPORT / BACK / SCREW HOLES ARE CENTERED ON GROOVE / $1\frac{1}{2}$ / #8 x 1" Fh WOODSCREW / 4 / SEE FIG. 8 / 1 / #8 x 1" Fh WOODSCREW

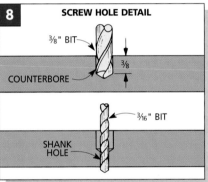

8 SCREW HOLE DETAIL / $\frac{3}{8}$" BIT / COUNTERBORE / $\frac{3}{8}$ / $\frac{3}{16}$" BIT / SHANK HOLE

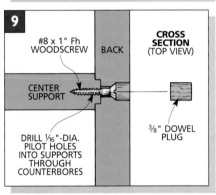

9 #8 x 1" Fh WOODSCREW / BACK / CROSS SECTION (TOP VIEW) / CENTER SUPPORT / DRILL $\frac{1}{16}$"-DIA. PILOT HOLES INTO SUPPORTS THROUGH COUNTERBORES / $\frac{3}{8}$" DOWEL PLUG

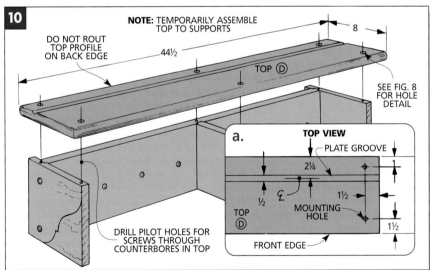

10 NOTE: TEMPORARILY ASSEMBLE TOP TO SUPPORTS / DO NOT ROUT TOP PROFILE ON BACK EDGE / $44\frac{1}{2}$ / TOP (D) / 8 / SEE FIG. 8 FOR HOLE DETAIL / DRILL PILOT HOLES FOR SCREWS THROUGH COUNTERBORES IN TOP

a. TOP VIEW / PLATE GROOVE / $2\frac{1}{4}$ / 1 / $\frac{1}{2}$ / $1\frac{1}{2}$ / TOP (D) / MOUNTING HOLE / $1\frac{1}{2}$ / FRONT EDGE

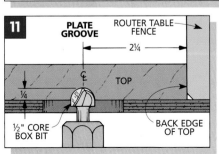

11 PLATE GROOVE / ROUTER TABLE FENCE / $2\frac{1}{4}$ / TOP / $\frac{1}{4}$ / $\frac{1}{2}$" CORE BOX BIT / BACK EDGE OF TOP

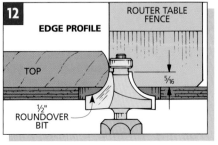

12 EDGE PROFILE / ROUTER TABLE FENCE / TOP / $\frac{5}{16}$ / $\frac{1}{2}$" ROUNDOVER BIT

ATTACH SUPPORTS

The next step is to assemble the supports and back temporarily in order to fit the top. This is done by screwing the pieces together (no glue yet).

LAYOUT. First, lay out the positions of the screws centered on the dadoes in the ends and back *(Figs. 6 and 7)*.

DRILL HOLES. All of the screw holes (except on the back) are counterbored for $\frac{3}{8}$" plugs that hide the heads of the woodscrews *(Fig. 8)*. Shank holes are then drilled the rest of the way through the counterbores.

Next, align the supports with the back, drill pilot holes, and screw the parts together *(Fig. 9)*.

TOP

The next step is to cut the top (D) to size *(Fig. 10)*. Note that the length of the top allows it to extend beyond the end supports $1\frac{1}{8}$" on both ends.

MOUNTING HOLES. Now you can drill counterbored holes to mount the top to the supports and back *(Fig. 10a)*.

PLATE GROOVE. If this shelf is used to display plates, a plate groove has to be cut to keep plates from sliding off. I used a $\frac{1}{2}$" core box bit on the router table *(Fig. 11)*. To prevent burn marks, rout the groove in two passes. Make the second pass very light and fast.

EDGE PROFILE. After routing the plate groove, rout bullnose profiles on the front edge and both ends of the top with a $\frac{1}{2}$" roundover bit *(Fig. 12)*. Rout the ends first and finish with the front edge, but leave the back edge square.

SHAPE SUPPORTS

Now the top is complete, but before mounting it, you'll need to unscrew the supports so you can cut the profile.

SAW PROFILE. I cut the profile to rough shape on a band saw *(Fig. 13)*. Then I smoothed the curves with a drum sander and a file.

CHAMFER EDGES. Next, the profiles of the curved edges are chamfered with a chamfer bit. Set the bit just high enough to leave a $\frac{1}{16}$"-wide chamfer *(Fig. 14)*.

Note: The inside corners (where the curve meets the shoulder) have to be cut with a chisel to blend them into the rest of the chamfered edges *(Fig. 14a)*.

ASSEMBLY. After all the supports are chamfered, the parts can be assembled.

Begin by sanding the surfaces smooth. Next, screw the back, supports, and top together. Then plug the screw holes with $^3/_8$" dowel plugs *(Fig. 15)*.

MOLDING STRIPS

After the shelf was assembled, I dressed it up with cove molding strips. Although these moldings can be bought, I made my own with two steps on the router table and table saw.

ROUT COVE. The first step in making the moldings is to rout coves on both edges of the molding stock (E) *(Step 1 in Fig. 16)*. When doing this, set the fence on the router table so the pilot on the cove bit is in line with the face of the fence. Next, raise the bit so the shoulder (above the cove) is $^1/_4$" thick *(Step 1 in Fig. 16)*. Then rout the cove on both edges of the molding stock.

CUT OFF MOLDINGS. To cut off the coved edges that become the moldings, lock the table saw rip fence $^3/_4$" from the blade. Then flip the stock over (so the coves face up) and rip the molding from the edges *(Step 2 in Fig. 16)*.

ATTACH MOLDINGS. After the moldings are cut, they're attached to the shelf. Begin by mitering the ends to fit. Then fasten the moldings in place with wire brads. (Don't glue them in place — they should be able to "move" as the top expands and contracts.)

To complete the shelf, it needs a bracket to hang it on the wall. The Shop Tip below has more about this. Then all that's left is to screw the pegs in place.

FINISH. The last thing to do is to apply a finish. I used a stain controller to prevent blotching. Then, after staining, I applied a couple of coats of varnish. ∎

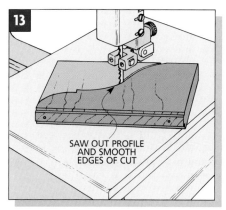

13 SAW OUT PROFILE AND SMOOTH EDGES OF CUT

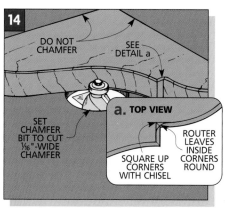

14 DO NOT CHAMFER — SEE DETAIL a — SET CHAMFER BIT TO CUT $^1/_{16}$"-WIDE CHAMFER

a. TOP VIEW — ROUTER LEAVES INSIDE CORNERS ROUND — SQUARE UP CORNERS WITH CHISEL

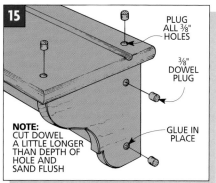

15 PLUG ALL $^3/_8$" HOLES — $^3/_8$" DOWEL PLUG — GLUE IN PLACE

NOTE: CUT DOWEL A LITTLE LONGER THAN DEPTH OF HOLE AND SAND FLUSH

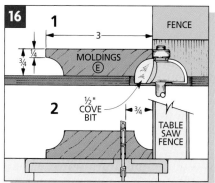

16 FENCE — 1 — 3 — $^1/_4$ — $^3/_4$ — MOLDINGS (E) — 2 — $^1/_2$" COVE BIT — $^3/_4$ — TABLE SAW FENCE

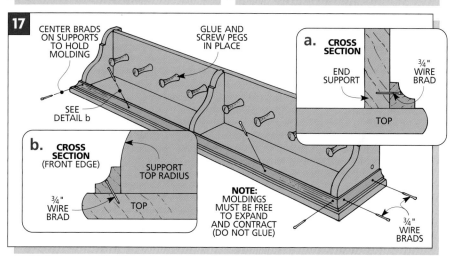

17 CENTER BRADS ON SUPPORTS TO HOLD MOLDING — GLUE AND SCREW PEGS IN PLACE — SEE DETAIL b

a. CROSS SECTION — END SUPPORT — $^3/_4$" WIRE BRAD — TOP

b. CROSS SECTION (FRONT EDGE) — SUPPORT TOP RADIUS — $^3/_4$" WIRE BRAD — TOP

NOTE: MOLDINGS MUST BE FREE TO EXPAND AND CONTRACT (DO NOT GLUE) — $^3/_4$" WIRE BRADS

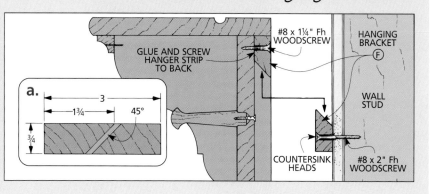

SHOP TIP . . . . *Beveled Hanging Bracket*

The shelf is hung on interlocking beveled strips. To make this hanging bracket (F), rip a piece of stock 3" wide (detail 'a' in drawing). Then rip this piece in half at a 45° angle.

One half of the strip is screwed to the back of the shelf just below the top (see drawing). The other half is screwed to the wall. (Make sure you screw into studs.)

a. 3 — $1^3/_4$ — 45° — $^3/_4$

GLUE AND SCREW HANGER STRIP TO BACK — #8 x $1^1/_4$" Fh WOODSCREW — HANGING BRACKET (F) — WALL STUD — COUNTERSINK HEADS — #8 x 2" Fh WOODSCREW

Step Stool

Instead of folding up, this stool has a step that slides easily into the base for convenient storage. Made of oak with exposed tenon joints, this weekend project adds a rustic appeal to your home.

Most step stools fold up when they're not in use. This may be pretty handy when it comes to storage, but not very convenient if you use the stool frequently. Setting one up always seems to take just a little longer and a little more patience than it really should.

The nice feature about this Step Stool is that instead of folding up, the step slides in and out of the front of the base. So it's ready to go at a moment's notice, without the hassle of unfolding and positioning it.

The step slides in a "track" in the base of the stool. And a system of pins

and stop blocks prevent the step from coming all the way out of the base. All this comes together to make the stool easy, safe, and convenient to use around the house or shop.

CURVES. Another nice feature about the stool is the series of curves added to all the pieces. These curves are easy to lay out and cut, with the help of a handy tip (see the Shop Tip on page 85).

SQUARE VERSION. But, you don't even have to cut the curves. If you'd prefer a version with straight lines and square steps, see the Designer's Notebook on page 89. In some ways, that version is even easier to build.

THROUGH MORTISES. One other feature that sets this Step Stool apart is the through mortise and tenon joinery. Letting the ends of the tenons show through the mortises on the sides highlights your skill and craftsmanship.

For step-by-step instructions on making this special joint, see the Joinery article on page 88.

MATERIALS. I chose oak for all the parts of this project. Along with making it solid and sturdy, the oak also gives the stool an honest, rustic look.

Adding to the charm of the stool is the finish. I chose a golden oak stain, then wiped on three coats of an oil finish.

EXPLODED VIEW

OVERALL DIMENSIONS:
16¾W x 14D x 16H (CLOSED, 24¼D OPEN)

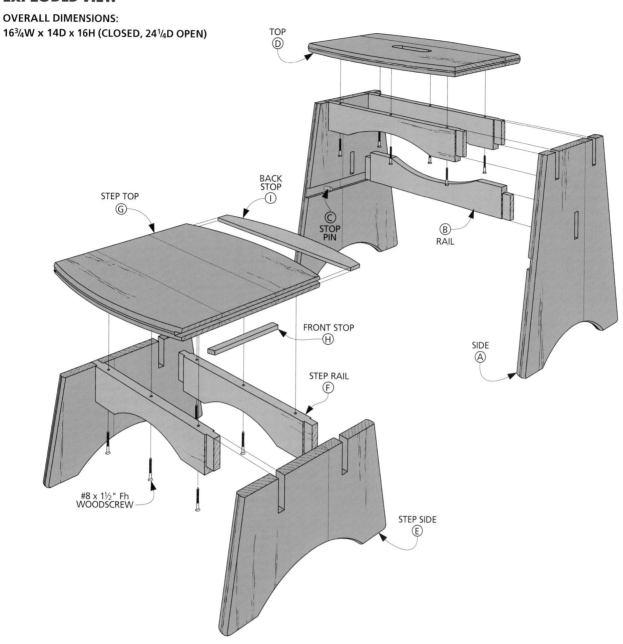

TOP
(D)

STEP TOP
(G)

BACK
STOP
(I)

STOP
PIN
(C)

RAIL
(B)

SIDE
(A)

FRONT STOP
(H)

STEP RAIL
(F)

#8 x 1½" Fh
WOODSCREW

STEP SIDE
(E)

MATERIALS LIST

WOOD

A	Sides (2)	¾ x 14 - 15¼
B	Rails (3)	¾ x 2½ - 16
C	Stop Pins (2)	¼ dowel x ⅞
D	Top (1)	¾ x 11⅜ - 16¾
E	Step Sides (2)	¾ x 14¼ - 7¼
F	Step Rails (2)	¾ x 2½ - 14¼
G	Step Top (1)	¾ x 14 - 15
H	Front Stops (2)	¼ x ½ - 5 rough
I	Back Stop (1)	¼ x 2 - 15

HARDWARE SUPPLIES
(12) No. 8 x 1½" Fh woodscrews
(2) No. 8 x ⅝" Fh woodscrews

CUTTING DIAGRAM

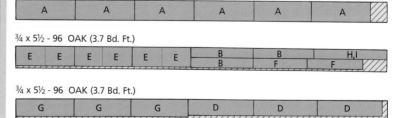

¾ x 5½ - 96 OAK (3.7 Bd. Ft.)

| A | A | A | A | A | A | |

¾ x 5½ - 96 OAK (3.7 Bd. Ft.)

| E | E | E | E | E | E | B | B | H,I |
| | | | | | | B | F | F |

¾ x 5½ - 96 OAK (3.7 Bd. Ft.)

| G | G | G | D | D | D |

NOTE: ALSO NEED SHORT LENGTH OF ¼" DOWEL FOR PART C.

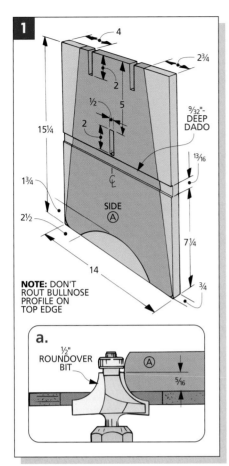

1

NOTE: DON'T ROUT BULLNOSE PROFILE ON TOP EDGE

a.
½" ROUNDOVER BIT
A
5/16

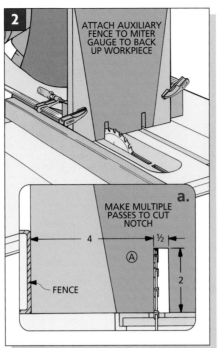

2

ATTACH AUXILIARY FENCE TO MITER GAUGE TO BACK UP WORKPIECE

a.
MAKE MULTIPLE PASSES TO CUT NOTCH
A
FENCE

BASE

The construction of both the step and the base is similar, but since the step is designed to fit closely inside the base, I started with the base and then built the step to fit.

The platform of the base is made up of five pieces — two sides and three rails (refer to *Fig. 3* on the next page). (A top is added later.) I started off by gluing up a couple ³/₄"-thick blanks for the sides (A) and then cut them to size (14" x 15¼") *(Fig. 1)*.

Note: If you're planning on building the square version of the stool, see the Designer's Notebook on page 89 before you go any further.

MORTISES. It's easiest to cut all the joinery on the sides while the blanks are still square. I began with the through mortises that will be used to join the sides with a set of rails.

The mortises at the top of each side piece are really notches — they're open at one end. I cut these on the table saw in a series of passes *(Figs. 2 and 2a)*.

But since the notches are the same distance from each side, I used my rip fence as a stop, flipping the piece

between passes. This ensured that they would be symmetrical.

Then to make the mortise in the center of each side piece, I drilled out most of the waste on a drill press and cleaned up the edges with a chisel. (For more on this, see page 88.)

Before cutting the sides to shape, I completed the "track" that the step slides in. This is nothing more than a dado cut on the inside face of each side piece *(Fig. 1)*. But when cutting this dado, pay close attention to the width. To keep the step from binding, it should be ¹/₁₆" wider than the thickness of the stock you will use to build the step. (I made trial cuts in a piece of scrap to "fine-tune" the width of the dado.)

With the joinery out of the way, the sides can be cut to their finished shape. I started by laying out the angles along the sides and the curves on the bottom of each piece *(Fig. 1)*.

To cut the curves, I used a band saw to cut away the waste, staying just outside the layout lines to avoid any mistakes. Then I sanded and planed the curved edges smooth.

The bottom corners of the base are also rounded. (This will prevent them from splintering if the stool is dragged across the floor.) For an easy, consistent way to lay out the rounded corners, refer to the Shop Tip at right.

To complete the sides, I routed a bullnose profile around each piece, except along the top edges (this is

where the top will sit). This is done with a router and a ½"-radius roundover bit that is set ⁵/₁₆" above the table *(Fig. 1a)*.

RAILS. Once the sides were complete, I began work on the three rails (B) that will connect them. These pieces are identical — the only difference is that the two top rails will be drilled for screws to attach them to the top of the stool *(Fig. 3)*.

The tenons on the rails need to match the thickness of the side pieces (³/₄"). (I made mine a hair longer and trimmed them flush after assembly, see page 88.) But the important thing is to make sure that the shoulder-to-shoulder distance is the same on all three rails (14½") *(Fig. 3c)*.

Once the tenons are cut, countersunk screw holes can be drilled in two of the rails *(Fig. 3c)*. This will provide a means of attaching the top.

CURVES. After drilling the screw holes, curves can be laid out on one edge of each rail *(Fig. 3c)*.

To cut the curves, again I used the band saw to bring them to rough shape and then sanded them smooth.

STOP PIN. There's one more step before gluing up the sides and rails. To prevent the step from being pulled completely out of the base, a ¹/₄"-dia. stop pin (C) is glued into a hole drilled in the dado on each side piece *(Fig. 3b)*. (This is just a piece of hardwood dowel.) These pins will limit the travel of the step. But more on this later.

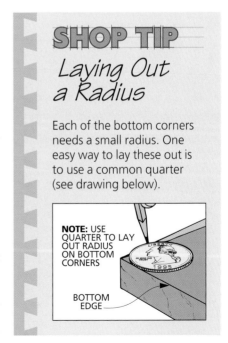

SHOP TIP

Laying Out a Radius

Each of the bottom corners needs a small radius. One easy way to lay these out is to use a common quarter (see drawing below).

NOTE: USE QUARTER TO LAY OUT RADIUS ON BOTTOM CORNERS

BOTTOM EDGE

ASSEMBLY. Gluing up the rails and sides is pretty straightforward. Just be sure to pay attention to the orientation and position of the rails.

The two rails that have screw holes fit at the top of the base. And while the curves on these two rails are facing *down*, the curve on the center rail should face *up (Fig. 3)*.

TOP. The last step to complete the base is to add a top (D). There's nothing tricky here — the top is just a ³⁄₄"-thick glued-up blank that's cut to size and shape *(Fig. 4)*.

Note: For a simple way to lay out the two shallow curves on the top, refer to the Shop Tip below.

After laying out the curves on top, I again used a band saw to cut them and then sanded them smooth.

To make it easier and more comfortable to lift the step stool, I made a cut-out in the center of the top *(Fig. 4a)*.

To make this cut-out, first I drilled two 1"-diameter holes (centered 3" apart). Then I cleaned out the waste in between with a jig saw.

And finally, before screwing the top to the base, I routed bullnose profiles on all the edges, including the inside of the hand cut-out *(Fig. 4b)*.

SHOP TIP

Laying Out Curves

Before cutting the curves on the top of the stool, you need a simple way to lay them out so you'll have a smooth line to cut along.

The best method I've found for doing this is to use a flexible hardboard scrap that bends evenly (see drawing). Then you can just trace the line with a pencil.

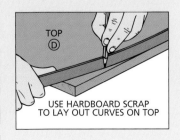

USE HARDBOARD SCRAP TO LAY OUT CURVES ON TOP

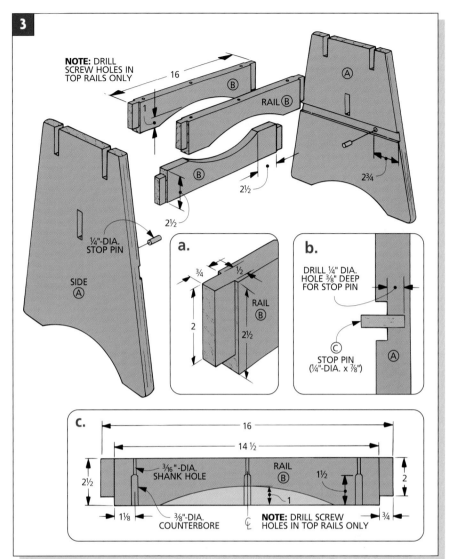

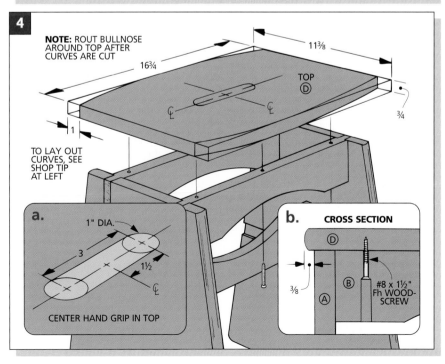

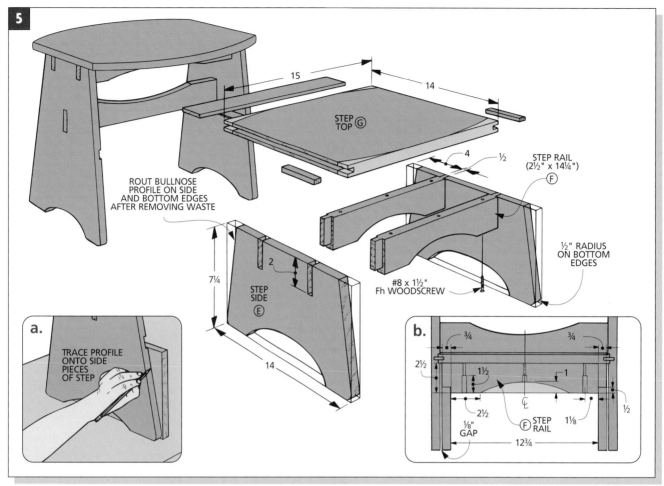

ROUT BULLNOSE
PROFILE ON SIDE
AND BOTTOM EDGES
AFTER REMOVING WASTE

15

14

STEP
TOP Ⓖ

4   ½

STEP RAIL
(2½" x 14¼")
Ⓕ

7¼

2

STEP
SIDE
Ⓔ

14

½" RADIUS
ON BOTTOM
EDGES

#8 x 1½"
Fh WOODSCREW

a.

TRACE PROFILE
ONTO SIDE
PIECES
OF STEP

b.

¾   ¾

2½

1½   1

2½   1⅛

⅛"
GAP

Ⓕ STEP
RAIL

12¾

½

6

FIRST: CUT SLOTS
ON ENDS OF TOP

TALL
AUXILIARY
FENCE

SECOND: RAISE
BLADE AND CUT
SLOT ON BACK
EDGE

a.

¼   END
SLOTS

b.

BACK
SLOT

2

7

BACK
STOP
Ⓘ

15

FRONT STOP
Ⓗ

5

STEP
TOP
Ⓖ

½

2

14   15

CUT STOPS
TO FIT IN
SLOTS IN ENDS
OF TOP

NOTE: FRONT
AND BACK STOPS
ARE CUT FROM
A SINGLE BLANK

STEP

With the base of the stool completed, building the slide-out step is simple. That's because the step is basically just a scaled-down version of the base. The only major difference is the stop system that is part of the top. But more on that a little later.

SIDES. Like I did with the base, I started out building the step by gluing up a couple of ¾"-thick blanks for the step sides (E) *(Fig. 5)*. Then after cutting these to size (7¼" x 14"), I cut the mortises for the rails.

Note: Again, if you're building the square version, refer to the Designer's Notebook on page 89.

The step sides (E) match the profile of the base sides. They're angled and have a curved cut-out at the bottom. So this time, I didn't have to do any measuring for the layout — I just traced them *(Fig. 5a)*.

After cutting the sides to shape and sanding the edges, I routed a bullnose profile on all but the top edges, to match the bullnose on the base.

RAILS. The step sides are joined by a pair of step rails (F). These pieces are cut to size and tenons are cut on the ends to fit the mortises in the sides. But since this distance will determine the final width of the step, the important thing to watch here is the shoulder-to-shoulder distance of the tenons ($12^3/4$") *(Fig. 5b)*.

After you've cut the tenons, dry-assemble the sides and rails to make sure the step fits between the sides of the base with the right amount of clearance. There should be a $1/8$" gap between the base sides and the step sides *(Fig. 5b)*.

Once I was satisfied with the fit of the step, I took it apart and drilled countersunk screw holes in the rails (to attach the step top). Then I cut out the curves on the bottom edge of each rail and sanded them smooth.

TOP. After gluing up the step sides and rails, I turned my attention to making a top for the step. Like the top on the base, the step top (G) starts off as a simple $3/4$"-thick glued-up blank *(Fig. 7)*. But the dimensions are slightly different (14" x 15").

The top uses a simple system of stops to limit the step's travel. When the step is pulled out, a back stop hits the stop pins and keeps the step from being pulled all the way out of the base. And when it's pushed back in, stops at the front of the top prevent the step from being pushed in too far.

These stops are all fitted into slots that are cut on the sides and back edge of the top *(Fig. 6)*.

To do this, first I cut the $1/4$"-wide slots on the ends of the top *(Fig. 6a)*. Then I raised the saw blade higher and cut a deeper slot along the back edge of the top *(Fig. 6b)*.

STOPS. The stops are cut from a single 2"-wide blank that is thicknessed to match the width of the slots in the edges of the top. I cut the two front stops (H) to width first, but I left them a little long (5") at this point.

The front stops ensure that the step will be centered in the base when it's pushed all the way in.

To determine the length and position of these stops, just slide the step top into the base, center it from front to back, and carefully insert the stops in the slots until they touch the stop pins *(Figs. 8 and 8a)*.

After marking the length of the stops, they can be removed, cut to size, and then glued back in place.

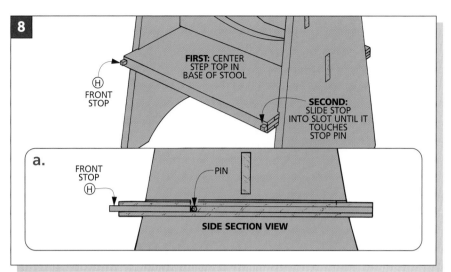

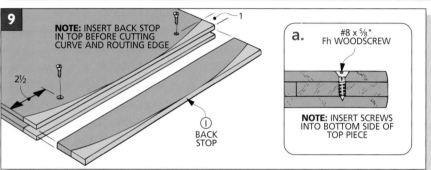

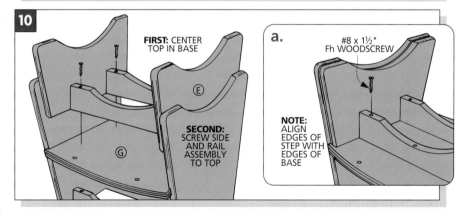

BACK STOP. The back stop (I) is a little different. It gets screwed in place rather than glued *(Figs. 9 and 9a)*. This way, you can remove it in order to get the step in and out of the base for finishing or repair.

Note: The back stop is screwed in place from the underside of the top.

After screwing the back stop in place, the curves can be laid out, cut, and sanded smooth.

Note: The curves on the step top are the same as those on the base top. For help in laying them out, refer back to the Shop Tip on page 85.

Then I routed the same bullnose profile on the front and back edges of the top.

ATTACHING THE TOP. When it came time to attach the top to the sides and rails of the step, I wanted to make sure that the sides of the step would line up with the sides of the base.

To do this, first I removed the back stop and centered the step top in the base. Then I marked the location of the screw holes on the underside of the top. Now the side and rail assembly can simply be glued and screwed to the step top *(Figs. 10 and 10a)*.

Finally, I added finish to the entire stool. To do this, I removed the back stop and step and then applied a golden oak stain. To top it off, I wiped on three coats of an oil finish. ∎

JOINERY........Through Mortise & Tenon

For the Step Stool shown on page 82, I decided to use through mortise and tenon joints. Making this joint isn't particularly complicated or difficult, but because the end of the tenon is exposed, it's more important to cut a clean, square mortise.

MORTISE

To do this, I start by laying out the mortise on the *outside* face of the workpiece (since this is the side that will be visible once the project is complete).

Note: For a project like the Step Stool, you want the mortises to be symmetrical. So keep this in mind as you're laying them out.

Then to avoid chipping out the edges of the mortise, I use a knife and a straightedge to lightly score the layout lines *(Fig. 1)*.

With the mortise laid out, the next step is to drill out the waste on a drill press. Here, I place a backer board underneath the workpiece to avoid

tearout *(Fig. 2.)* And to make sure all the holes line up evenly, I attach a fence to my drill press table.

Once the bulk of the waste has been removed from the mortise, the sides of the mortise can be squared up with a chisel. But to avoid tearout on the inside face of the workpiece, I work from *both* sides *(Figs. 3 and 4)*.

TENON

Of course, making the mortise is only half the battle. It's just as important to cut a nice, tight-fitting tenon (that will give you the smooth, seamless look that really makes the joint stand out).

To do this, I start by cutting my workpiece slightly longer than necessary (about $\frac{1}{16}$") rather than cutting it to fit from the start.

By doing this, what I'm actually doing is making the length of the tenon a hair longer than the depth of the mortise. This way, I can simply pare the end flush with a chisel after the project is

assembled *(Fig. 5)*. Then it's much easier to get a perfect fit.

To lay out the tenon, I take measurements directly from the mortise. Then when cutting the tenon, I make it a little fat and sneak up on the final size until I get a good, snug fit.

Finally, I take the time to number each mortise and tenon (to make the assembly of the project a little easier).

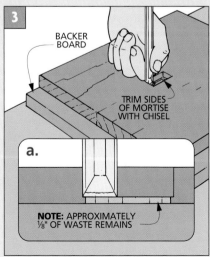

1

NOTE: LAY OUT MORTISE ON OUTSIDE FACE OF WORKPIECE

SCORE LAYOUT LINES WITH UTILITY KNIFE

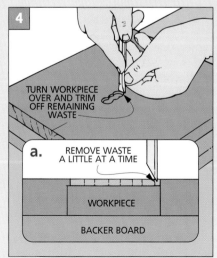

2

FENCE

FORSTNER BIT

DRILL SERIES OF OVERLAPPING HOLES TO REMOVE WASTE

BACKER BOARD

a.

WORKPIECE

BACKER BOARD

TO PREVENT TEAROUT, MOVE BACKER BOARD AND WORKPIECE TOGETHER

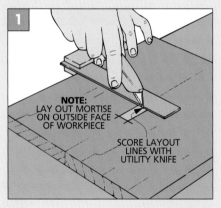

3

BACKER BOARD

TRIM SIDES OF MORTISE WITH CHISEL

a.

NOTE: APPROXIMATELY ⅛" OF WASTE REMAINS

4

TURN WORKPIECE OVER AND TRIM OFF REMAINING WASTE

a. REMOVE WASTE A LITTLE AT A TIME

WORKPIECE

BACKER BOARD

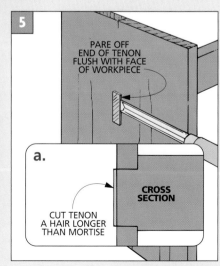

5

PARE OFF END OF TENON FLUSH WITH FACE OF WORKPIECE

a.

CROSS SECTION

CUT TENON A HAIR LONGER THAN MORTISE

DESIGNER'S NOTEBOOK

You don't have to spend a lot of time or add parts to the Step Stool for a different appearance. By straightening the edges and building with pine, you'll end up with more of a country look.

CONSTRUCTION NOTES:

■ To make the stool square, the main difference is in the sides (A) and step sides (E). They are cut to the same size, with the same taper as on the curved stool, but instead of curves, the sides now have squared profiles that are parallel to the edges *(Fig. 1)*.

Note: I decided to use pine for this version to give it more of a country feel (and make it lighter weight).

■ To make the profiles on the sides, first lay out two holes on each piece *(Fig. 2)*.

■ Then lay out lines connecting the holes and edges. The lines need to be *parallel* to the outside edges of the sides *(Fig. 2)*.

■ Now drill the holes and cut along the lines to form the profiles.

■ Add a ¹⁄₂" radius to each bottom corner of the pieces to match those in the profiles (refer back to the Shop Tip on page 84 for help with this).

■ Now you can complete the joinery for the sides and step sides as before.

■ The only other difference in this stool is that the top (D) and step top (G) are narrower with straight edges *(Fig. 3)*. And each corner of these pieces is rounded like the bottoms of the sides.

Note: The back stop (I) will end up straight as well, when the edge of the step top is cut off.

MATERIALS LIST

CHANGED PARTS

D	Top (1)	³⁄₄ x 9¹⁄₂ - 16³⁄₄
G	Step Top (1)	³⁄₄ x 12³⁄₈ - 15

SQUARE STOOL

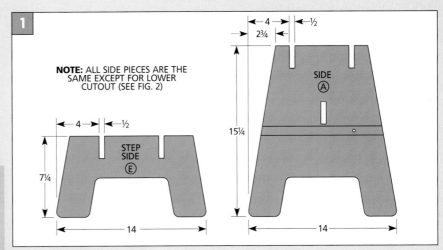

1

NOTE: ALL SIDE PIECES ARE THE SAME EXCEPT FOR LOWER CUTOUT (SEE FIG. 2)

STEP SIDE (E)

4 ¹⁄₂ 7¹⁄₄ 14

SIDE (A)

4 ²³⁄₄ ¹⁄₂ 15¹⁄₄ 14

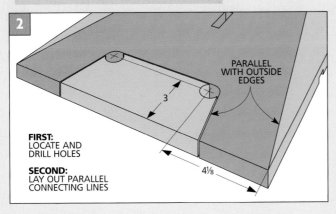

2

PARALLEL WITH OUTSIDE EDGES

3

4¹⁄₈

FIRST: LOCATE AND DRILL HOLES

SECOND: LAY OUT PARALLEL CONNECTING LINES

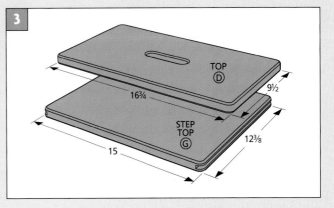

3

TOP (D)

9¹⁄₂

16³⁄₄

STEP TOP (G)

12³⁄₈

15

IN THE SHOP

It's always nice when a shop project can be built in a day or two — leaving more time to build furniture projects. That's definitely the case in this section.

For instance, easy to build projects like the sandpaper storage rack, the drill bit case, and the saw blade rack keep supplies front and center while protecting your valuable accessories. The stacking sawhorses and utility ladder provide a boost when you need it most and then can be easily stored out of the way. Finally, the joiner's mallet is an easy project to build with many satisfying features.

Shop Tote

A unique "split" handle design provides a handy grip for each tray and allows you to stack them on top of each other. The dividers are great for keeping all your tools and fasteners organized.

There's plenty of storage for stuff in my shop. But the other day while walking back and forth between my workbench and one of those storage cabinets, I realized that what I really needed was a way to gather everything up and carry it all to where I'm working.

What I came up with is not another tool box. Instead I made something a little different — it's a small Shop Tote that works great for organizing and carrying around hardware, hand tools, or other small items (see photo above).

TWO TRAYS. At first it looks like it's a fairly deep box with a centered handle. But on closer inspection, you'll find that

there are actually two small trays in my Shop Tote — one tray on top of the other.

Lift up the top tray by the sides and you'll see that "half" of the handle comes along with it. The other "half" of the handle is built into the bottom tray. I know what you're thinking — why? Well, this way each tray has its own handle. When the trays are stacked up, the handles combine to form a heavy-duty grip for the entire tote.

DIVIDERS. In addition to the unique handle design, the tote also features a set of built-in dividers. The short dividers allow you to customize each tray to help organize its contents.

EXPLODED VIEW

OVERALL DIMENSIONS:
$10^{1}/_{16}$W x 14L x $7^{1}/_{2}$H

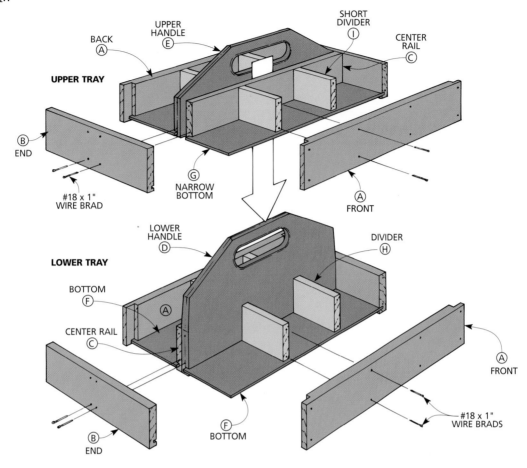

CUTTING DIAGRAM

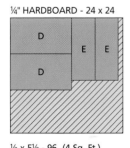

1/4" HARDBOARD - 24 x 24

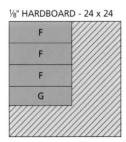

1/8" HARDBOARD - 24 x 24

1/2 x 5 1/2 - 96 (4 Sq. Ft.)

TRAY PARTS

Since the basic parts of the upper and lower trays are identical, I started with blanks wide enough to make both trays *(Fig. 1)*. Then I trimmed the individual pieces to finished width later.

FRONT, BACK, AND ENDS. All of the blanks are the same width (height) — 5$\frac{1}{8}$". But their lengths are different. First, cut the blanks for the front and back pieces (A). Then add a rabbet on each end to receive the end pieces *(Figs. 1 and 1a)*. Now you can cut the blanks for the ends (B).

CENTER RAILS. Next, make a blank for the two center rails (C) *(Fig. 1)*. To find the length of this blank, measure the distance between the shoulders of the rabbets on a front blank (13").

CUT TO WIDTH. Now you can rip all of the tray pieces (A, B, and C) to their finished widths (2$\frac{1}{2}$"). Then set these pieces aside; they're used later.

HANDLES

After the tray pieces are cut to size, you can turn your attention to the handles. I decided to use hardboard for the handles because of its stability.

HARDBOARD. To make each handle, I glued up a blank made from two layers of $\frac{1}{4}$"-thick hardboard *(Fig. 2)*.

Each handle blank is the same length (13"). The lower handle (D) is 7$\frac{1}{2}$" tall. But since the upper handle (E) rests on top of the lower tray, it's 5" tall.

HANDLE SHAPE. To make sure the handle shapes match, I fastened the blanks together with a piece of carpet tape and laid out the shape on top *(Figs. 2 and 2a)*. Then with the blanks still taped together, cut out the shape.

Now you can separate the pieces and round over only the holes and top edges on a router table *(Figs. 3 and 3a)*.

LOWER TRAY

Next start on the lower tray. It uses the taller (7$\frac{1}{2}$") of the two handles *(Fig. 4)*.

CUT GROOVES. The first step is to cut grooves for the tray bottoms that are added later. These $\frac{1}{8}$"-wide grooves are cut on the inside bottom edge of each lower tray piece (including the handle) *(Figs. 4 and 4a)*.

TAPER HANDLE. To make it easier to slide the upper tray down over the handle of the lower tray when it's

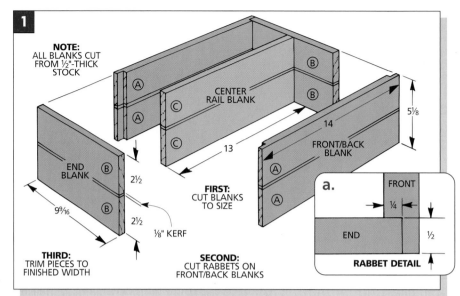

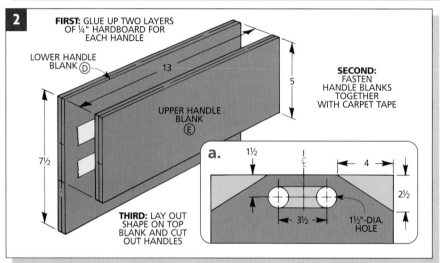

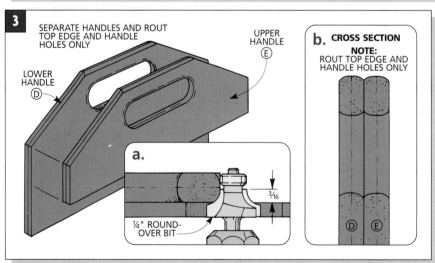

assembled, I sanded slight tapers on the ends of the handle *(Fig. 4)*.

TRAY BOTTOMS. Now determine the size of the tray bottoms *(Fig. 4)*. To do this, first dry-clamp the tray together.

Then position the center rail (C) and handle (D) so they're centered on the width of the tray.

Next, measure each of the openings and add $\frac{1}{2}$" to both the length and the width. Now cut two $\frac{1}{8}$"-thick hardboard bottoms (F) to size *(Fig. 4)*. (In my case, they're $4\frac{1}{2}$" wide and $13\frac{1}{2}$" long.)

ASSEMBLY. After the bottoms have been cut to size, all that's left is to assemble the lower tray. Start by gluing the center rail to the handle so the grooves on each are facing out *(Fig. 4)*. Then apply glue to the remaining tray parts and nail the tray together.

UPPER TRAY

To complete the upper tray, first cut $\frac{1}{8}$"-wide grooves in all of the tray pieces for the hardboard bottoms *(Fig. 5a)*.

TRAY BOTTOMS. To determine the size of the tray bottoms, I again dry-clamped the tray. Only this time, I clamped it up around the handle of the lower tray. This does two things.

First, it ensures that the sides and ends of the upper tray will align with those on the lower tray. And second, it positions the upper handle and center rail in the correct positions for the handle of the lower tray to slip through.

Note: To make sure there's enough clearance for the upper tray to slide over the handle, insert a paper shim between the handle and the center rail before nailing it in place *(Fig. 6)*.

Although the length of both bottom pieces is the same ($13\frac{1}{2}$"), their widths are different. The narrow bottom (G) that fits on the center rail side is $\frac{1}{2}$" narrower than the other side (4"). The other bottom (F) is $4\frac{1}{2}$" wide *(Fig. 5)*.

ASSEMBLY. With the bottoms cut to size, the upper tray can now be glued, clamped, and nailed together on top of the lower tray *(Fig. 6)*.

DIVIDERS

Now add the dividers *(Fig. 7)*. Cut them from $\frac{1}{2}$"-thick stock to fit inside the tray.

The dividers (H) for the lower tray and one side of the upper tray are the same — $2\frac{1}{8}$" high (wide) and 4" long. But the short dividers (I) for the other side of the upper tray are only $3\frac{1}{2}$" long.

When the dividers are cut to size, position each one in the tray and glue and nail them in place *(Fig. 7)*. ■

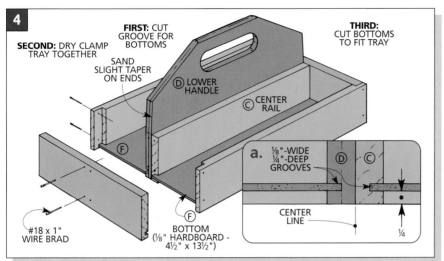

4 **FIRST:** CUT GROOVE FOR BOTTOMS · **SECOND:** DRY CLAMP TRAY TOGETHER · SAND SLIGHT TAPER ON ENDS · **THIRD:** CUT BOTTOMS TO FIT TRAY · (D) LOWER HANDLE · (C) CENTER RAIL · (F) · **a.** $\frac{1}{8}$"-WIDE $\frac{1}{4}$"-DEEP GROOVES · (D) (C) · CENTER LINE · $\frac{1}{4}$ · #18 x 1" WIRE BRAD · (F) BOTTOM ($\frac{1}{8}$" HARDBOARD - $4\frac{1}{2}$" x $13\frac{1}{2}$")

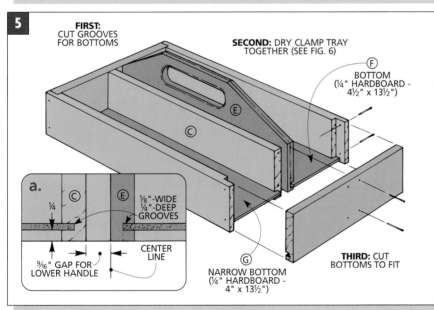

5 **FIRST:** CUT GROOVES FOR BOTTOMS · **SECOND:** DRY CLAMP TRAY TOGETHER (SEE FIG. 6) · (F) BOTTOM ($\frac{1}{4}$" HARDBOARD - $4\frac{1}{2}$" x $13\frac{1}{2}$") · (E) · (C) · **a.** (C) $\frac{1}{4}$ · (E) $\frac{1}{8}$"-WIDE $\frac{1}{4}$"-DEEP GROOVES · CENTER LINE · $\frac{9}{16}$" GAP FOR LOWER HANDLE · NARROW BOTTOM ($\frac{1}{4}$" HARDBOARD - 4" x $13\frac{1}{2}$") · (G) · **THIRD:** CUT BOTTOMS TO FIT

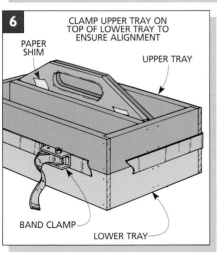

6 CLAMP UPPER TRAY ON TOP OF LOWER TRAY TO ENSURE ALIGNMENT · PAPER SHIM · UPPER TRAY · BAND CLAMP · LOWER TRAY

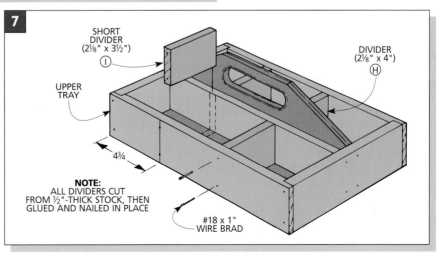

7 SHORT DIVIDER ($2\frac{1}{8}$" x $3\frac{1}{2}$") (I) · UPPER TRAY · $4\frac{3}{4}$ · DIVIDER ($2\frac{1}{8}$" x 4") (H) · **NOTE:** ALL DIVIDERS CUT FROM $\frac{1}{2}$"-THICK STOCK, THEN GLUED AND NAILED IN PLACE · #18 x 1" WIRE BRAD

Sandpaper Storage

This storage unit brings your sandpaper supply out of the drawer and places it right where you need it most — front and center. Build a single unit or "gang" them together to create a spot for each grit.

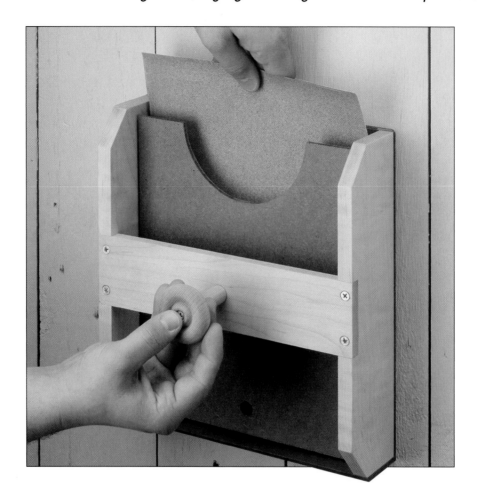

The workbench drawer where I kept my sanding supplies just wasn't working out. Besides the fact it was stuffed so full I couldn't find what I needed, and all of my supplies were getting damaged.

Because of the humidity in my shop, sheets of sandpaper had curled up at the edges. And the backs on my rolls of adhesive-backed sandpaper had collected so much dust and dirt that they wouldn't stick any more.

To solve both problems, I built a pair of simple Sandpaper Storage units: a press for storing sheets of sandpaper (see photo above) and a roll dispenser to hold rolls of adhesive-backed sandpaper (for more on this, see page 100).

SPRING-LOADED PRESS. To keep sheets of sandpaper flat, I made a simple press that mounts on the wall. It's just an open box with a spring-loaded plate that applies pressure against the sandpaper.

Depending on how much space you can spare in your shop, you can build a single press to hold a variety of grits of sandpaper or you could build a row of press storage units. This way, you'll end up with a place for each grit. That not only makes it easier to find the right grit, but it also allows you to have a

better idea of how much is left (so you don't run out). For more on how to group several presses together, see the Designer's Notebook on page 99.

ROLL DISPENSER. I also came up with another way to store all my rolls of adhesive-backed sandpaper. This roll dispenser provided me with a quick way to measure and cut strips of sandpaper to the exact length needed. Here again, you can make a single storage unit or "gang" several together for storing additional rolls. The Woodworker's Notebook beginning on page 100 provides complete instructions on how to build this dispenser.

EXPLODED VIEW

OVERALL DIMENSIONS:
10¼W x 5½D x 11½H

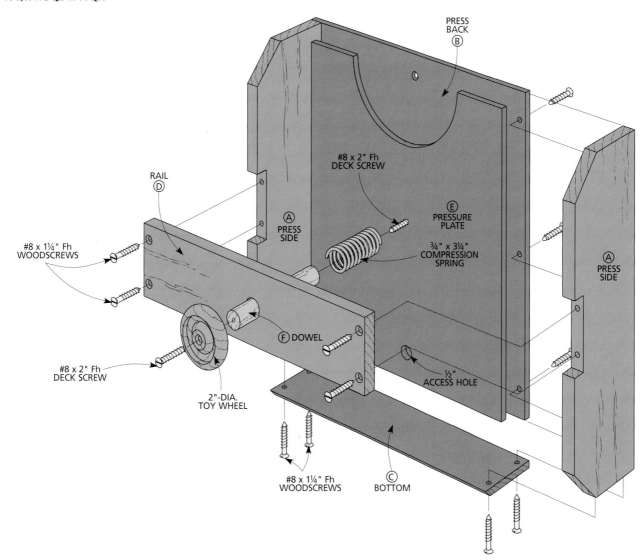

PRESS
BACK
Ⓑ

#8 x 2" Fh
DECK SCREW

Ⓔ
PRESSURE
PLATE

¾" x 3¼"
COMPRESSION
SPRING

RAIL
Ⓓ

Ⓐ
PRESS
SIDE

Ⓐ
PRESS
SIDE

#8 x 1¼" Fh
WOODSCREWS

Ⓕ DOWEL

½"
ACCESS HOLE

#8 x 2" Fh
DECK SCREW

2"-DIA.
TOY WHEEL

#8 x 1¼" Fh
WOODSCREWS

Ⓒ
BOTTOM

MATERIALS LIST

PRESS
A Press Sides (2) ½ x 3½ - 11¼
B Press Back (1) ¼ hdbd. - 10¼ x 11¼
C Bottom (1) ¼ hdbd. - 10¼ x 2½
D Rail (1) ½ x 2½ - 10¼
E Pressure Plate (1) ¼ hdbd. - 9⅛ x 10¾
F Dowel (1) ⅝ dowel x 4

HARDWARE SUPPLIES
(14) No. 8 x 1¼" Fh woodscrews
(2) No. 8 x 2" Fh deck screws
(2) No. 8 x 1¾" Fh woodscrews
(1) ¾" x 3¼" compression spring
(1) 2"-dia. toy wheel

CUTTING DIAGRAM

½ x 5½ - 48 (1.8 Sq. Ft.)

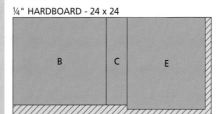

A	A	D

¼" HARDBOARD - 24 x 24

B	C	E

NOTE: PART F IS CUT FROM A
6" LENGTH OF ⅝" DOWEL

BOX

To keep sheets of sandpaper flat, I made a simple press that mounts on the wall. It's just an open box with a spring-loaded plate mounted on the front.

SIDES. I began by making two sides (A) *(Fig. 1)*. These are just $1/2$"-thick pieces of hardwood with the outside corners cut at an angle. To accept a rail that's added later, cut a notch that's centered on the outside edge of each side.

BACK. The sides are held together with a hardboard back (B) *(Fig. 1)*. Besides adding rigidity to the sides, attaching the back creates an opening for full-sized sheets of sandpaper. After drilling a pair of mounting holes in the back, it's simply screwed in place so it's flush with the sides.

BOTTOM. To keep sandpaper from falling out of the press, there's also a $1/4$" hardboard bottom (C) attached to the sides *(Fig. 2)*. The bottom gets beveled along the front edge to match the angle of the sides. Once it's cut to size, go ahead and screw it in place *(Fig. 2a)*.

SPRING-LOADED PRESS

Once the box is complete, you can start building the spring-loaded press.

Using the press is simple. When you pull the handle back, the plate com-presses a spring *(Fig. 4)*. Releasing the handle pushes the spring against the plate, which presses the sandpaper flat.

RAIL. To make this work, a hardwood rail (D) is added to the front of the press. It's ripped to width to fit into the notches cut earlier in the sides *(Fig. 2)*.

Now drill a centered hole in the rail. The hole guides a dowel that will be attached to the plate later. This keeps the plate centered in the press as it moves in and out.

To complete the rail, just drill a pair of holes in each end for screws that will be used to fasten it to the sides. But don't attach it yet. The rail is added later when you assemble the press.

PRESSURE PLATE. Next, you can add a hardboard pressure plate (E) *(Fig. 3)*. The plate applies pressure against the sandpaper when the press is at "rest."

To keep the plate from binding, cut it to fit inside the box with $1/16$"-wide gaps around the sides and bottom. A curved opening in the top makes it easy to pull out the sandpaper *(Fig. 3a)*.

Also, drill a hole near the bottom of the pressure plate *(Fig. 3)*. When the press is assembled, it provides access to the bottom hole in the back that's used to mount the press to the wall.

DOWEL. There's just one more thing to do before you assemble the press. That's to attach a dowel (F) to the pressure plate. In addition to providing a way to pull the pressure plate away from the sandpaper, the dowel supports the compression spring *(Fig. 3)*.

The dowel is held in place with a single deck screw added through the back of the pressure plate. Since a deck screw has a straight shank and coarser threads along the entire shank, it's less

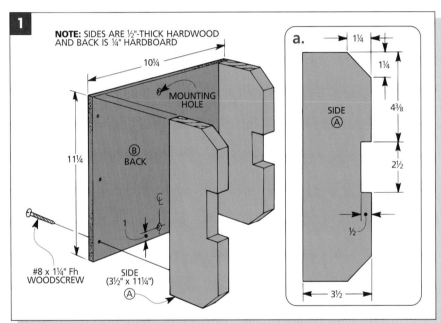

NOTE: SIDES ARE $1/2$"-THICK HARDWOOD AND BACK IS $1/4$" HARDBOARD

10¼

MOUNTING HOLE

B BACK

11¼

C

1

#8 x 1¼" Fh WOODSCREW

SIDE (3½" x 11¼") A

a.

1¼

1¼

SIDE A

4⅜

2½

½

3½

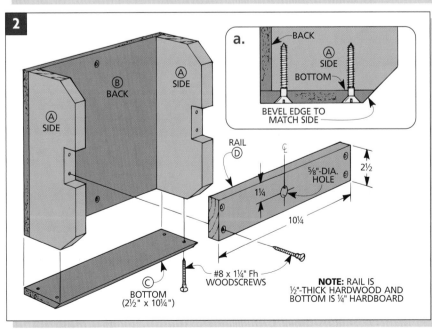

A SIDE

B BACK

A SIDE

A SIDE

a.

BACK

A SIDE

BOTTOM

BEVEL EDGE TO MATCH SIDE

RAIL D

⅝"-DIA. HOLE

2½

1¼

10¼

C BOTTOM (2½" x 10¼")

#8 x 1¼" Fh WOODSCREWS

NOTE: RAIL IS $1/2$"-THICK HARDWOOD AND BOTTOM IS $1/4$" HARDBOARD

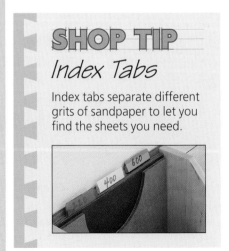

SHOP TIP
Index Tabs

Index tabs separate different grits of sandpaper to let you find the sheets you need.

likely to pull out when it's screwed into the end grain of the dowel.

ASSEMBLY. Now you should be ready to assemble the press. The best way I found to do this is to lay the box on its back so the opening faces up.

Start by setting the pressure plate in the opening and slipping the compression spring down over the dowel. Then use the rail to compress the spring as you fit it into the notches you've cut in the sides. (You'll need to hold the rail down as you screw it in place.) Also, to make it easy to pull the plate back, I screwed a 2"-dia. toy wheel onto the end of the dowel (*Fig. 3*).

MOUNT PRESS. Finally, it's just a matter of mounting the sandpaper press to the wall (*Fig. 4*) and loading it with sandpaper (see the Shop Tip far left).

Note: If you have a lot of sheet sandpaper, you may want to "gang" several sandpaper presses together (refer to the Designer's Notebook below). ∎

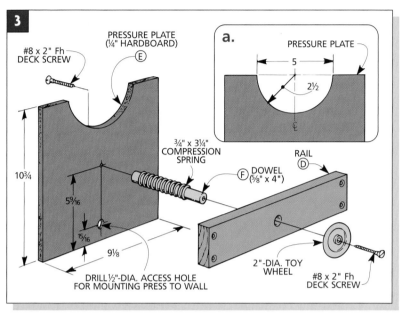

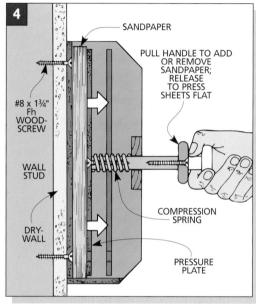

DESIGNER'S NOTEBOOK

A group-mounted press can stretch your storage options to include several grits and types of sandpaper.

GROUP-MOUNTED PRESS

■ You can build a group-mounted version of the sandpaper press that will hold several grits of sandpaper (see drawing). The back (B), bottom (C), and rail (D) are each longer than the originals.

■ Now they're "ganged" together to make it easier to select the grit you need. You can even use this version to store a variety of different types of sandpaper.

MATERIALS LIST		
CHANGED PARTS		**HARDWARE SUPPLIES**
A Press Sides (4)	½ x 3½ - 11¼	(24) No. 8 x 1¼" Fh woodscrews
B Press Back (1)	¼ hdbd. - 11¼ x 29¾	(6) No. 8 x 1¾" Fh woodscrews
C Bottom (1)	¼ hdbd. - 2½ x 29¾	(6) No. 8 x 2" Fh deck screws
D Rail (1)	½ x 2½ - 29¾	(3) ¾" x 3¼" compression springs
E Pressure Plates (3)	¼ hdbd. - 9⅛ x 10¾	(3) 2"-dia. toy wheels
F Dowels (3)	⅝ dowel x 4	

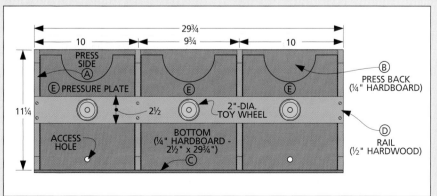

WOODWORKER'S NOTEBOOK

A Roll Dispenser for adhesive-backed sandpaper keeps everything clean and within easy reach. And with a roll stored in the dispenser, it's easy to tear off a strip the exact length you need.

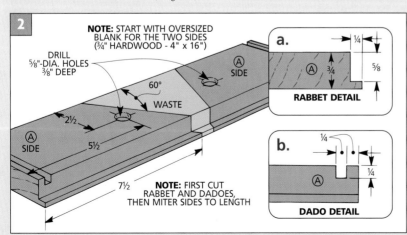

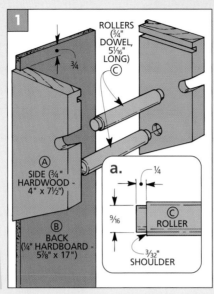

1

ROLLERS (3/4" DOWEL, 5 1/16" LONG)
Ⓒ

3/4

SIDE (3/4" HARDWOOD - 4" x 7 1/2") Ⓐ

BACK (1/4" HARDBOARD - 5 7/8" x 17") Ⓑ

a.

1/4

9/16

Ⓒ ROLLER

3/32" SHOULDER

MATERIALS LIST

ROLL DISPENSER

A	Sides (2)	3/4 x 4 - 7 1/2
B	Back (1)	1/4 hdbd. - 5 7/8 x 17
C	Rollers (2)	3/4 dowel x 5 1/16
D	Lid (1)	1/4 hdbd. - 3 3/4 x 5 1/8
E	Guide Block (1)	3/4 x 2 5/8 - 1 1/2
F	Upper Cleat (1)	3/4 x 1 1/2 - 6 1/8
G	Lower Cleat (1)	3/4 x 1 - 6 1/8

HARDWARE SUPPLIES
(4) No. 8 x 1 3/4" Fh woodscrews
(2) No. 6 x 1/2" Rh woodscrews
(1) Hacksaw blade (6 1/8" long)

ROLL DISPENSER

■ In addition to holding a roll of adhesive-backed sandpaper, this dispenser provides a quick way to measure and cut strips of sandpaper to the exact length you need. Make a single unit or "gang" several together.

■ The dispenser primarily consists of two 3/4"-thick hardwood sides that support a pair of rollers *(Fig. 1)*. The upper roller holds a roll of sandpaper. And the lower roller guides the sandpaper out the bottom (refer to *Fig. 7*).

■ The sides (A) are fairly small pieces, so start with an oversized blank *(Fig. 2)*. A rabbet in the back edge accepts a hardboard back *(Fig. 2a)*. And there's a dado near each end for a lid *(Fig. 2b)*.

■ After drilling two shallow holes that will hold the lower roller, the sides are simply mitered to final length.

■ To make the upper roller removable (and keep it from slipping out as you pull out the sandpaper), there's an angled slot in each side *(Fig. 1)*. Use carpet tape to attach the sides together temporarily *(Fig. 3)*. Then drill a hole to form the end of the slot and remove the waste with a band saw *(Fig. 3a)*.

■ With the sides complete, you can add the back (B) *(Fig. 1)*. It's sized so the distance from the bottom edge to a cutter that's added later will cut a piece of sandpaper to fit a half-sheet sander.

■ The next step is to make the two rollers (C) *(Fig. 1)*. They're just hardwood dowels with a tenon cut at each

end. The tenons allow the dowels to fit loosely in the angled slots at the top and the holes in the sides of the dispenser *(Fig. 1a)*. The tenons *and* the loose fit allow the rollers to spin freely as you pull out a strip of sandpaper. (For more on cutting tenons on dowels, see the Shop Tip on the next page.)

■ At this point, you're ready to glue the sides to the back. Just remember to slip the lower roller in place first (no glue) so it's trapped between the sides.

■ When the glue dried, I added a hardboard lid (D) *(Fig. 4)*. It keeps dust in the shop from settling on the exposed adhesive on the sandpaper. To make it easy to install a new roll, the lid slides in and out of the dadoes in the sides.

■ Besides the lid, you'll also need to add two small guide blocks *(Fig. 4)*. Along with the lower roller, they keep sandpaper from curling back around the roll. And they provide an opening for your fingers to pull out the sandpaper.

2

NOTE: START WITH OVERSIZED BLANK FOR THE TWO SIDES (3/4" HARDWOOD - 4" x 16")

DRILL 5/8"-DIA. HOLES 3/8" DEEP

60°

WASTE

Ⓐ SIDE

2 1/2

Ⓐ SIDE

5 1/2

7 1/2

NOTE: FIRST CUT RABBET AND DADOES, THEN MITER SIDES TO LENGTH

a.
1/4
Ⓐ
Ⓐ 3/4
5/8
RABBET DETAIL

b.
1/4
Ⓐ
1/4
DADO DETAIL

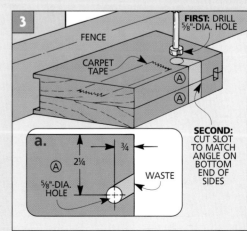

3

FENCE

CARPET TAPE

Ⓐ
Ⓐ

FIRST: DRILL 5/8"-DIA. HOLE

SECOND: CUT SLOT TO MATCH ANGLE ON BOTTOM END OF SIDES

a.
Ⓐ 2 1/4
3/4
5/8"-DIA. HOLE
WASTE

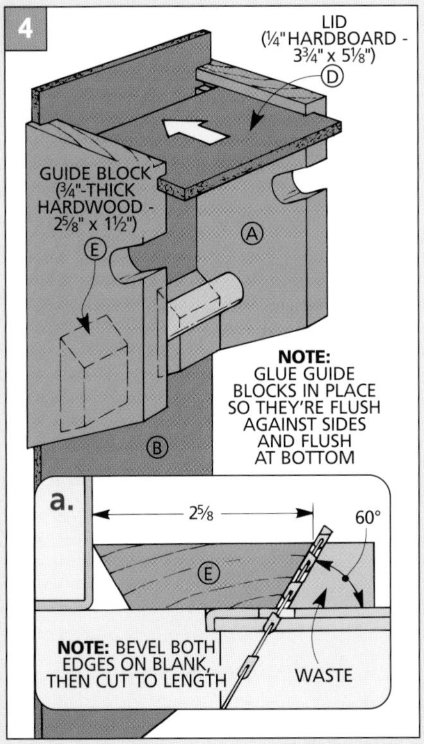
4
LID
(¼" HARDBOARD - 3¾" x 5⅛")
D
GUIDE BLOCK
(¾"-THICK HARDWOOD - 2⅝" x 1½")
E
A
B
NOTE:
GLUE GUIDE BLOCKS IN PLACE SO THEY'RE FLUSH AGAINST SIDES AND FLUSH AT BOTTOM
a.
2⅝
60°
E
NOTE: BEVEL BOTH EDGES ON BLANK, THEN CUT TO LENGTH
WASTE

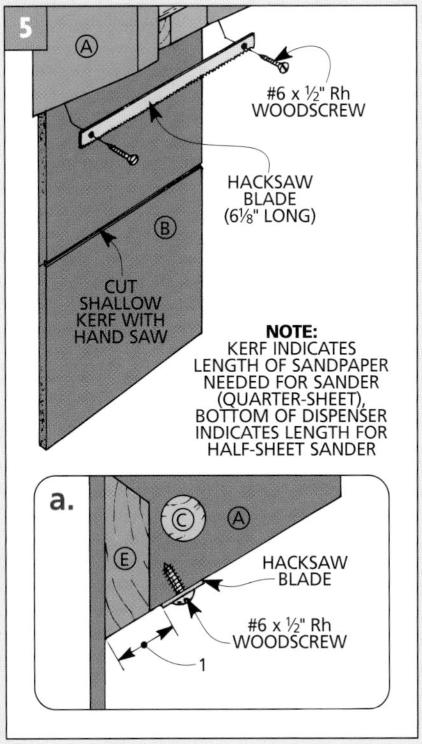
5
A
#6 x ½" Rh WOODSCREW
HACKSAW BLADE (6⅛" LONG)
B
CUT SHALLOW KERF WITH HAND SAW
NOTE:
KERF INDICATES LENGTH OF SANDPAPER NEEDED FOR SANDER (QUARTER-SHEET), BOTTOM OF DISPENSER INDICATES LENGTH FOR HALF-SHEET SANDER
a.
C
A
E
HACKSAW BLADE
#6 x ½" Rh WOODSCREW
1

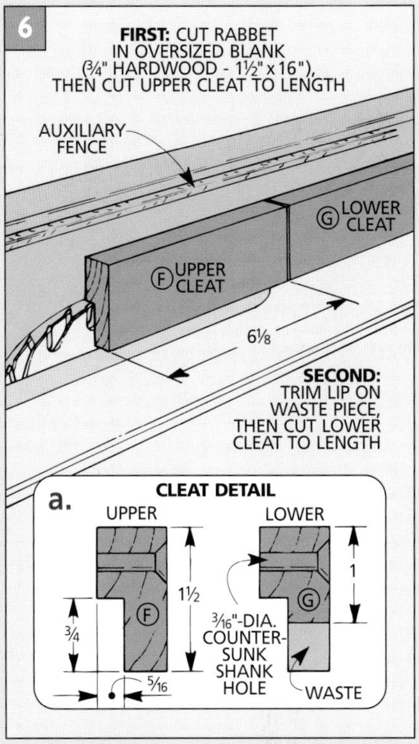
6
FIRST: CUT RABBET IN OVERSIZED BLANK (¾" HARDWOOD - 1½" x 16"), THEN CUT UPPER CLEAT TO LENGTH
AUXILIARY FENCE
G LOWER CLEAT
F UPPER CLEAT
6⅛
SECOND: TRIM LIP ON WASTE PIECE, THEN CUT LOWER CLEAT TO LENGTH
a.
CLEAT DETAIL
UPPER
LOWER
1½
1
¾
F
G
3⁄16"-DIA. COUNTER-SUNK SHANK HOLE
5⁄16
WASTE

■ To make it easy to weave a strip of sandpaper around the lower roller, there's a bevel on the top of the guide blocks. A bevel on the bottom matches the angle on the sides *(Fig. 4a)*.

■ Here again, it's safest to start with a long blank for the guide blocks. Then bevel both edges before cutting the guide blocks (E) to length *(Fig. 4a)*.

■ To cut the sandpaper to length, screw a shortened hacksaw blade to the angled end of each side *(Figs. 5 and 5a)*.

■ Once the hacksaw blade is attached, you can cut a shallow kerf in the back that shows how far to pull out the sandpaper for a sander that uses a quarter sheet. The bottom edge is for a half-sheet sander.

■ Now all that's left is to mount the dispenser to a wall. It's held in place by two hardwood cleats that are designed so you can easily remove the dispenser and carry it to where you're working.

■ What makes this work is each cleat is rabbeted to form a lip that holds the dispenser in place. To provide clearance when you remove the dispenser (or hang it up), the lip on the lower cleat is shorter than the one on top *(Fig. 7)*.

■ To make both cleats at once, use an extra-long blank and cut a rabbet that's the same width as the one required for the upper cleat *(Figs. 6 and 6a)*. After cutting the upper cleat (F) to length, trim the lip on the remaining piece and cut the lower cleat (G) to length.

■ Finally, drill holes in the hardwood cleats and screw them to the wall. Be sure to space the screws to hit studs.

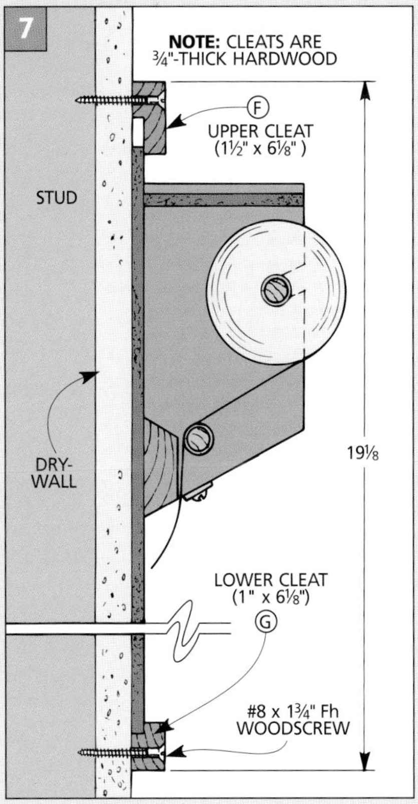
7
NOTE: CLEATS ARE ¾"-THICK HARDWOOD
F
UPPER CLEAT (1½" x 6⅛")
STUD
DRY-WALL
19⅛
LOWER CLEAT (1" x 6⅛")
G
#8 x 1¾" Fh WOODSCREW

SHOP TIP . . . . *Round Tenons*

I used a table saw and dado blade to cut the tenons on my dowels. An auxiliary fence on both the miter gauge and rip fence helps.

The diameter of the tenon is determined by the height of the dado blade. Set the rip fence for the length of the tenon (detail 'a').

To make the cut, hold the miter gauge in place with the dowel against the auxiliary fence as you rotate it forward (see drawing).

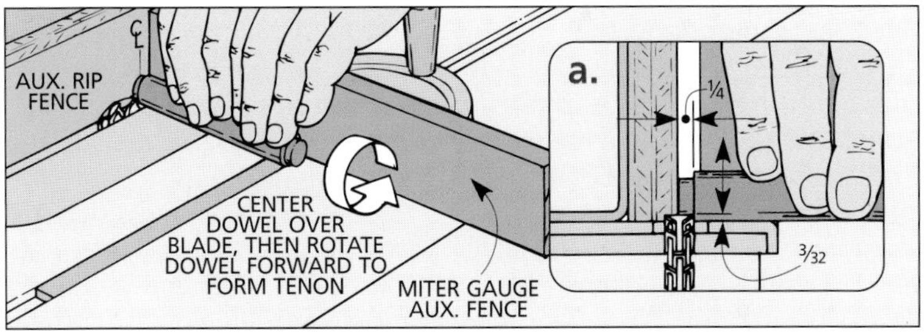
AUX. RIP FENCE
CENTER DOWEL OVER BLADE, THEN ROTATE DOWEL FORWARD TO FORM TENON
MITER GAUGE AUX. FENCE
a.
¼
3⁄32

Saw Blade Rack

This rack is so simple to build it should only take a couple of hours to complete. But the protection it provides will help your table saw blades last a lifetime. Plus, it keeps your blades close at hand.

Many of the woodworking shops I've been in have the table saw blades simply hung on a nail. The problem with this is the teeth can knock against each other and you risk damaging an expensive carbide tip. And somehow, you always end up needing the blade that's on the bottom of the stack.

This Saw Blade Rack takes care of both of these problems. The blades are always right at hand, and the teeth are protected. And since it hangs on the wall, it doesn't take up much space.

SLEEVES. The unique feature of this rack is the sleeves that the saw blades slide into. They tilt forward so the blades are easy to pull out and slide back in. But getting the sleeves set at the correct angle in the rack took some thought.

My first thought was to cut a series of angled dadoes in the sides of the rack. But this would have required a special indexing jig. And simply screwing them between the sides would also have been a bit awkward.

SUPPORT PINS. So to hold the sleeves at the proper angle, I borrowed a common shelving technique — support pins. I added small dowels to the inside of the rack. Then I cut grooves on the ends of the sleeves. This way, they simply slide over the pins.

CONSTRUCTION. Building the rack couldn't be simpler. It's just a box made from low-cost 1x6 pine. I used rabbets to join the rack sides to the top and bottom and routed a groove to hold a hardboard back. A couple of backing strips provide extra support for the screws used to attach the rack to the wall

Each saw blade sleeve is just a three-layered hardboard sandwich. To make the triangle-shaped spacers for the sleeves, I used a simple sled that serves two purposes: to help in cutting the spacers to size, and as an alignment guide for drilling holes for the pins that hold the sleeves together.

EXPLODED VIEW

OVERALL DIMENSIONS:
12½W x 4¼D x 27H

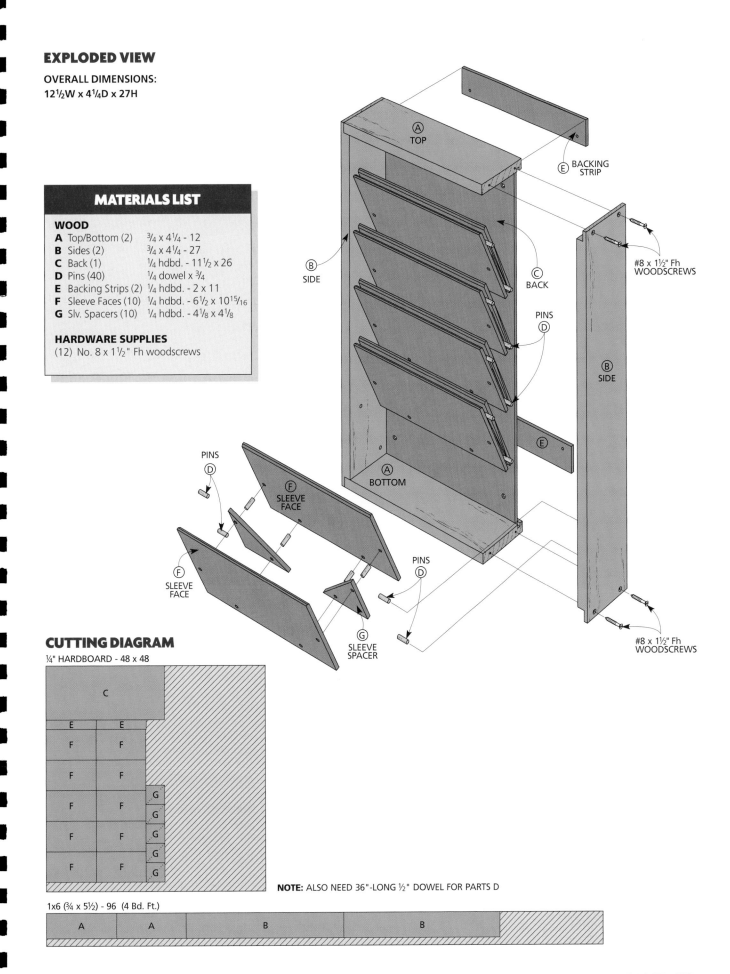

MATERIALS LIST

WOOD

A	Top/Bottom (2)	¾ x 4¼ - 12
B	Sides (2)	¾ x 4¼ - 27
C	Back (1)	¼ hdbd. - 11½ x 26
D	Pins (40)	¼ dowel x ¾
E	Backing Strips (2)	¼ hdbd. - 2 x 11
F	Sleeve Faces (10)	¼ hdbd. - 6½ x 10¹⁵/₁₆
G	Slv. Spacers (10)	¼ hdbd. - 4⅛ x 4⅛

HARDWARE SUPPLIES

(12) No. 8 x 1½" Fh woodscrews

CUTTING DIAGRAM

¼" HARDBOARD - 48 x 48

NOTE: ALSO NEED 36"-LONG ½" DOWEL FOR PARTS D

1x6 (¾ x 5½) - 96 (4 Bd. Ft.)

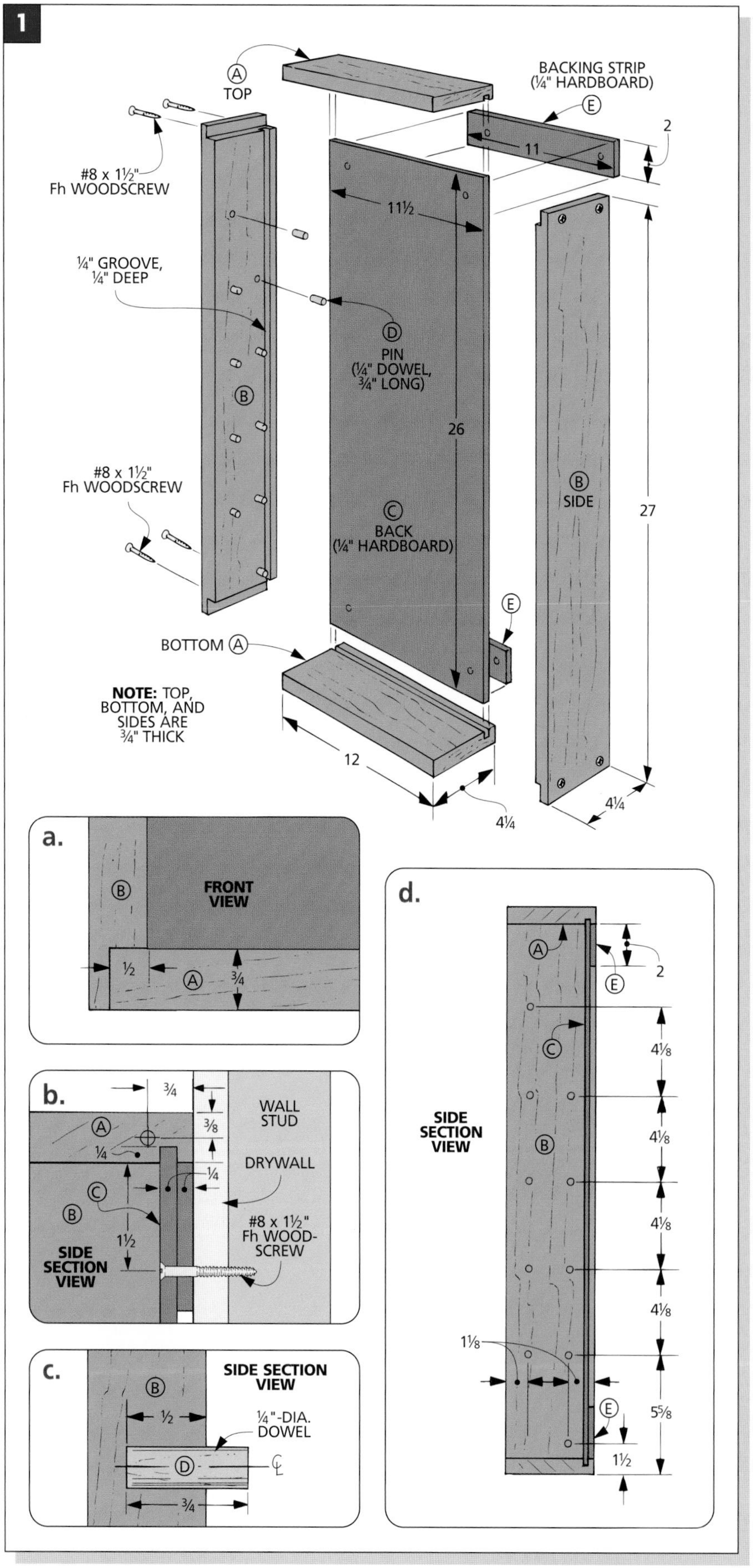

1

Ⓐ
TOP

BACKING STRIP
(¼" HARDBOARD)

Ⓔ

2

#8 x 1½"
Fh WOODSCREW

11

11½

¼" GROOVE,
¼" DEEP

Ⓐ

Ⓓ
PIN
(¼" DOWEL,
¾" LONG)

26

Ⓑ

#8 x 1½"
Fh WOODSCREW

Ⓒ
BACK
(¼" HARDBOARD)

Ⓑ
SIDE

27

Ⓔ

BOTTOM Ⓐ

NOTE: TOP,
BOTTOM, AND
SIDES ARE
¾" THICK

12

4¼

4¼

a.

Ⓑ

FRONT VIEW

½   Ⓐ   ¾

b.

¾

Ⓐ   ⅜

¼

Ⓒ   ¼

Ⓑ   1½

SIDE SECTION VIEW

WALL STUD

DRYWALL

#8 x 1½"
Fh WOOD-SCREW

c.

Ⓑ

½   ¼"-DIA. DOWEL

Ⓓ   ₵

¾

d.

SIDE SECTION VIEW

Ⓐ

Ⓔ   2

Ⓒ

4⅛

Ⓑ

4⅛

4⅛

4⅛

1⅛

Ⓔ   5⅝

1½

To build the Saw Blade Rack, I started with the rack assembly. This includes the ¾"-thick top and bottom (A) that are trapped between a couple of rabbeted sides (B) *(Figs. 1 and 1a)*.

After all the pieces are cut to size and the side pieces are rabbeted, you'll need to cut a groove in each piece to hold a ¼"-thick hardboard back *(Fig. 1b)*. Then dry-assemble the rack and cut the back (C) to size.

But before you glue the rack together, it's best to drill a series of holes for the ¼"-diameter support pins (D) *(Figs. 1c and 1d)*. Then you can cut a ¾"-long pin from a ¼" dowel to glue into each hole.

With the rack put together, I glued two ¼" hardboard backing strips (E) to the back *(Fig. 1)*. These strips simply support the back when it's time to screw the rack to the wall.

SLEEVES. Now you can turn your attention to building the sleeves for the blades. Each one is a sandwich of three layers of ¼" hardboard.

I started by cutting two rectangular sleeve faces (F) for each sleeve *(Fig. 2)*. I made mine ¹/₁₆" shorter than the width of the rack opening (10¹⁵/₁₆"). Then to make it easy to slide the saw blades into the sleeves, I chamfered only the inside edge of each face *(Fig. 2a)*.

Next, I worked on the sleeve spacers (G) *(Fig. 2)*. These end up as triangle-shaped pieces that allow the saw blade to slide between the sleeve faces. But they start out as 4⅛"-square blanks that I made from ¼" hardboard *(Fig. 3)*. (One square blank of hardboard will make two triangular spacers.) And to cut the blank into spacers, I made a simple sled *(Figs. 3 and 3a)*.

The base of the sled is a 4" x 12" scrap piece of plywood. By gluing a couple of fences in place on the base, the sled will hold the spacer blanks at the right angle *(Fig. 3)*.

Note: I used a hardboard blank to make it easier to position the fences when gluing them to the sled. Just line up opposing corners of the blank along the edge of the base *(Fig. 3)*.

Now the spacer blanks are ready to be cut into triangles. But when positioning the rip fence, set it so the blade cuts through the center of the square *(Fig. 3)*. (This means your first pass will trim off the edge of the sled.)

With the spacers cut to size, the sleeves can be assembled. But since glue makes the pieces slide, I decided to use more pins (D).

To do this, first I drilled $\frac{1}{4}$"-diameter holes for the pins in all four pieces of each sleeve. To ensure that all the pieces lined up, I used the sled again, only this time I clamped it to the drill press table *(Fig. 4)*. After drilling the first hole in each corner, flip the workpiece over and drill the second *(Fig. 4a)*.

Note: With the face pieces, drill the holes at the bottom edge (the one without the chamfer).

Now, after you've cut some more $\frac{3}{4}$"-long dowel pins, the sleeves can be glued together. Just keep in mind that the chamfered edges on the face pieces should face each other.

At this point, all that's left is to cut a centered groove on each end of the sleeve *(Fig. 5)*. Set your dado blade to size this groove so that it fits over the pins inside the rack assembly *(Fig. 6)*. Then to complete the rack, screw it to the wall and slide the sleeves into place. ■

This shop-built rack is a handy way to store and protect your table saw blades. Plus, the bottom of the rack provides a convenient place to set an arbor wrench when it's not being used.

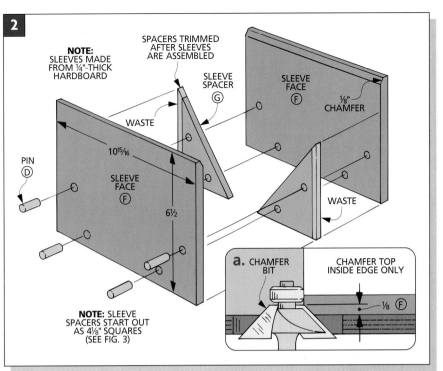

2

NOTE: SLEEVES MADE FROM $\frac{1}{4}$"-THICK HARDBOARD

SPACERS TRIMMED AFTER SLEEVES ARE ASSEMBLED

SLEEVE SPACER G

SLEEVE FACE F

$\frac{1}{8}$" CHAMFER

WASTE

$10^{15}/_{16}$

SLEEVE FACE F

PIN D

$6\frac{1}{2}$

WASTE

NOTE: SLEEVE SPACERS START OUT AS $4\frac{1}{8}$" SQUARES (SEE FIG. 3)

a. CHAMFER BIT

CHAMFER TOP INSIDE EDGE ONLY

$\frac{1}{8}$ F

3

BLANK FOR SLEEVE SPACER G

SLED

NOTE: SPACER BLANKS START OFF $4\frac{1}{8}$" x $4\frac{1}{8}$"

a. TOP VIEW

12

SLED

4

45° 4 FENCE

4

DRILL $\frac{1}{4}$"-DIA. ALIGNMENT HOLES IN ALL SLEEVE PIECES

SLED

a. TOP VIEW

SLED

$\frac{1}{2}$ $2\frac{3}{4}$

FLIP PIECE AFTER DRILLING FIRST HOLE

5

ASSEMBLED SLEEVE

DADO BLADE

CUT CENTERED GROOVE TO FIT OVER PINS IN RACK

a. ASSEMBLED SLEEVE

$\frac{1}{4}$" DADO BLADE

$\frac{1}{4}$

6

NOTE: GROOVES ALLOW SLEEVES TO BE POSITIONED AT PROPER ANGLE ON PINS

Stacking Sawhorses

A system of interlocking tabs and notches make these sawhorses sturdy, as well as versatile. They're short enough to make it easy to work on a large project, or they can be stacked to raise it off the floor.

Aren't the sawhorses a little short? That was the question I heard most often as I was building this set of Stacking Sawhorses. Actually, there are two answers to that question — yes and no. Let me explain.

First of all, the sawhorses *are* short. Each one stands in at only 17" tall. That's why one person in our shop suggested we call them saw "ponies" instead. And this low height would be fine if all they are only going to be used for is to support a sheet of plywood for an assembly table.

But it only takes a second to make the sawhorses "taller." You simply stack one sawhorse on top of another. This raises the top sawhorse to a height of 30".

That provides a comfortable working height for most jobs (see photo). But if you need a lower work surface (when assembling a large project for instance), simply unstack the sawhorses.

STORAGE. Once the job is completed, storing the sawhorses isn't a problem either. You can tuck a whole stack of them in a corner of the shop (see the photo on page 111).

TAB AND NOTCH. But as much as I appreciate the convenience of these

sawhorses, the thing that impresses me even more is how sturdy they are — even when they're stacked together. The secret is a system of interlocking tabs and notches that prevents them from moving from side to side or from end to end (see inset photo).

PLYWOOD. You won't need a lot of material to build these sawhorses. In fact, I made four complete sawhorses from a single sheet of 'AC' fir plywood.

REPLACEABLE TOP. To make the sawhorses even more durable, you can add a replaceable top that stays put *without* clamps. To learn more, see the Designer's Notebook on page 110.

EXPLODED VIEW

OVERALL DIMENSIONS:
15½W x 24½D x 17H

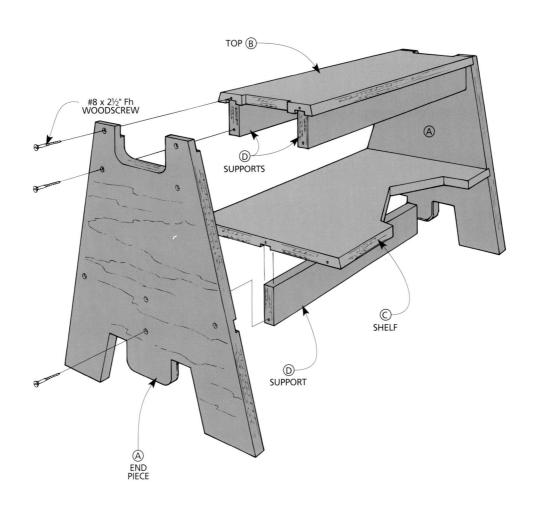

#8 x 2½" Fh
WOODSCREW

TOP Ⓑ

Ⓐ

Ⓓ
SUPPORTS

Ⓒ
SHELF

Ⓓ
SUPPORT

Ⓐ
END
PIECE

MATERIALS LIST

WOOD
A End Pieces (8)   ¾ ply - 17 x 15½
B Tops (4)   ¾ ply - 7¼ rgh. x 23½
C Shelves (4)   ¾ ply - 12¼ rgh. x 23½
D Supports (12)   ¾ ply - 2½ x 23

HARDWARE SUPPLIES
(64) No. 8 x 2½" Fh woodscrews
Note: The quantities listed above are for four sawhorses.

CUTTING DIAGRAM

¾" PLYWOOD - 48 x 96

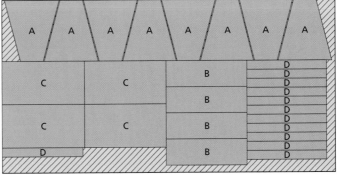

TEMPLATE

The key to these Stacking Sawhorses is the M-shaped pieces on the ends. Altogether, there are eight of these pieces. And the tab on one piece needs to fit the notch in another like the pieces of a jigsaw puzzle.

To produce a good fit, I began by making a template. This template ensures that all eight pieces are identical. And it speeds up the process of making the end pieces.

LAY OUT TEMPLATE. The template starts out as a piece of $1/4$" hardboard that's cut to the same width ($15\frac{1}{2}$") and height (17") as the end pieces *(Fig. 1)*.

To provide a firm footing, the end pieces taper gradually from a wide base to a narrow top. So in order to duplicate this taper, you'll need to lay out an angled line on each side of the template.

The next step is to mark the location of the tab and notch. It's important that they're the exact same size and shape.

PATTERN. An easy way to accomplish this is to make a pattern from a piece of posterboard and use it to lay out both the tab and the notch *(Fig. 1a)*. To position the pattern accurately on the template, draw a centerline on each one and align the marks.

FEET. Now all that's left is to lay out the two "feet" at the bottom of the template. The lines that form the inside edges of these feet are parallel to the angled sides. But before drawing these lines, you'll need to establish the outside corner of the "ear" on each side of the tab.

CUT TO SHAPE. At this point, it's just a matter of cutting the template to shape. The goal is to make the edges of the template as smooth as possible. That's because they'll be used to guide a flush trim bit when the end pieces are routed to shape.

To cut the straight, angled sides of the template, I used a simple jig on the table saw (refer to the Shop Jig box on page 109). The jig allowed me to cut right up to the layout line. But you'll need to cut the tab and notch with a band saw (or jig saw). When you cut the tab and notch, just be sure to stay about $1/8$" to the waste side of the line and then sand up to the mark.

LAY OUT END PIECES. Once the template is complete, you can use it to lay out the end pieces. It's possible to get all eight pieces from a 17"-wide strip cut from a full sheet of plywood. But there's not a lot of "extra" material, so be careful not to leave too much waste.

To do this, I started by positioning the template $1/4$" in from the end to lay out the first piece *(Fig. 2)*. Then, to lay out each remaining piece, simply turn the template end for end.

Note: It's a good idea to leave a $3/8$" space between layout lines. This way, you can use a jig saw to separate them without cutting into either piece.

CONSTRUCTION

At this point, the basic groundwork for the set of Stacking Sawhorses is complete. Now it's just a matter of cutting the end pieces to final shape and connecting them with the top, shelf, and supports (refer to the Exploded View drawing on page 107).

REMOVE WASTE. The first step is to remove the bulk of the waste from the area inside the notch and around the tab. There's no need to lay out these areas. Just stick the template to each end piece (A) with carpet tape and use a band saw (or jig saw) to rough out the basic shape *(Fig. 3)*.

There's one thing to watch here while you rough out the template — be sure that you don't accidentally cut into the edge of the hardboard template. I make it a point to stay at least $1/8$" away from the edge. This will leave you a

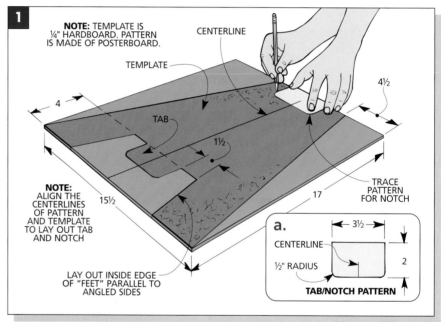

1

NOTE: TEMPLATE IS $1/4$" HARDBOARD. PATTERN IS MADE OF POSTERBOARD.

CENTERLINE

TEMPLATE

TAB

$4\frac{1}{2}$

4

$1\frac{1}{2}$

TRACE PATTERN FOR NOTCH

NOTE: ALIGN THE CENTERLINES OF PATTERN AND TEMPLATE TO LAY OUT TAB AND NOTCH

$15\frac{1}{2}$

17

LAY OUT INSIDE EDGE OF "FEET" PARALLEL TO ANGLED SIDES

a.

CENTERLINE

$1/2$" RADIUS

$3\frac{1}{2}$

2

TAB/NOTCH PATTERN

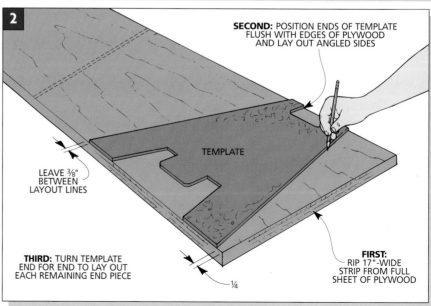

2

SECOND: POSITION ENDS OF TEMPLATE FLUSH WITH EDGES OF PLYWOOD AND LAY OUT ANGLED SIDES

TEMPLATE

LEAVE $3/8$" BETWEEN LAYOUT LINES

THIRD: TURN TEMPLATE END FOR END TO LAY OUT EACH REMAINING END PIECE

$1/4$

FIRST: RIP 17"-WIDE STRIP FROM FULL SHEET OF PLYWOOD

U sing a template to make all of the end pieces for the Stacking Sawhorses ensures each one is identical to the next one. This is important if you're looking for a stable surface, especially when you're working on large projects. But there is a small "catch." That's because, in order to get the sawhorses to fit together nice and tight, each side of the template needs to be cut at the exact same angle.

To accomplish this, I made a taper sled for the table saw to cut the sides of the end pieces on. It consists of two parts: a plywood base and a wood stop (see the drawing at right).

REFERENCE EDGE. The idea here is to create a *reference edge* on the base of the taper sled that indicates the path of the table saw blade. This reference edge is then used to position the template for cutting the sides.

To establish the taper sled's reference edge, start by ripping the plywood base to a width of 16" (see *Step 1* in the drawing above). Then, without moving the rip fence, align one of the layout lines on the top of the template with this edge (*Step 2*).

ATTACH STOP. Before making a cut, you'll need a way to keep the template

THIRD: SCREW STOP TO BASE SO IT'S SNUG AGAINST TEMPLATE

FIRST: CUT BASE 16" WIDE

STOP (¾" HARDWOOD - 1½" x 12")

WASTE

TEMPLATE

WASTE

FOURTH: PUSH SLED AND TEMPLATE THROUGH BLADE

SECOND: ALIGN LAYOUT LINE ON TEMPLATE WITH EDGE OF BASE

from sliding around on the jig base. So to do this, simply butt the stop snug against the bottom edge of the template and screw it to the base (*Step 3* in drawing). Then you can turn on the table saw and push the sled and the workpiece through the blade (*Step 4*).

FLIP TEMPLATE. This takes care of the first side of the end piece. But now is where you'll have a slight problem. Flipping the template over to cut the

opposite side hides the layout lines that you already marked on the template. That's the nice thing about the stop. It makes it easy to duplicate the angle that's already cut.

To do this, just place the bottom edge of the template against the stop. Then, after aligning the corner at the bottom of the template with the reference edge, you can easily cut the angle on the second side.

small amount of material that can be removed quickly and easily.

ROUT TO SHAPE. Now all that's left is to rout the legs to shape. To do this, the end piece is routed to final shape with a flush trim bit mounted in the router table (*Fig. 4*). The idea here is to adjust the height of the bit carefully so the bearing rides against the edge of the template. This way, the cutting edge of

the bit trims the end piece perfectly flush with the template.

But there's only one problem here. The router bit will leave the *inside* corners of the end piece slightly rounded. That's okay for the corners of the notch. But the corners of the "ears" around the tab will need some additional work.

FILE CORNERS. To allow the tab on the top sawhorse to fit all the way down into

the notch of the one below, you'll need to clean up these corners. A few strokes with a file is all it takes to get them nice and straight (*Fig. 4a*).

CHAMFER TAB. While you're at it, it's a good idea to file a slight chamfer on the *inside* of the tab (*Fig. 4a*). This will make it a lot easier for the tab to slip down into the notch when you need to stack the sawhorses.

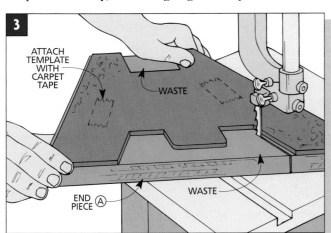

3

ATTACH TEMPLATE WITH CARPET TAPE

WASTE

END PIECE (A)

WASTE

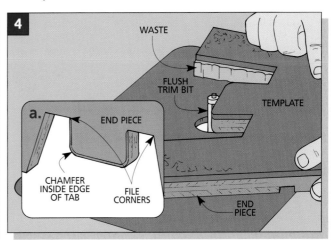

4

WASTE

FLUSH TRIM BIT

TEMPLATE

a.

END PIECE

CHAMFER INSIDE EDGE OF TAB

FILE CORNERS

END PIECE

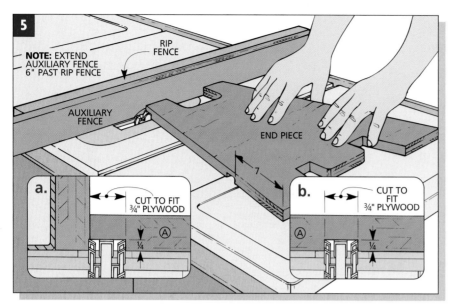

5

NOTE: EXTEND AUXILIARY FENCE 6" PAST RIP FENCE

RIP FENCE

AUXILIARY FENCE

END PIECE

7

a. CUT TO FIT ¾" PLYWOOD

Ⓐ

¼

b. CUT TO FIT ¾" PLYWOOD

Ⓐ

¼

JOINERY

After repeating the process of laying out, cutting, and shaping all of the remaining end pieces, you can start to concentrate on the joinery that's used to assemble the sawhorses.

Most sawhorses have a tendency to rack, especially after they've seen a lot of use. So to provide sturdy support for the top portion of the sawhorse, the top sits in a rabbet in the top edge of each end piece. And to strengthen the shelf, it fits into a dado. Finally, three plywood supports help to strengthen the entire assembly.

AUXILIARY FENCE. But before cutting either the rabbets or dadoes into the side pieces, I attached a long auxiliary

DESIGNER'S NOTEBOOK

Extend the life of the Stacking Sawhorses with a replaceable top.

CONSTRUCTION NOTES:

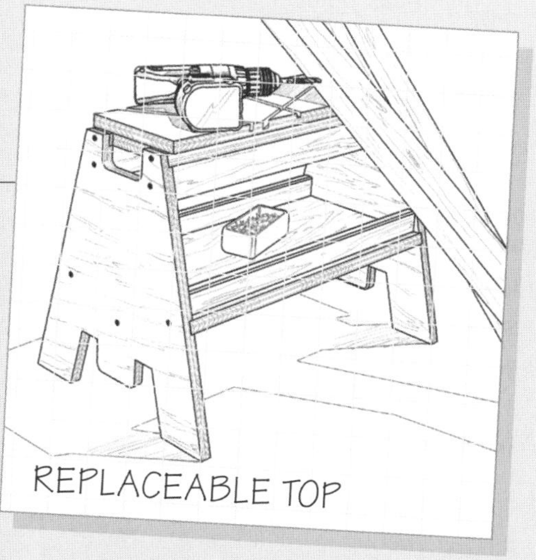

■ The tops of the sawhorses are only ¾" thick, so it would be easy to accidentally saw through them. I built a replaceable top to keep this from happening.

Start by cutting the replaceable top (E) to size. It's slightly wider than the sawhorse top, but the length is the same *(Figs. 1 and 2).* (This leaves the

notch exposed so the sawhorses can still be stacked up.)

■ Next, I cut a slot in the top (A) to make room for an alignment key *(Fig. 2a).* (This slot also doubles as a handhold.)

To make the slot, drill two 1¼"-dia. holes *(Fig. 2b).* Now use a jig saw to remove the waste between the holes.

■ Next, make a key (F) *(Fig. 2a).* Sand the sides of the key until it just slides into the handhold and then rout a ⅛" roundover around one face.

■ Attach the key to the underside of the top with glue only (no screws) *(Fig. 2).*

■ Then I added two tray retainers to the shelf. This way you can store tools while

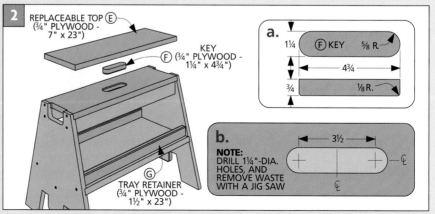

REPLACEABLE TOP

you work or store the replaceable top when it's not in use. Just cut the tray retainers (G) to size and rout ⅛" roundovers on the top edges *(Figs. 1 and 2).* Then position them on the shelf and glue and screw them in place.

MATERIALS LIST

NEW PARTS

E	Replaceable Top (1)	¾ ply - 7 x 23
F	Key (1)	¾ ply - 1¼ x 4¾
G	Tray Retainers (2)	¾ ply - 1½ x 23

HARDWARE SUPPLIES

(8) No. 8 x 1¼" Fh woodscrews

1 CROSS SECTION

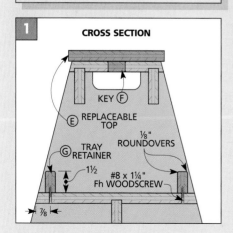

KEY Ⓕ

Ⓔ REPLACEABLE TOP

⅛" ROUNDOVERS

Ⓖ TRAY RETAINER

1½

#8 x 1¼" Fh WOODSCREW

⅞

2 REPLACEABLE TOP Ⓔ
(¾" PLYWOOD - 7" x 23")

KEY
Ⓕ (¾" PLYWOOD - 1¼" x 4¾")

a.

1¼ Ⓕ KEY ⅝ R.

4¾

¾ ⅛ R.

b.

3½

NOTE: DRILL 1¼"-DIA. HOLES, AND REMOVE WASTE WITH A JIG SAW

Ⓖ TRAY RETAINER (¾" PLYWOOD - 1½" x 23")

fence to the rip fence on the table saw *(Fig. 5)*. The auxiliary fence is just a scrap piece of wood that extends about 6" past the end of the rip fence.

This fence allows you to "bury" the blade when cutting the rabbet *(Fig. 5a)*. And it also provides continuous support for the bottom edge of the end piece as you cut the dado *(Fig. 5b)*.

TOP AND SHELF. Once the ends have been completed, the next step is to add a plywood top (B) and shelf (C) below it *(Fig. 6)*. The long edges of these pieces are beveled to match the angle of the end pieces.

Ripping the bevels on the shelf is easy. The trick is to get the beveled edges to fit flush with the end pieces once the sawhorse is assembled.

The best way I found to do this is to rip the shelf pieces to rough width first. Then I sneak up on the final width by making a series of bevel cuts on each side, removing a small amount of material with each pass.

CUT GROOVES. In addition to the bevels, you'll also need to cut two grooves in the top and a single groove in the shelf. These grooves will accept the three support pieces that are added later.

RECESS. Before assembling the sawhorses, there's one more thing to do. That's to cut a shallow recess in each end of the top. Once the sawhorse is assembled, the recess provides clearance for the tab to fit down in the notch.

To lay out this recess accurately, it's easiest to set the top in place in the rabbets cut into the end pieces *(Fig. 6a)*. Then, after attaching a tall fence to the miter gauge, make several passes over a dado blade to cut the recess *(Fig. 6b)*.

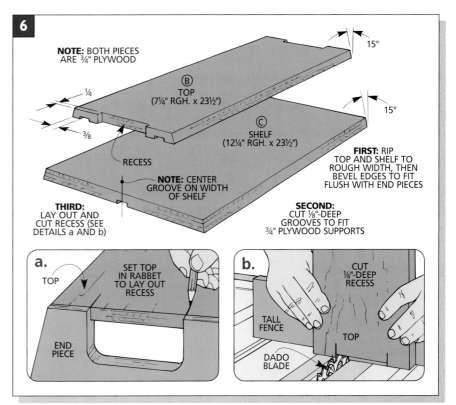

SUPPORTS. To help strengthen the sawhorse, I added three plywood supports (D) *(Fig. 7)*. Two of these supports fit in the grooves cut in the top. And there's a single support set into the groove below the shelf.

You can go ahead and rip these supports to final width. But it's best to dry-assemble the sawhorse before cutting them to final length.

ASSEMBLY. Now you're ready to assemble the sawhorses. The top and shelf of each one are glued and screwed to the end pieces *(Fig. 7)*. And the supports are glued into the grooves and secured with screws driven into the ends *(Fig. 7a)*. ∎

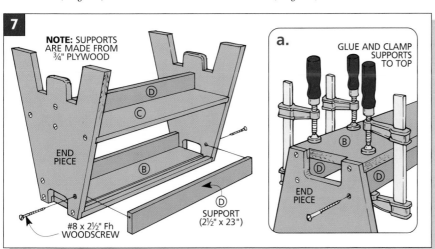

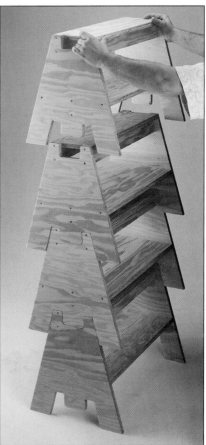

When it's time to "stable" your sawhorses, they don't take up much floor space. Just stack all four sawhorses together for storage.

Drill Bit Case

Keep your twist drill bits right at your fingertips with this pocket-size case featuring a flip-open lid. Made with wood and hardboard you've salvaged from the scrap bin, it keeps bits protected and organized.

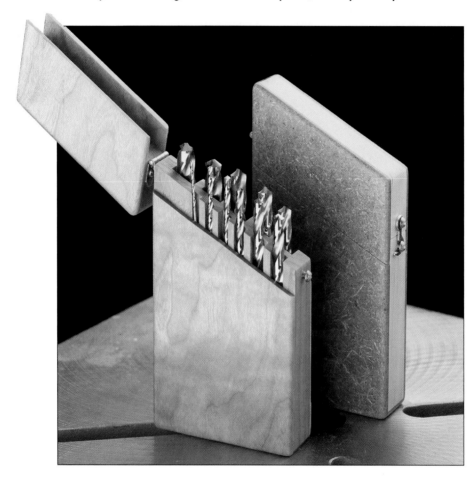

When I decided to make this Drill Bit Case, I knew I'd take some ribbing from the guys in the shop. After all, why make a case when you can go down to the hardware store and buy one? One reason is that this case gave me a perfect opportunity to use up some of the small scrap pieces I had lying around. Plus, it's a good example of what can be done in just a few hours in the shop. And it sure looks better than any store-bought case.

MATERIALS. To build the case, I used scrap pieces of maple and ⅛"-thick hardboard. But you could make it entirely out of a hardwood like cherry (see photo). I

like the contrast of the hardboard against the lighter colored maple, but remember this is a scrap project.

Note: If you decide to make the case sides from cherry or another hardwood, I've provided a tip that will make resawing a little easier (see the Shop Tip box on page 114).

CONSTRUCTION. The insides of the case start out as a piece of 12"-long hard maple. The case itself is less than 6" tall (including the lid), but I left it long for a reason. That's because these are small pieces, so the extra length makes it easier to cut all the grooves and recesses for the drill bits.

One other thing. When it came time to add the hinge and the small hook, I found it paid to take a little extra time. The small brass screws tend to twist off real quick (especially in the hard maple) if you don't drill starter holes first. To find sources for this hardware, go to page 126.

MAKE EXTRAS. After you're finished building one of these cases, I'd be willing to bet that you'll be spending a lot more time digging around the scrap bin than usual. In fact, I didn't just stop with one case. I made a couple extra to hold not only my twist bits, but all of my brad point drill bits as well.

EXPLODED VIEW

OVERALL DIMENSIONS:
$2^7/_8$W x 1D x $5^{13}/_{16}$H

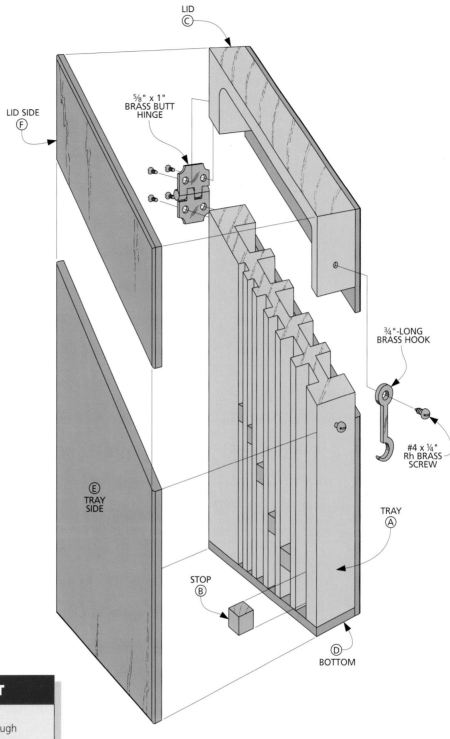

LID
Ⓒ

⅝" x 1"
BRASS BUTT
HINGE

LID SIDE
Ⓕ

¾"-LONG
BRASS HOOK

Ⓔ
TRAY
SIDE

#4 x ¼"
Rh BRASS
SCREW

TRAY
Ⓐ

STOP
Ⓑ

Ⓓ
BOTTOM

CONSTRUCTION

The Drill Bit Case is designed to hold eleven twist bits ranging in size from $^1/_{16}$" to $^3/_8$" in $^1/_{32}$" increments. To provide room for that many bits in a pocket-size case, I started with a $2^7/_8$"-wide blank (*Fig. 1*).

CORE PIECES. Since these bits "stairstep" up in length as the diameter increases, I cut the blank at an angle to match the line formed by the tips of the bits. This produces two core pieces — one for a tray to hold the bits, and the other for a lid (*Fig. 1*).

Note: The core pieces for the lid *and* the tray should each be cut *extra* long to make them easier to work with.

TRAY. Now work can begin on the tray (A). To create a "pocket" for each bit, I cut a series of grooves in the tray *slightly* deeper and wider than the diameter of the bits (*Figs. 2 and 2a*). Then I went ahead and trimmed the tray to its finished length (*Fig. 3*).

STOPS. If you take a look at the various drill bits that you're making this case for, you'll see that a $^1/_{16}$" drill bit is shorter than a $^3/_8$" bit. So to keep short bits from dropping to the bottom of the tray, I added six "stops." The stops (B) are just pieces of wood that are sized to fit each groove and then glued into the grooves under the end of each bit (*Fig. 4*).

The idea is to locate the stops so all the bits extend up the same amount. By placing the end of one of the longer bits flush with the bottom of the tray, you

can use the tip as a gauge to raise the short bits to the correct height (*Fig. 4*). Start by placing the largest short bit ($^7/_{32}$") at the front and working your way back to the smallest bit ($^1/_{16}$") (*Fig. 4*).

LID CORE. After installing the stops, work can begin on the core piece for the lid (C). To provide clearance for the bits

when the lid is closed, a recess needs to be cut in the bottom (angled) end of the lid core (*Fig. 5*).

WRAP CASE. The next step is to fit the lid to the tray. To do this, the case is "wrapped" with $^1/_8$"-thick hardboard.

Note: You can also use thin strips of hardwood. To learn about an easy way

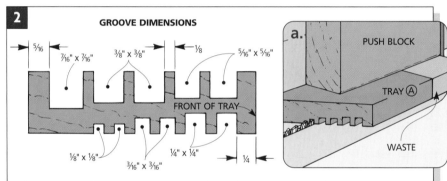

1

CORE PIECE FOR LID

$^3/_4$

WASTE

$2^7/_8$

WASTE

62°

CORE PIECE FOR TRAY

6

12

WASTE

NOTE: BLANK IS LEFT LONG TO MAKE IT EASIER TO ADD GROOVES FOR BITS

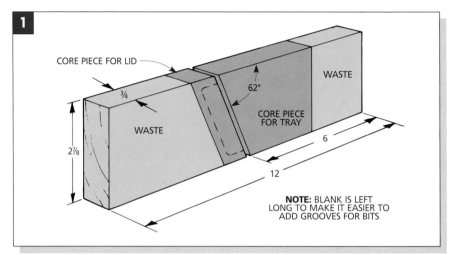

2

GROOVE DIMENSIONS

$^5/_{16}$ $^7/_{16}$" x $^7/_{16}$" $^3/_8$" x $^3/_8$" $^1/_8$ $^5/_{16}$" x $^5/_{16}$"

FRONT OF TRAY

$^1/_8$" x $^1/_8$" $^3/_{16}$" x $^3/_{16}$" $^1/_4$" x $^1/_4$" $^1/_4$

a.

PUSH BLOCK

TRAY Ⓐ

WASTE

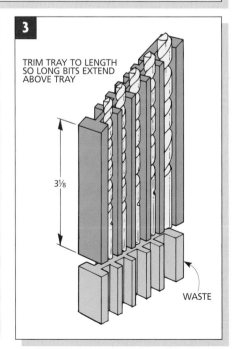

SHOP TIP .... Two-Step Resawing

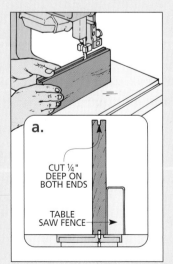

a.

CUT $^1/_4$" DEEP ON BOTH ENDS

TABLE SAW FENCE

I used both a table saw and band saw for resawing the boards for the sides of the Drill Bit Case. This method is most useful with boards that are too wide to cut all the way through on the table saw.

Start by using the table saw to score the two edges of the board with cuts that are about $^1/_4$" deep (see detail 'a'). Then, to finish resawing the board, switch to the band saw (see drawing). The scored cut lines on each edge of the board act as "guides" to keep the band saw blade on track.

This method works well because it usually results in boards of uniform thickness (which means there will be less final planing needed).

3

TRIM TRAY TO LENGTH SO LONG BITS EXTEND ABOVE TRAY

$3^1/_8$

WASTE

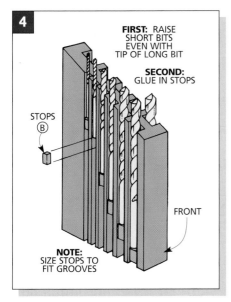

4

FIRST: RAISE SHORT BITS EVEN WITH TIP OF LONG BIT

SECOND: GLUE IN STOPS

STOPS
(B)

NOTE: SIZE STOPS TO FIT GROOVES

FRONT

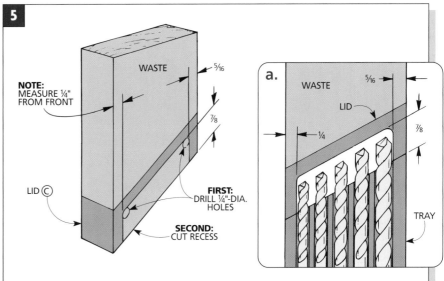

5

NOTE: MEASURE ¼" FROM FRONT

WASTE

⁵⁄₁₆

⁷⁄₈

LID (C)

FIRST: DRILL ¼"-DIA. HOLES

SECOND: CUT RECESS

a.

WASTE

⁵⁄₁₆

LID

¼

⁷⁄₈

TRAY

to resaw these thin pieces, see the Shop Tip box on the facing page.

The bottom (D) is cut to fit and glued on first *(Fig. 6)*. Then the sides can be added. I started with a long blank for each side of the case and cut the side pieces at an angle to match the core pieces that were cut earlier.

ATTACH SIDES. Attaching the sides to the two tray pieces is easy. They're just glued in place. The trick is locating the sides so the lid fits down snug over the tray like the top on a shoebox.

To do this, a narrow shoulder is formed by attaching the tray sides (E) ³⁄₈" below the top of the tray *(Fig. 6)*.

The lid sides (F) extend the same amount below the lid. This creates a lip that allows the lid sides to "seat" over the end of the tray.

FINAL DETAILS. To complete the case, the top of the lid is trimmed to match the angle of the side pieces *(Fig. 6)*. Then, I used some sandpaper to soften the sharp edges on all the parts.

Finally, I installed a hinge and a small hook *(Figs. 7 and 8)*. (For mail order sources, see page 126.)

Note: To make sure that the brass screws didn't twist off, I drilled starter holes first, then added the screws. ∎

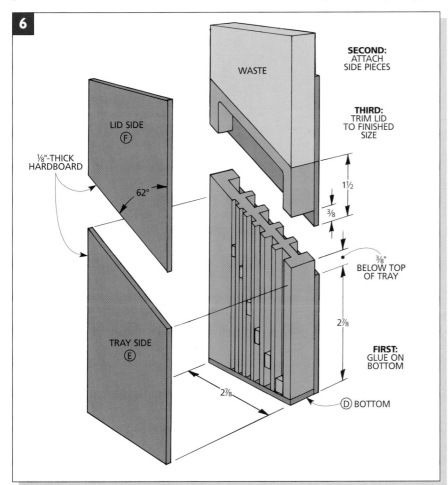

6

SECOND: ATTACH SIDE PIECES

WASTE

THIRD: TRIM LID TO FINISHED SIZE

LID SIDE
(F)

⅛"-THICK HARDBOARD

62°

1½

³⁄₈

³⁄₈"
BELOW TOP
OF TRAY

2⅞

FIRST: GLUE ON BOTTOM

TRAY SIDE
(E)

2⅞

(D) BOTTOM

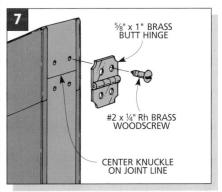

7

⁵⁄₈" x 1" BRASS BUTT HINGE

#2 x ¼" Rh BRASS WOODSCREW

CENTER KNUCKLE ON JOINT LINE

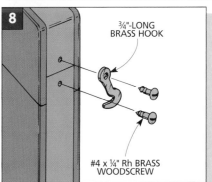

8

¾"-LONG BRASS HOOK

#4 x ¼" Rh BRASS WOODSCREW

Utility Ladder

Now you can build a sturdy folding step ladder that won't wobble, is strong enough for two people, and has a built-in tray for holding tools or even a gallon can of paint.

Every time I use a rickety step ladder, I promise myself I'm going to build one that's sturdy. There's only one problem — this requires cutting perfectly-matched angled dadoes for the rungs. So when I decided to make this Utility Ladder, I started by coming up with a simple way to do this.

The first set of angled dadoes is easy; the trick is cutting a second set. All it takes is a simple shop-made angle gauge (see the Shop Jig box on page 120) and an even simpler technique. To learn how I did it, see the article on page 119. Then I set out on my mission to build a better Utility Ladder.

WIDER LEGS. Since my main goal was to eliminate any chance of wobble, the ladder legs are 33% wider than legs on a store-bought ladder.

And there's stiffer bracing than you'll find on most ladders. In fact, I beefed up the support underneath each of the ladder rungs. To do this, I ripped some pieces of 1x6 for rung supports.

BRACES. Plus, I was able to add a lot of strength to the braces that hold the ladder open by adding on a backing that's made from 1/4"-thick hardboard. The braces swing out of the way to allow you to fold up the ladder when it's not in use (see photo). A long threaded rod

serves as a pivot for the braces. And a notch cut in one end allows the brace to slip over the threaded rod. Finally, a pair of wing nuts holds everything in place.

TRAY. While I was at it, I added a tray on top to keep tools and materials handy. I sized it so a gallon can of paint fits just right (see photo on page 120). And so two people can work off the ladder at the same time, it has rungs on both sides.

MATERIALS. I decided to use Douglas fir for the ladder parts. Its strength to weight ratio makes it a good choice for this type of project.

Now when I need a ladder in my shop, I know I can climb in confidence.

EXPLODED VIEW

OVERALL DIMENSIONS:
$25\frac{1}{2}$W x $41\frac{15}{16}$D x $41\frac{1}{2}$H

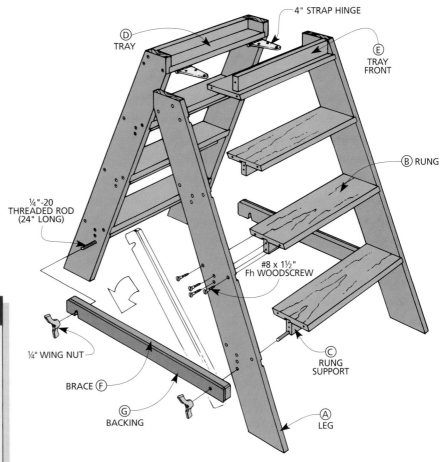

4" STRAP HINGE

D TRAY

E TRAY FRONT

B RUNG

¼"-20 THREADED ROD (24" LONG)

#8 x 1½" Fh WOODSCREW

¼" WING NUT

BRACE F

G BACKING

C RUNG SUPPORT

A LEG

MATERIALS LIST

WOOD

A	Legs (4)	$\frac{3}{4}$ x $4\frac{3}{4}$ - 48 rough
B	Rungs (6)	$\frac{3}{4}$ x $5\frac{1}{2}$ rough - 20
C	Rung Supports (6)	$\frac{3}{4}$ x $2\frac{1}{2}$ - $19\frac{1}{2}$
D	Trays (2)	$\frac{3}{4}$ x $5\frac{1}{2}$ rough - 20
E	Tray Fronts (2)	$\frac{3}{4}$ x $1\frac{1}{2}$ rough - $19\frac{1}{2}$
F	Braces (2)	$\frac{3}{4}$ x 2 - 32 rough
G	Backing (2)	¼ hdbd. - 2 x 32 rgh.

HARDWARE SUPPLIES

(60) No. 8 x 1½" Fh woodscrews
(2) 4" strap hinges w/ screws
(4) ¼" plastic wing nuts
(2) ¼"-20 x 24" threaded rods

CUTTING DIAGRAM

1x6 (¾ x 5½) - 96 DOUGLAS FIR (Two Boards @ 4 Bd. Ft.)

A	A

NOTE: ALSO NEED 4½" x 34" PIECE OF ¼" HARDBOARD FOR BACKING (G)

1x6 (¾ x 5½) - 96 DOUGLAS FIR (4 Bd. Ft.)

C	C	C	F
C	C	C	F

1x6 (¾ x 5½) - 72 DOUGLAS FIR (Two Boards @ 4 Bd. Ft.)

B	B	B	

1x6 (¾ x 5½) - 72 DOUGLAS FIR (4 Bd. Ft.)

D	D	E
		E

The Utility Ladder consists of two identical leg assemblies hinged at the top and held apart by a pair of braces (refer to the Exploded View on page 117). I began work on the ladder by making the leg assemblies.

LEG ASSEMBLIES. Each leg assembly consists of two legs that are mirror images of each other. They're made up of three rungs with a support under each rung, and a tray in place of a top rung (once again, see the Exploded View drawing on page 117).

The first step is to cut four legs (A) to finished width and rough length (refer to *Fig. 2*). Then cut a 22° miter on each end of each leg.

EAR. Next, to allow the leg assemblies to butt up against each other once the hinges are added, the top (inside) ear of each leg is cut at 90° *(Fig. 3a)*.

TEMPLATE. Now a set of angled dadoes is cut for the rungs. To ensure the dadoes align, make a template from a scrap piece of ¼" hardboard *(Fig. 1)*. Then use the template to lay out the angled dadoes carefully *(Fig. 3)*.

I also used the template to lay out the holes for attaching the rungs and supports to the legs *(Fig. 3)*.

USING THE TEMPLATE. To use the template, start by laying it on the inside face of one of the legs, keeping it flush at the ends. Then scribe or mark a line at the top, mark an "X" to indicate the waste area, and slide the template up to mark the next dado.

DADOES. Once everything is laid out, drill countersunk pilot holes and cut the angled dadoes *(Fig. 3b)*. (To learn more about how I cut the angled dadoes for the Utility Ladder, see the Technique box on the next page.)

RUNGS AND TRAY. Each leg assembly is held together with three rungs (B) and a tray (D) (once again, refer to the Exploded View on page 117 and *Fig. 2*). To allow the ladder to fold up, the rungs and trays are bevel ripped to match the slope of the legs *(Fig. 4a)*.

Note: Be sure to bevel only the outside edge of the two trays (refer to *Fig. 5a* on page 120).

Also, I cut a groove in the bottom face of each rung to accept the supports that are added next *(Fig. 4)*. Just

remember, there's no need to cut a groove in the tray — that's because it's not intended to be used as a top step.

SUPPORTS. Once the grooves have been cut, you can glue and screw the rungs to the legs. Then to strengthen each rung, cut a rung support (C) to fit between the legs.

Note: The bottom supports each have a groove cut in them for a threaded rod that's added later *(Fig. 4a)*.

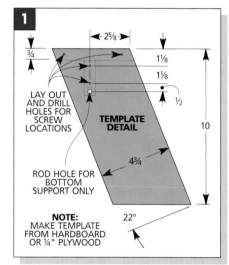

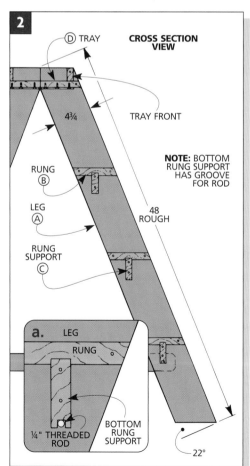

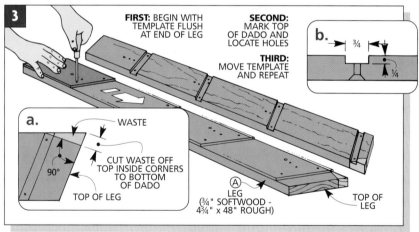

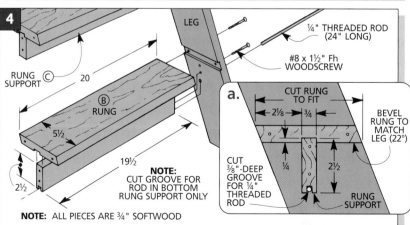

TECHNIQUE .... *Angled Dadoes*

It's not that complicated to cut one set of angled dadoes. The trick is to cut a second set that's a mirror image of the first.

That's because after you cut dadoes in one piece, you need to adjust the angle of the miter gauge to cut matching dadoes in the other. And if both angles aren't *exactly* the same, chances are good the dadoes won't align.

So when building a project like the Utility Ladder, I use a simple technique that aligns the dadoes. All it takes is two things: an accurate layout and a shop-made angle gauge to set your miter gauge.

Note: For more on how I made an angle gauge and how to use it, see the Shop Jig article on page 120.

LAYOUT

When laying out the angled dadoes, there are several things you can do to build in accuracy.

GANG PIECES. First, it helps to "gang" the leg pieces together and then lay out the dadoes carefully on both pieces at once (*Fig. 1*). Just be sure to clamp the pieces together with the ends flush. And be sure the sides that will be dadoed are facing each other.

SINGLE LINE. Another way to ensure accuracy is to use a *single* line to lay out each dado. This way, you'll be able to adjust the dado blade to whatever width you want without affecting the accuracy of the layout. To avoid cutting the wrong side of the line, don't forget to mark the waste area with an "X."

SIDES. Once the edges are marked, you can lay out the sides. This is where the angle gauge comes in handy. After using it to set the angle on a bevel gauge, just transfer the angle to the outside face of each workpiece (*Fig. 1*).

CUT DADOES

With the layout complete, you're ready to cut the dadoes. As with any dado (angled or straight), there are a couple of preliminaries to take care of first.

WIDTH OF CUT. For starters, adjusting the width of cut. What you're after is to adjust the width of the blade to match the thickness of the piece that will fit in

the dado. The only way I've found to get a snug fit is to make a test cut, check it, and readjust the blade if needed.

FENCE. Also, to prevent chipout on the edge of the workpiece, I attached an auxiliary fence to the miter gauge.

Note: Make sure the auxiliary fence is long enough to extend past the blade when you tilt the miter gauge (*Fig. 2*).

ADJUST ANGLE. Now adjust the angle of the miter gauge to cut the first set of dadoes. The angle gauge makes quick work of finding the exact setting (see the Shop Jig article on page 120).

But even with the correct angle, you still need a way of aligning the workpiece to the blade so the dadoes end up exactly where you want them.

NOTCH. To do this, cut a notch in the fence to use as a reference and extend a line up from the side of the notch (*Figs. 2a and 2b*).

Note: If the notch is too tall, the edge of the workpiece will chip out when the blade cuts through. So cut the notch so its height equals the depth of the dado. The best way to do this is to make a pass with the blade set low, then sneak up on the final depth of cut.

MATCHING DADOES. Now set the miter gauge to the correct angle and cut one set of dadoes. Then readjust the miter gauge to cut the matching dadoes (*Fig. 2*).

Note: Before cutting the second set of dadoes, cut a new notch in the fence.

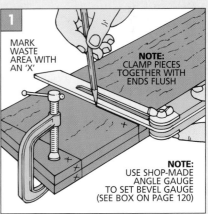

1

MARK WASTE AREA WITH AN 'X'

NOTE: CLAMP PIECES TOGETHER WITH ENDS FLUSH

NOTE: USE SHOP-MADE ANGLE GAUGE TO SET BEVEL GAUGE (SEE BOX ON PAGE 120)

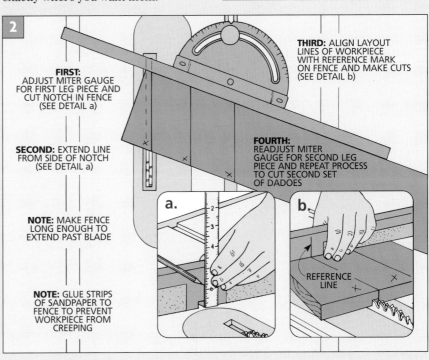

2

FIRST: ADJUST MITER GAUGE FOR FIRST LEG PIECE AND CUT NOTCH IN FENCE (SEE DETAIL a)

SECOND: EXTEND LINE FROM SIDE OF NOTCH (SEE DETAIL a)

NOTE: MAKE FENCE LONG ENOUGH TO EXTEND PAST BLADE

NOTE: GLUE STRIPS OF SANDPAPER TO FENCE TO PREVENT WORKPIECE FROM CREEPING

THIRD: ALIGN LAYOUT LINES OF WORKPIECE WITH REFERENCE MARK ON FENCE AND MAKE CUTS (SEE DETAIL b)

FOURTH: READJUST MITER GAUGE FOR SECOND LEG PIECE AND REPEAT PROCESS TO CUT SECOND SET OF DADOES

a.

b.

REFERENCE LINE

Making an angle gauge is easy. I made mine using a scrap piece of ³/₄"-thick MDF. (A piece of ³/₄"-thick plywood would also work for the gauge.)

First I cut a groove in each side to accept the bar of the miter gauge (see drawing). And then one end of the jig is cut to the desired angle of the dadoes that you'll be cutting (see drawing). (In my case, this was 22°.)

To learn more about using the jig, see the photos below.

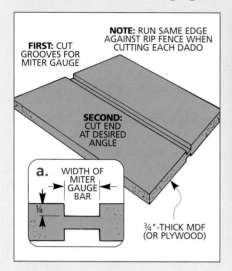

FIRST: CUT GROOVES FOR MITER GAUGE

NOTE: RUN SAME EDGE AGAINST RIP FENCE WHEN CUTTING EACH DADO

SECOND: CUT END AT DESIRED ANGLE

a. WIDTH OF MITER GAUGE BAR

¼

³/₄"-THICK MDF (OR PLYWOOD)

First Angle Setting. *To set the first angle, hold the miter gauge upside down, pivot the head so it's tight against the end, and lock it in place.*

Second Angle Setting. *Flipping the angle gauge over and repeating the process automatically sets the miter gauge to the exact opposite angle.*

TRAY. Now, go ahead and form the tray by adding the two tray fronts (E) *(Fig. 5)*. The fronts are just two short pieces of softwood that are cut to length to make them fit. Then they're ripped to width so they're flush with the tops of the legs. Now the two leg assemblies can be joined together with a pair of 4" strap hinges *(Figs. 5 and 5a)*.

Note: Line up the barrel of each hinge so it's centered between the trays.

BRACING

Now finish everything up by building the part of the ladder that makes it so sturdy. To prevent the legs from splaying apart during use, a brace (F) is added to each side *(Fig. 6)*. The braces pivot on 24"-long threaded rods that fit in the grooves cut earlier in the bottom rung supports. To find the length of the braces, measure between the rods and add 2½" *(Fig. 6)*. Then to strengthen each brace, I laminated it with a backing (G) made from ¼"-thick hardboard.

NOTCH. Finally, a notch is cut on the end of each brace to allow it to slip over the threaded rod *(Fig. 6a)*. To locate the notch, unfold the legs and measure between the rods. Then transfer this distance to the brace, drill a hole, and remove the waste. Now slide the braces over the rods and add the wing nuts. ■

The built-in tray at the top of this sturdy Utility Ladder is a great place for laying your tools and supplies or even a gallon can of paint.

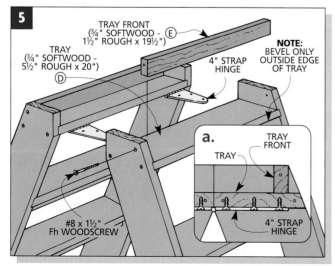

5

TRAY FRONT (³/₄" SOFTWOOD - 1½" ROUGH x 19½") Ⓔ

TRAY (³/₄" SOFTWOOD - 5½" ROUGH x 20") Ⓓ

4" STRAP HINGE

NOTE: BEVEL ONLY OUTSIDE EDGE OF TRAY

a. TRAY FRONT

TRAY

4" STRAP HINGE

#8 x 1½" Fh WOODSCREW

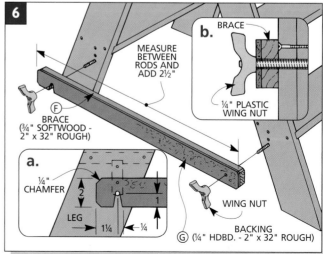

6

MEASURE BETWEEN RODS AND ADD 2½"

b. BRACE

¼" PLASTIC WING NUT

BRACE (³/₄" SOFTWOOD - 2" x 32" ROUGH) Ⓕ

a. ¼" CHAMFER

2

LEG

1¼   ¼

1

WING NUT

BACKING Ⓖ (¼" HDBD. - 2" x 32" ROUGH)

Joiner's Mallet

The secret to this well-balanced shop-made mallet is the two "pockets" in the laminated head. Lead weights are used to fill these pockets in the core pieces and provide extra striking force.

There's something very satisfying about using a tool that you've crafted yourself. And this Joiner's Mallet is no exception. Every time I pick it up I enjoy its heft and balance, especially the way the handle fits my hand. That's something you just can't get from a store-bought tool.

Now let's think about when you use a Joiner's Mallet. At times, I like to use a mallet to help with chopping the waste from dovetails or mortises. That's where the solidness of this mallet comes in real handy. That heft is the result of two round "pockets" I drilled in the head and filled with lead sinkers (see the

Exploded View on page 122). The sinkers are glued in place with epoxy.

At other times, a mallet comes in handy to help coax a tenon into a too-tight mortise. So to prevent the mallet head from marring the surface of a workpiece, I glued a thick piece of leather onto each end. They also help to soften the blow. (For sources of weights and leather, see page 126.)

MATERIALS. There's another nice thing about building your own hand tools — it's okay to make it as attractive as it is useful. For instance, I really like the look of the contrasting hardwoods that I used for the handle and head of

the mallet. I ended up using hard maple for the blanks that make up the head. But I didn't choose it just for its good looks. Hard maple is strong enough to stand up to years of use.

The handle is special too. It's made from straight-grained walnut, and I made sure to pick a piece that was free of knots and flaws. The last thing I wanted was to have the handle break.

WEDGES. There's one last interesting detail here — the wedges (see photo above). Once again, they look good, but more importantly, they "lock" the head to the handle. To learn how to make the wedges, see page 125.

EXPLODED VIEW

OVERALL DIMENSIONS:
5¾W x 1¾D x 12H

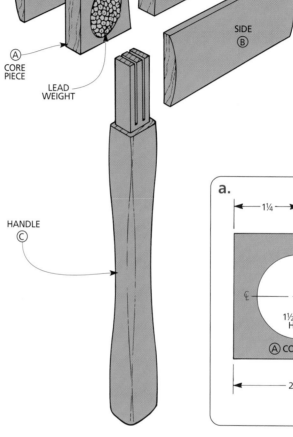

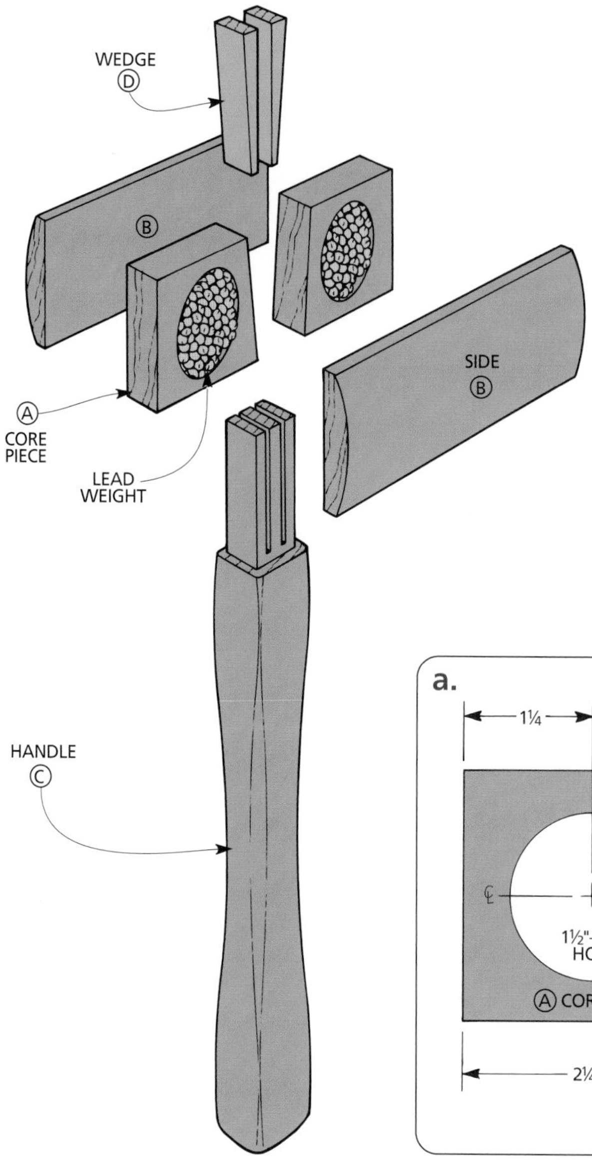

WEDGE
Ⓓ

SIDE
Ⓑ

CORE
PIECE
Ⓐ

LEAD
WEIGHT

HANDLE
Ⓒ

CUTTING DIAGRAM

¾ x 5 - 18 (.6 Bd. Ft.)

A		D
B		

1 x 2 - 14 (.2 Bd. Ft.)

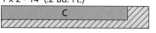

C

MATERIALS LIST

WOOD
A Core Pieces (2) ¾ x 2¼ - 2¼
B Sides (2) ½ x 2¼ - 5½
C Handle (1) 1 x 1¼ - 12
D Wedges (2) ⅛ rgh. x ¾ - 2¼

HARDWARE SUPPLIES
(10 oz.) 3/0 split-shot fishing sinkers

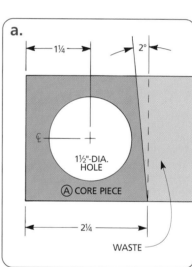

a.

1¼

2°

¢

1½"-DIA.
HOLE

Ⓐ CORE PIECE

2¼

WASTE

1

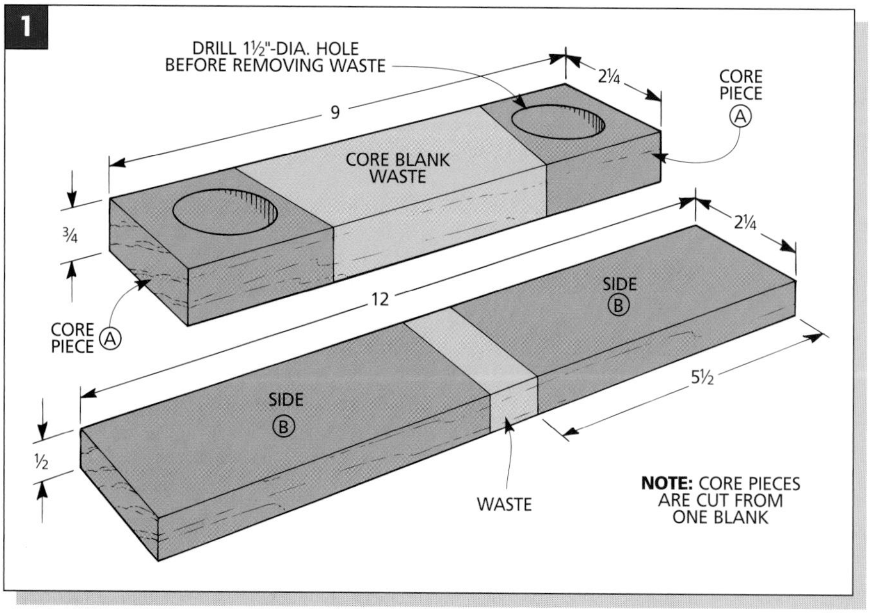

DRILL 1½"-DIA. HOLE
BEFORE REMOVING WASTE

9

2¼

CORE
PIECE
Ⓐ

CORE BLANK
WASTE

¾

CORE
PIECE Ⓐ

12

2¼

SIDE
Ⓑ

SIDE
Ⓑ

5½

½

WASTE

NOTE: CORE PIECES
ARE CUT FROM
ONE BLANK

MALLET HEAD

The first step in building the Joiner's Mallet is to make the head. The head consists of two core pieces (A) and two side pieces (B) (see the Exploded View above). The core pieces are drilled to make the "pockets" and then shaped on the table saw to form the tapered mortise for the handle.

CORE BLANK. To make the two core pieces (A), start by cutting a 2¼"-wide core blank from ¾"-thick stock *(Fig. 1)*. (I used hard maple for both the core and the sides because of its durability.) I cut the blank extra long so I could safely drill the pockets and cut the short core pieces to length.

POCKETS. With the blank cut to rough size, go ahead and lay out hole

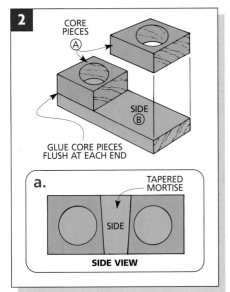

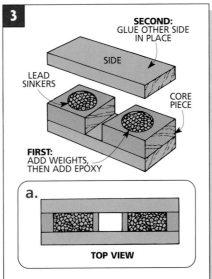

The laminated construction technique used for the head of the Joiner's Mallet, combined with the lead weights added to the pockets, creates a mallet with excellent balance and heft.

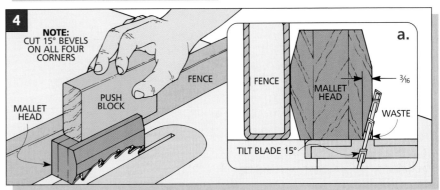

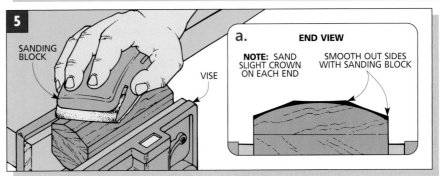

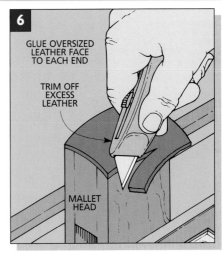

locations on both ends of the blank (see detail 'a' in the Exploded View at left). Then, drill the $1\frac{1}{2}$"-dia. holes at each end of the core piece.

CUT TO LENGTH. Once the holes are drilled, the next step is to cut the core pieces to length. You'll notice these are cut at a slight angle (2°) to form a tapered mortise for the handle (see detail 'a' in Exploded View). To do this, set your miter gauge at 2° and cut the core pieces off the blank *(Fig. 1)*.

SIDES. With the core pieces cut to length, work can begin on the $\frac{1}{2}$"-thick sides (B). (Here again, to provide contrast, I used hard maple.) Each side is cut the same width as the core pieces ($2\frac{1}{4}$") and $5\frac{1}{2}$" long *(Fig. 1)*.

GLUE-UP. Once the sides are cut, the mallet head can be glued up. To do this, first glue the two core pieces to one of the side pieces *(Fig. 2)*.

Note: Make sure the tapered edges of the core pieces face in to form the tapered mortise *(Fig. 2)*.

The next step is to fill the pockets in the core pieces with lead weight *(Fig. 3)*. I used small lead fishing sinkers for this (mine were 3/0 size split-shot). This size makes it easy to pack them tight in the pockets.

And then to keep the sinkers from rattling, I poured in some quick-setting epoxy (see photo above). When the epoxy has dried completely, glue the remaining side piece in place *(Fig. 3a)*.

SHAPE HEAD. The next step is to shape the head. I curved the sides of the mallet by first cutting 15° bevels on all four corners *(Figs. 4 and 4a)*. (Make sure to use a push block when cutting the bevels on the short pieces that form the head of the mallet.)

Then I used a sanding block to shape the sides of the mallet head to a smooth curve *(Figs. 5 and 5a)*.

Next, sand slight "crowns" on both ends of the head.

LEATHER. Finally, I glued a leather face to both ends of the mallet head. I decided to use contact cement here. Start by applying two coats to a couple of oversized pieces of leather and to the ends of the mallet. Then press the leather in place and trim off the excess *(Fig. 6)*. For ideas on where to find leather, see Sources on page 126.

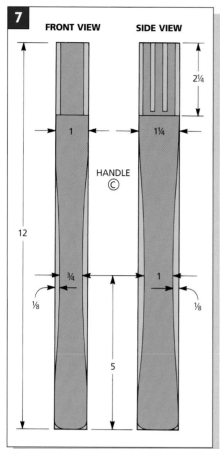

7

FRONT VIEW   SIDE VIEW

2¼

1

1¼

HANDLE
©

12

¾

1

⅛

⅛

5

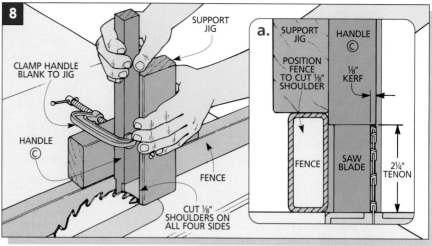

8

CLAMP HANDLE
BLANK TO JIG

HANDLE
©

SUPPORT
JIG

FENCE

CUT ⅛"
SHOULDERS ON
ALL FOUR SIDES

a. SUPPORT
JIG

HANDLE
©

POSITION
FENCE
TO CUT ⅛"
SHOULDER

⅛"
KERF

FENCE

SAW
BLADE

2¼"
TENON

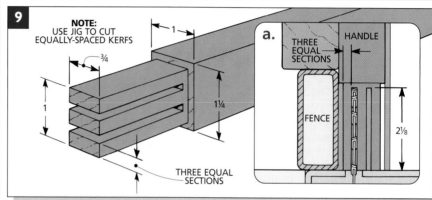

9

NOTE:
USE JIG TO CUT
EQUALLY-SPACED KERFS

1

¾

1

1¼

THREE EQUAL
SECTIONS

a.

THREE
EQUAL
SECTIONS

HANDLE

FENCE

2⅛"

MALLET HANDLE

I used a piece of straight-grained walnut for the handle (but any contrasting hardwood will do). Just be sure to choose a piece that is free of knots and flaws of any kind. The overall length of the handle (C) is 12". The width and thickness are determined by the size of the mortise in the mallet head.

HANDLE BLANK. To determine the size of the mallet handle blank, first measure the mortise at the bottom (narrowest part) of the head. Then to allow

for ⅛" shoulders on all four sides, add ¼" to each measurement and cut the blank to these dimensions *(Fig. 7)*. (In my case, the handle blank starts out 1" thick and 1¼" wide.)

CUT TENON. After the blank is cut to size, the next step is to cut the tenon (leaving ⅛" shoulders). To do this, I used the table saw and a simple jig to support the blank *(Figs. 8 and 8a)*.

The jig is just a scrap piece of 2x4 that's cut in two and screwed together to form a cross *(Fig. 8)*. It rides on both the rip fence and the table top to sup-

port the cut. And I also used a C-clamp to hold the workpiece steady while I was making the cut.

WEDGE KERFS. With the tenon cut on the end of the blank, the next step is to cut the kerfs for the wedges that hold the head in place *(Fig. 9)*. To prevent the handle from splitting, cut the saw kerfs ⅛" less than the length of the tenon (2⅛") *(Fig. 9a)*.

Position the rip fence so the 1"-wide tenon will be divided into three equal parts *(Figs. 9 and 9a)*.

SHAPE HANDLE. Now that the kerfs are cut, the handle can be shaped to fit your hand (refer to *Fig. 7*). To do this, I used a file to get the handle to rough shape *(Fig. 10)*. As you can see, to make it easy to work on the blank, I used a bar clamp to hold it securely while I worked on it. The bar clamp is then placed in a bench vise to lift the piece above the workbench. Once you've filed the blank to rough shape, use a scraper or sandpaper to remove the file marks.

I chose to use maple for the wedges and I made sure to orient the grain to run parallel to the sides of the wedge (see *Fig. 1* in the Technique box above right). Orienting the grain like this

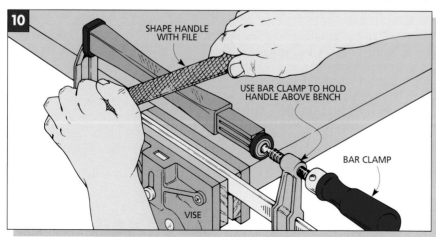

10

SHAPE HANDLE
WITH FILE

USE BAR CLAMP TO HOLD
HANDLE ABOVE BENCH

BAR CLAMP

VISE

To hold the head securely in place, the wedges have to be tapered. That means the narrow end of the wedge is cut to match the width of the kerf in the handle. This ensures the wedges won't bottom out in the kerfs before the handle is tight in the mallet head.

SET UP. To cut these small wedges safely, I use a two-step process and an oversized piece of hardwood scrap for the blank. To do this, start by positioning the rip fence on your table saw.

Adjust the rip fence so the distance between the blade and the fence is the same as the width of the kerf in the handle. Then, tilt the blade to match the taper of the mortise (2°) and push the blank along the fence (*Fig. 1*).

To cut the wedges to length (and prevent them from binding against the blade), position the rip fence so they fall to the left of the blade (*Fig. 2*).

Note: The wedges are cut 1/8" longer than the kerf in the handle. This allows you to trim them off for a perfect fit.

Once the wedges are cut to fit the kerfs in the handle, you'll need to trim them to width (3/4" in my case). To do this, I used a fine-toothed back saw to cut the wedges to final width (*Fig. 3*).

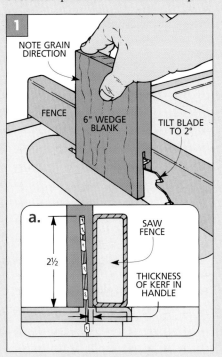

1 NOTE GRAIN DIRECTION — FENCE — 6" WEDGE BLANK — TILT BLADE TO 2°

a. 2½ — SAW FENCE — THICKNESS OF KERF IN HANDLE

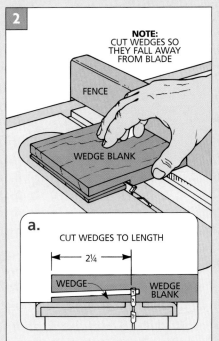

2 NOTE: CUT WEDGES SO THEY FALL AWAY FROM BLADE — FENCE — WEDGE BLANK

a. CUT WEDGES TO LENGTH — 2¼ — WEDGE — WEDGE BLANK

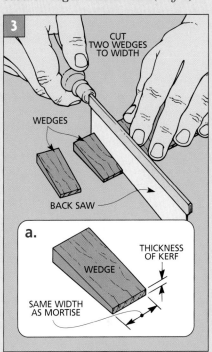

3 CUT TWO WEDGES TO WIDTH — WEDGES — BACK SAW

a. THICKNESS OF KERF — WEDGE — SAME WIDTH AS MORTISE

helps prevent the wedges from breaking off when they're driven into the handle (*Fig. 11*). The wedges need to be cut to the right length. (To learn more about an easy way to cut the wedges, see the Technique box above.)

ASSEMBLY

Once the wedges are cut to size, the mallet can be assembled. To do this, first apply glue to the handle tenon and slide it into the mortise formed in the mallet head (*Fig. 11*).

Then, apply glue to the wedges and drive them into the handle. The trick here is to gently tap in both of the wedges at the same time. To do this, I placed a scrap block over both wedges to tap them in together.

Finally, use a sharp chisel to trim the wedges flush with the head and then finish sand the mallet (*Fig. 11a*). ■

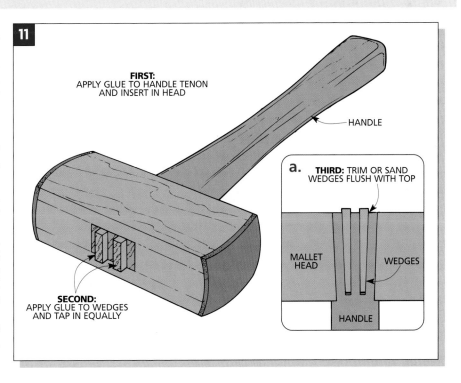

11 FIRST: APPLY GLUE TO HANDLE TENON AND INSERT IN HEAD — HANDLE

SECOND: APPLY GLUE TO WEDGES AND TAP IN EQUALLY

a. THIRD: TRIM OR SAND WEDGES FLUSH WITH TOP — MALLET HEAD — WEDGES — HANDLE

One of the first things we take into consideration when designing projects at *Woodsmith* is whether hardware is affordable and easy to find. Does it complement the project and is it appropriate? Is it affordable? But, most important, is it commonly available?

You'll probably be able to find most of the hardware and supplies for the projects in this book at your local hardware store or home center. Two additional good sources for some of the supplies in this book are craft stores and hobby shops. Sometimes, though, you may have to order hardware through the mail. If that's the case, we've tried to find reputable sources with toll-free phone numbers and web sites (see the Mail Order Sources box at right).

In addition, *Woodsmith Project Supplies* offers hardware for one of the projects in this book (see below).

Note: We *strongly* recommend that you have all of your hardware and supplies in hand *before* you begin building any project in this book. There's nothing more discouraging than completing a project and then finding out that the hardware you ordered for it doesn't fit or is no longer available.

WOODSMITH PROJECT SUPPLIES

At the time this book was printed, the following project supply kit was available from *Woodsmith Project Supplies*. The kit includes hardware, but you must supply any lumber or finish. For current prices and availability, call toll free:

1-800-444-7527

Picture Frame Clock
(pages 34-41)

This kit contains four rare-earth magnets, a $2^3/4$" quartz clock fit-up with brass bezel, the spring catch, brass hinges, and screws. You'll need to supply the veneer and acetate sheet.

..................................No. 7512120

KEY: TL12

MAIL ORDER SOURCES

Some of the most important "tools" you can have in your shop are your mail order catalogs. The ones listed below are filled with special hardware, tools, finishes, lumber, and supplies that can't be found at many local hardware stores or home centers. You should be able to find many of the supplies for the projects in this book in one or more of these catalogs. Many even offer online ordering.

Note: The information below was current when this book was printed. Time-Life Books and August Home Publishing do not guarantee these products will be available nor endorse any specific mail order company, catalog, or product.

THE WOODSMITH STORE

2625 Beaver Avenue
Des Moines, IA 50310
800–835–5084
Our own retail store with tools, jigs, hardware, router bits, Shaker pegs, books, and finishing supplies. We don't have a catalog, but we do send out items mail order.

ROCKLER WOODWORKING & HARDWARE

4365 Willow Drive
Medina, MN 55340
800–279–4441
www.rockler.com
A very good catalog of hardware, including hinges, coat hooks, spring catches, and keyhole hangers. Accessories include gallery spindles, quartz clock movements, and brad drivers. You'll also find a wide variety of Shaker pegs, wood plugs and wheels, plus veneer and inlay supplies.

WOODCRAFT

560 Airport Industrial Park
P.O. Box 1686
Parkersburg, WV 26102-1686
800–225–1153
www.woodcraft.com
Almost everything you'd need, from layout to hardware to finishing supplies. A good selection of carbide-tipped blades, carving tools, hinges, and router bits, plus quartz clock movements and brad drivers.

LEE VALLEY TOOLS LTD.

P.O. Box 1780
Ogdensburg, NY 13669-6780
800–871–8158
www.leevalley.com
Several catalogs actually, with tools and hardware. In the hardware catalog you'll find carving tools, a good variety of router bits, Shaker pegs, butt hinges, brass screws, brad drivers, graphite transfer paper, and rare-earth magnets.

THE WOODWORKER'S CHOICE

2 The Professional Drive
West Jefferson, NC 28694
800–892–4866
www.thewoodworkerschoice.com
A great online store with a full selection of hardware and supplies. Find carbide-tipped blades, finishing supplies, plastic T-knobs, rare-earth magnets, and router bits.

CONSTANTINE'S

1040 E. Oakland Park Blvd.
Ft. Lauderdale, FL 33334
954–561–1716
www.constantines.com
One of the original woodworking mail order catalogs. Find brass hinges, hooks, screws, spring catches and escutcheon pins. You'll also find a good selection of dowels, inlay, veneer, wooden wheels and plugs, and Shaker pegs. They also carry brad drivers for frames.

INDEX

AUGUST HOME
PUBLISHING COMPANY

President & Publisher: Donald B. Peschke
Executive Editor: Douglas L. Hicks
Project Manager: Craig L. Ruegsegger
Creative Director: Ted Kralicek
Art Director: Doug Flint
Senior Graphic Designers: Robin Friend, Chris Glowacki
Assistant Editors: Joel Hess, Joseph E. Irwin
Graphic Designer: Vu Nguyen
Design Intern: Matt O'Gara

Designer's Notebook Illustrator: Chris Glowacki
Photographer: Crayola England
Electronic Production: Douglas M. Lidster
Production: Troy Clark, Minniette Johnson
Project Designers: Chris Fitch, Ryan Mimick, Ken Munkel, Kent Welsh
Project Builders: Steve Curtis, Steve Johnson
Magazine Editors: Terry Strohman, Tim Robertson
Contributing Editors: Vincent S. Ancona, Jon Garbison, Brian McCallum,
Bryan Nelson
Magazine Art Directors: Todd Lambirth, Cary Christensen
Contributing Illustrators: Harlan Clark, Mark Higdon, David Kreyling,
Erich Lage, Roger Reiland, Kurt Schultz, Cinda Shambaugh, Dirk Ver Steeg

Corporate V.P., Finance: Mary Scheve
Controller: Robin Hutchinson
Production Director: George Chmielarz
Project Supplies: Bob Baker
New Media Manager: Gordon Gaippe

For subscription information about
Woodsmith and *ShopNotes* magazines, please write:
August Home Publishing Co.
2200 Grand Ave.
Des Moines, IA 50312
800-333-5075
www.augusthome.com/customwoodworking

Woodsmith® and *ShopNotes*® are registered trademarks of August Home
Publishing Co.

TIME
LIFE
BOOKS

Direct Holdings Americas Inc.

Weekend & Evening Projects

ISBN 0-7835-5961-5

10 9 8 7 6 5 4 3 2